BECOME #1
IN
SELLING!

First Edition

BECOME #1 IN SELLING!

FIRST EDITION
Copyright © 1996 by
Thomas A. Lisk, LHD

Library of Congress Catalog Card Number: 96-94021

Cover design by Michael Slone

Cover photo of the globe courtesy of the National Space and Aeronautics Administration

ISBN 0-7880-0666-5
PRINTED IN U.S.A.

ACKNOWLEDGMENTS

This book exists because of thousands of people I have met from my audiences and seminars; and because of my customers, mentors and the great salespeople I have encountered. They have inspired and encouraged me. Some of their successes confirmed the principles I write about and the stories I share. Hundreds have shaped my knowledge.

I would also like to thank God who really is first in my life and without whose teaching and inspiration, this book would not have been started, let alone finished.

To David Gambol, Ph.D., Mrs. Miracol and Kathy Edwards, thanks for your patience with me with the first manuscript.

To Valerie Wilson for your typing and a little editing.

To my most important mentors (many of you are mentioned), may this help your caring live on.

To my staff and wife Lorna who help make our company very effective in our ability to serve our customers.

To our initial publisher, Fairway Press, thank you for helping create a quality product. Thousands can and will benefit due to our partnership.

To Louann and Mary who worked diligently and precisely on the final manuscript to prepare it for publishing.

Thank you all.

Readers: *Your comments and questions to:*

> Thomas A. Lisk, LHD
> The Thom Lisk Group
> 1112 Firth Ave.
> Worthington, OH 43085
> (614) 841-1776 • Fax: (614) 846-1377

CONTENTS

Contents

INTRODUCTION

You can BECOME more than you are today, in all areas of life, and BECOME #1 IN SELLING with the important help in this book. The book is more than most books in that it provides a system and how-to's for setting and reaching goals and more success. Because I am often hired as a motivational speaker or teacher, as well as a sales educator, and business management, marketing or human resources/potential consultant, the book touches on the whole person, and picture. Fine tune your skills and improve your performance with these proven ideas.

I have seen salespeople go from last to first, and that includes me, when properly directed and motivated. Regardless of your experience level, there is much in these pages that can benefit you, if your mind and heart are open. Open yourself to these truths and apply them with love. I did and became #1 in selling in two giant companies in two different industries before age 28. This book will pay dividends.

Do you want more money? More job satisfaction? A more significant life? Better family relationships? More time to pursue personal goals? The answers to these needs and much more is yours for the reading. I give live in-house seminars, workshops and keynote or banquet speeches where we custom tailor the ideas further to your needs.

A complete reading is recommended along with answering all the questions. Some companies will use this for all their salespeople, one chapter a week, as a sales training program. Great *results* will be forthcoming if management holds people accountable for implementation, or if you can hold yourself accountable for the goals you establish. I guarantee this will help.

You can look at the bibliography and index in the back of the book to get a better overview if needed. This will save you time.

Remember "he who serves best (will) profit most." I hope this helps you so that all your dreams do come true!

This page contains the twelve most persuasive words published by Yale University. If you think you can list all twelve, drop me a note for a free prize. Thank you.

CHAPTER 1

Mining For Gold!

YOUR GOLD MINE

Recently, I visited what was once the **most productive** gold mine in Southern California. Stonewall mine was named after President Stonewall Jackson and was owned by the governor of California during its heyday. (*You* have a potential gold mine!)

It closed about the same time my grandmother was born, 1888. An entire community *bustled with activity* when the mine was producing. When the gold eventually was all mined, the town went bust! Today, there are few signs of the **prosperity** the area once enjoyed in the hills of East Central San Diego County.

I lived not far from there for nearly a year. One day I was out driving when I came upon this **treasure** of the past. How many great sales opportunities have you missed in your own back yard? Your "Acres of Diamonds" or Gold!

So it often is with the sales careers of many of America's salespeople. Some Become #1 in Selling, but burn out, or get promoted beyond their level of maximum effectiveness, or the company cuts territories, changes the rules, or something else goes wrong, preventing them from maintaining their #1 status. So few make *all* the right moves and reach all their dreams. Why was I able to earn over $60,000 in one year at age 23 in 1973?

This chapter lays a foundation upon which specific building blocks for your success are given. Your problems are really only challenges for wise decisions, opportunities to prosper, or situations for growth.

WHY ARE YOU LIVING?

Become 🌸👤 in Selling!

Some years ago, a ***regional sales manager*** was in the Pittsburgh International Airport about to board a small plane for Altoona, Pennsylvania. He phoned the salesperson who was to meet him at the airport to confirm his arrival time before they made sales calls together.

The salesperson wanting to help and maximize time asked the regional manager to change planes to a Johnstown commuter plane. The first customer they were to see was in Johnstown, maybe 30 miles from Altoona. The regional sales manager changed planes. Later in the day, he learned the plane to Altoona which he was about to board crashed and everyone was killed!

Would you recognize a phone call from God or God-inspired directions if you received them? Spiritual values are mentioned throughout in this book because they are better than gold. That regional sales manager is your author, and he is dedicated to helping you become a gold hearted person and #1 in selling.

SELL YOURSELF

All great salespeople know you must **first sell yourself!** You do this in very subtle ways, always remembering what some call the **Golden Rule**, *"Do unto others as you would have them do unto you."* I would like to emphasize that *"Do unto others the way they want done unto them"* is the key that will bring you more gold. My friend, Art Fettig, and others, call this the **PLATINUM RULE.**

My younger brother Greg is an excellent dentist and salesperson. He has become #1 in his chosen career field in Pickerington, Ohio. He installs lots of gold in his customers' mouths. It is your mouth that will bring gold to you. Your words are a reflection of your heart or your subconscious.

Dr. Greg Lisk and his staff are *friendly* professionals with their patients. Their patients know they are highly *qualified and really care.* And these *satisfied customers* then make *recommendations to others* who become patients. Referrals!

It can be as **easy** for any salesperson working to Become #1 in Selling! Your customers recognize you as an expert problem solver, who, just like the doctor, really does care. The professional salesperson is *well prepared*, knowing the product, service, ideas, and company (and himself/herself) **better** than his/her competitor knows what they sell. The #1 pro *knows* God, also.

And the pro knows the customer and why he or she may or may not buy, thereby, adjusting the presentation as needed. He also anticipates objections and brings them up before the prospect or customer does.

Since I was #1 in selling for two large companies and in my market niche with my own company, I believe, by God's grace, I can teach you how-to's for Becoming #1 in Selling.

Many great **mentors** in selling have accelerated my understanding of people and the sales and marketing process . . . mentors who are or were #1 in selling. Behavioral psychology and common sense are included, with the many how-to's. Consider HOW TO WIN BY INFLUENCING AND SERVING PEOPLE. More importantly, do your customers know you care?

People do not care how much you know until they know how much you care about them! Never criticize others!

A College Education or Ph.D. in Selling!

I like to think of this book as my dissertation paper for my Doctorate in Selling . . . DR. THOM LISK. That has a nice sound to it. However, we all know, no college or university awards a Ph.D. in the *most valuable career field*, the oldest career field, the most populated career field, **the highest paying career field,** at times, the most frustrating career field, and the most rewarding career field, SELLING.

The first bound manuscript of this book was presented to Dr. Otto H. Reese who bestowed upon me an Honorary Doctorate of

Become 🐾 **in** *Selling!*

Humane Letters Degree from his Christian college and seminary. Another book was finished at this retreat site, too. When I walked the aisle to receive the diploma, wore the purple colors over the robe, and moved the tassel from one side to the other, I thought of YOU, my reader. You need this help. What **award** can you **see yourself** receiving?

> **The greatest gift you can give another (including a customer) is to see that person as the person they can become.** When you can do that, you can not only better see yourself as the person you can become, you can become who you desire.

Greg was not born a dentist. I was not *born a professional salesperson*, speaker, business consultant, or writer. Some pastors believe their profession is the most rewarding. You must think selling is the **most beneficial.**

This book gives you a concise understanding, and an added appreciation for selling. Today, among my many accomplishments, I am very proud of my skills and accomplishments as a **master salesperson.** How about you? I want to *raise* your self-esteem and self-image. You must be glad you are a salesperson! You will *earn more gold*! You can serve and give more! Then you not only will have success, you will have a *significant life.*

Do not let anyone ever again make you feel insignificant. **You** are **important**!!!

Selling can have similar characteristics with other professions. And all **professionals** sell.

Three common denominators are:

    ☞   **Body of knowledge**

    ☞   **Language & terminology**

    ☞   **Structural procedures**

We will discuss these three further as we proceed. However, first, let me share with you a personal story. My personal stories have applications for you. My story can be similar to your story.

EUREKA!

A man took me to the San Diego airport for a flight to Seattle, Washington in a church van. I was drawn back in my memory to 1969 when I first joined The Eureka Company (Eureka means *I found it!*). Eureka is what the gold miners exclaimed when they discovered gold . . . . E U R E K A ! !

You will be saying . . . Eureka!! as you read this book and apply what is taught. Or, after attending one of our seminars, one good idea from them will more than make up for your investment. EUREKA!!. And, that is what you want your customers to say about you, your products, your services, **"I found it!!"**

That's exactly what I was saying when I first joined the company. I had two brief sales jobs after graduating from High School in June 1968 while pursuing a college education. And that is all they were to me . . . . . jobs! You need to see selling as a *career choice*. Or, if not, at least a critical part of your **career** position description. The second position for Woolco Department Stores, a division of F.W. Woolworth, saw me labor in the domestic department, selling many items, including vacuum cleaners. The lessons I learned! **Learn where you are now planted.**

This led to my meeting with Scott MacLeod, Branch **Profit** Center Manager, at Eureka. He made sales calls on Woolco. I was "lucky" to meet Scott. What is your Profit and/or Loss? *WITH THE CORRECT ATTITUDE, YOU ALWAYS PROFIT!*

My first sales job was direct in home sales for Electro Hygiene, a company similar to Electro Lux and Kirby. I have met many great sales people who **worked** their way through college, as I was, with some kind of direct in-home sales opportunity funding their education and living expenses. I was no exception. I had additional

incentive: I was married at 18, a father at 19! Some would call this a **handicap**. To me it was a **blessing**. The correct attitude!

When I began my sales career, I was like a friend described one sales person. . . like an Alaskan duck: **HUMOR:** "Whatever he didn't knock over, he messed up." Another friend depicted: "Not only didn't he know anything, he didn't even suspect anything!"

Scott offered me the position that helped me "escape" the confinement of retail sales work. I was so elated! I was willing to take a pay cut. After all, I would call on retail stores, develop **RELATIONSHIPS**, as Scott did, and work for this (now #1) manufacturer, wholesaling to the retailers. How did you begin?

My **aptitude** and attitude would help me to eventually Become #1 in Selling for this giant company. Someone also believed in me who told me, **"YOU ARE TERRIFIC!"**

And how can you Become #1 in Selling? *You can*, in any industry, selling any product, service, idea, company or yourself, if you are given the proper opportunity with a **great** product or service. You can learn how to *out sell* all others, including your **competition**. Then, you can apply your knowledge and succeed.

THANKFULNESS

All salespeople that Become #1 in Selling are **thankful**, no matter what.

I really didn't know that early on. However, due to my circumstances, anyone would have been thankful.

Little could I conceive then that I could go from earning $640 a month to $4,600 plus a month in income in 4 years with Eureka. I found it! Actually, in 1973, at age 23, I **earned $61,940.17**. YOU CAN FIND IT TOO! *What can you achieve?*

Today, these 1973 dollars would be equivalent to $200,000 per year or more. Recently, I spoke to Frank Wobst, Chairman and CEO of Huntington Banc Shares, Inc. Business First reports his **annual income at *over 1.4 million dollars*!** You can have this kind of income, too, if you BELIEVE YOU CAN.

Does this get your ATTENTION? SALES PEOPLE MUST GET AND MAINTAIN THE ATTENTION OF THOSE THEY ARE SELLING. I will use **methods** of doing that throughout this book. I am **demonstrating** some of the principles as I proceed. Do you do that? SHOW AND TELL TO SELL!!

FOCUS OR DIE

If I can do it, so can you. I have helped many others *Become #1 in Selling* so I know I can help you. You must want to Become #1 in Selling and receive **proven blueprints**.

Just recently, during a concentrated period in May through August, I served a great salesperson so he could improve further. The last month during the period I was his consultant, he had his **best month** in the 15-year history of his work in his industry. John is very *focused and disciplined.* He is #1 in his niche! He is thankful and gives credit to God. John knows that in any sales business, we must **focus or die!**

To Become #1 in Selling, he became the #1 SERVANT to a very select market segment. So can you. **It's really simple, but not easy.**

Let me assert that we have helped salespeople selling the most complex and high tech products Become #1 in Selling. So, please don't think, "I'm too good or too successful to need this book, teachings or reminders."

It's the great salespeople who are always the most open to learning how to improve!

We all need to go back to the basics periodically. Never lose sight of the basics. Focus as long as needed in the right basics until it becomes habit. Selling yourself is basic.

As this book proceeds chapter by chapter, **more sophisticated** procedures, techniques, ideas and blueprints will be presented; however, I write for you who really wants to . . .

BECOME YOUR BEST!

Become 🏃 *in* *Selling!*

   These **solutions**, this *system*, these *plans*, and ideas WORK, if you work them!

   EXCELLENCE in selling is doing all the RIGHT THINGS RIGHT! Ask yourself constantly,

        ☛   What Is Currently Going Right?

        ☞   What Is Not Quite Right?

        ☛   What Would Make It Right?

   My *MENTOR* with Eureka, Scott MacLeod, taught me at age 19 the essence of the Tom Peters' research synopsis in the books *"A Passion for Excellence"* and *"In Search for Excellence"*: ***"He who serves best profits most!"*** *(King David from the Proverbs)*

Neuro Association Conditioning

   Neuro Association Conditioning is designed to make you feel *change will be pleasurable.*

   Therefore, because people can associate the **new behavior** with a *positive benefit*, people gladly change!

   Many *companies* have a 90-day probationary period for new employees. Make certain you hire (or are) the right person. *Company owners or CEO'S, make more certain you help people understand the behaviors you desire and the rewards to them. then they will be more concerned with the rewards for the company.* My first adult mentor, Scott, did that very well.

   Making better decisions brings better results.

   Scott helped interrupt the **patterns of my lifestyle**, so I would never want to go back to my old ways! Is that what you need to Become #1 in Selling? Who do you see yourself becoming?

SERVICE CUSTOMERS BETTER

Understand the **need** to *service existing customers, better.*

Do you see clearly the areas in which you must improve or change? If not, I trust you will, by the end of this book.

My father, a great journalist and public relations executive (mom was a fabulous school teacher), first taught me how to sell at the family vegetable stand. My dad was a great guy! My story, like yours I hope, has a very **happy and prosperous** ending. Dad had a scholarship towards college journalism named in his honor. Recently, the honor is given to an outstanding graduating senior from his high school alma mater in Hilliard, Ohio.

Hal Lisk taught me how to "MAKE SURE THE CUSTOMER GETS MORE THAN HIS MONEY'S WORTH." When they wanted a pound of our CHOICE tomatoes, he would **always insist** that we weigh out more than a pound. He would check every ear of corn to *insure* that it was fresh and ripe.

WEED YOUR SALES GARDEN

At the time Dad was public relations director for the Ohio Chamber of Commerce was when I learned the most on that vegetable stand. And, oh yes, we had to help plant, harvest, weed, and clean the produce before our weekend **capitalistic** efforts. Learning how to give change to Varena Ward and our other regular customers was **fun**, and also, I got a percentage of the profits. Do you have weeds in your sales or prospect patch?

> **If you aren't having FUN at work, you are either doing it wrong, or it may not be for you!**

People came from miles around to get Lisk's Choice Tomatoes, as the road side sign read. Dad insisted on DEVELOPING A *QUALITY* PRODUCT AND DELIVERING EXCELLENT CUSTOMER SERVICE. I hope I never forget those early positive lessons. Only now, many years after his passing away, do I fully appreciate what he did for me. **Great salespeople appreciate others NOW.**

We used many **tools** to produce a bumper crop. Sales people need tools just like any other professional. Part of the tools are the words in our LANGUAGE: mentors, objections, prospecting, sales styles, closing, etc. And these days: E-Mail, INTERNET, fax on demand, customer data base. Mike McKinley, recent president of the National Speakers Association, has called them "Tools for Transforming Tomorrow."

Dad gave me a STRUCTURED PROCEDURE for hoeing the garden, tying the tomatoes to the stakes, and for merchandising the produce. **Sales people need to adhere more to structured procedures, and they need leaders who can give them the RIGHT procedures, technology, and ideas.**

Dad had a BODY OF KNOWLEDGE that I did not know or understand or appreciate when I began. So many people die with their music still in them! I pray that does not happen to you, or to me! SALES PEOPLE NEED TO ACQUIRE THE BODY OF KNOWLEDGE FROM GREAT MENTORS TO ELIMINATE TRIAL AND ERROR, AND TO BECOME WISER SALES PEOPLE.

You are terrific! In my seminars, I often ask people to affirm themselves, **"I am terrific!"** Positive thoughts and words are wonderful tools.

USE THINGS, SERVE PEOPLE!

Selling Christmas cards door to door to relatives and teachers at school as I was growing up caused me to analyze why people buy. The dialogue I developed at age 12 as a young businessman would help me begin to understand how to Become #1 in Selling! And, of course, creating the orders was only a small part of the job. Once I got their deposit, I then had to: **place** the orders; **deliver** the product when they arrived; **collect** the balance of the money; this is when I'd get my . . . you guessed it . . . PROFITS! I WAS

TAUGHT TO PUT *PEOPLE FIRST*, THEN PROFITS WOULD FOLLOW. PROFIT IS NOT A FOUR-LETTER (OR DIRTY) WORD!

PASSION

We need to examine our values and beliefs, to live with more passion. **PASSION**, I found at an early age, brings more profits. Some describe it as **enthusiasm**, however, there is a difference and a place for both. You need both in selling.

Think with me about teachers who most **impacted** your life. They had a passion for their subject. They sold an **interest**, they **created** a desire to learn, and to do homework! Each of us could probably count on one hand those who permanently impacted and **influenced** our lives for the better as young people growing up. Who have been your great teachers or managers/leaders (mentors or coaches) as an adult?

THE BIKE WRECK LESSON

Early one evening 2 boys put a bike beside the road in a ditch near a farm home, and made it to look like a kid had a terrible wreck. They shined a flashlight on the "bike wreck" so the motorist driving by would not miss it. The clothing stuffed with straw had no head! The first car screeched to a halt. The kids laughed from their vantage point in the corn field where they could not be seen.

The driver was told that something was real which really was not. MANY **FEARS ARE ILLUSIONS** that when faced and properly dealt with can UNLOCK YOUR APTITUDE AND ATTITUDE TO BECOME A BETTER PERSON SO YOU CAN BECOME #1. The kind of selling described in the prior paragraph has no place in your business life or mine. Sometimes, it is helpful to know what not to do, so doing the RIGHT things becomes more obvious and you become more motivated to . . . **just do it!**

Become **in Selling!**

. This is why great athletes watch videos of their performances to evaluate where to improve. SALES PEOPLE NEED TO EVALUATE THEIR SALES PRESENTATIONS FOR THE SAME REASONS, DON'T THEY?

PEOPLE LOOK FOR QUALITY, VALUE, EXCELLENT SERVICE, A FAIR PRICE . . . NOT ILLUSIONS!

Honesty has always been a hallmark of a person who Becomes #1 in Selling.

GREAT SALESPEOPLE ACTUALLY *EARN RESPECT* FROM THEIR CUSTOMERS BY ADMITTING WHEN THEY OR THEIR COMPANY ARE WRONG, OR WHEN THEY DON'T KNOW THE ANSWER TO THE CUSTOMER'S OR PROSPECT'S QUESTION OR PROBLEM. Especially so when they work to *find the answer* or the solution.

Scott advised me to tell the customers or prospects I called on that not only was I (obviously) new with the company, but also "at age 19, I am already married, my wife and I have a baby boy (Todd), and I hope to finish my college education at Ohio State University at night."

Key: People actually want to help people who sincerely and humbly ask properly. It became obvious that I was "GOING THE EXTRA MILE." Do your **customers want you to succeed**?

Like most large sales organizations, we had salespeople, branch managers, 13 regional managers, 4 divisional sales managers, then the KING (at least that's how he was referred to), Red Connell, Vice President of Sales & Marketing. Each branch was its own Profit Center.

Red taught me . . .

THE CUSTOMER IS KING . . . OR . . . QUEEN!

I was asked to meet with Chuck Breckheimer, regional sales manager, over dinner before I was hired. Chuck was in charge of parts of six states. He was from Fairport, New York, a suburb of Rochester, we were told. This all seemed very exciting to me.

12

Chuck had been a champion tennis player as a teenager and young man. We could discuss our various athletic accomplishments, I planned.

GREAT SALESPEOPLE KNOW HOW TO FIND POINTS OF COMMON INTEREST WHEN DEVELOPING RAPPORT WITH OTHERS. Chuck was a master at this. Over dinner, my wife and I felt as if we were being "adopted" into their corporate family. She commented that Chuck was quite a **gentleman**. If he knew how to treat a new sales person this good, I concluded that he can make the *customer feel like a king or queen.*

Could I foresee that almost exactly 4 years later, this outstanding sales leader would need to take an early retirement, and I would be asked at age 23, to replace this legend? I was asked to become the youngest regional sales manager in this now 86-year old company's history! This and some of my other #1 records still stand, I have been told.

INTEGRITY

It was obvious Chuck was a man of *integrity.* Although I didn't understand at the time how important integrity is in a sales career, I knew who had integrity and who didn't. Have you set a **goal** to be known as a man or woman of integrity? Phoning people when you know you will be late as an example, is an act of integrity. It is the right thing to do. **No excuses**, please! And how about your ethics? We must be **ethical**. Today, I observe that all *great* salespeople, leaders, managers, and company owners or corporate executives strive to know and do what is right. Some selfishly crunch others, rather than serve them to succeed. Great does not describe them.

When I married, so did my cousin Ted to one of my classmates, Mary Ellen Brown. Ted joined the Marines. I was chairman of the organizing committee for our 25th high school class reunion and was reminded of these "good old days." I married a girl named Linda from the 1967 class before us. It is interesting to **study** how lives have changed in 25 years since high school. And, although a college education is often a prerequisite for **open doors** in business, and in many sales careers, we see that those who did not graduate from college (or high school) or those who are immigrants sometimes become the most successful.

And many C students Become #1 in Selling and many rise to the **very top** in their chosen career fields. Why?

DETERMINATION

It is because they have lots of determination and do not give up. They also have faithfulness, honesty and integrity--attributes that must be at the heart of a sales career. The Marine motto . . . "Semper Fideleus," means "always faithful." You must cultivate those attributes in the same manner that you cultivate the personality and health habits that will help you live well and live long, as advised by experts.

You **learn** more through your failures than through your success. Failure is not failure at all in many cases. It is a learning experience.

It was said by one great mentor, "The successful person is willing to do what the unsuccessful person will not do!" The tragedy is the unsuccessful usually know what to do, but does not do it or enough of it. They need **motivation**!

This book, *"Become #1 in Selling!"* gives you **blueprints** for success not only in selling but also in life. You must use them as your guide.

BLUEPRINTS FOR BUILDING YOUR BUSINESS

This is the name of our complete sales system which we customize for individuals, companies, and industries today.

Scott MacLeod, Chuck Breckheimer and Walt Maerke could not make the sales for me at Eureka. I had to accept their counsel, direction, experience and ideas, become *disciplined* in my daily planning and actions, and build positive relationships while accepting their proven blueprints for my business. You must do this, too.

FIND OUT WHAT THEY WANT. . . AND WHY THEY WANT IT!

Have you heard the saying, "Talk is cheap?" Actually talk is not cheap. Our talk will make or break us as salespeople! Or anyone, even those who **think** they are not selling. Words shape the future!

What is more important than talk to a master salesperson? And what kind of talk or words are best? And how must we structure our sentences and our presentations?

I will answer all these and other questions and as we proceed.

Now, however, I'd like to **assert** that I was taught as a young salesperson that LISTENING is more important than speaking. Later I will give you specific rules for better listening and speaking, so you can *Become #1 in Selling*.

Think of the art of selling like the profession of a great physician.

A doctor *does not* manipulate us to accept his diagnosis and take his prescription. The physician asks all the right questions as he or she **examines** the patient before offering the prescription for the illness. My beautiful and very intelligent second wife (and last, I pray!) Lorna, has helped me to understand this further. She was the young widow of a doctor. (Two of her oldest sons, my stepsons, recently graduated from medical school, and her third son is in medical school.)

You can become a sales doctor offering your products or services as **your prescriptions**. Remeber the foregoing as you find out what customers want and why they want it.

BUILDING TRUST

Remember when you were courting your wife (or husband)? Or when you went on a first date?

Become 🐛 **in** *Selling!*

Before the first good night kiss, there was a lot of dialogue back and forth. She asked the young man a lot of questions verbally, and some only with her eyes and heart before giving that first kiss. Why?

"I can **trust** you, can't I?" women say non-verbally, don't they? (tie down questions). Customers are saying the same thing. To gain trust, you must be trustworthy. This is of prime importance to cultivate in your personal life. Then it will be carried over into your business life.

I don't know about you, but reading the opposite sex properly helped me to fine tune certain sales approaches so I could *Become #1 in Selling* early in life.

Those of you who are parents can relate to this, too. My daughter, Erin, who is 22 has BUYER'S RESISTANCE because she has had a steady boyfriend whom she trusts for over three years. She is very *focused and knows what she wants*, characteristics for success. During her first year at Otterbein College, she was on the dean's list. Today she is in the school of Allied Medicine at Ohio State University. If I were the dean of your sales college, I will reward you for learning this material. Please study this book as if you were taking a college **prerequisite**. Answer all questions correctly at the end of each chapter and you *will succeed* more. I trust you to do so.

I was always one of the best athletes in school. Academically, I had excelled in grade school (straight A's), and later, when I wanted to, and when I did not have other priorities, pressures and interests. Salespeople can be distracted or, maybe, the reward is not a **sufficient** motivator any longer. Managers must be willing to **change** to keep people motivated and continually build trust.

COKE BOTTLE TOMMY

My nickname in first grade was "4 eyes," or "Coke Bottle Tommy." These names were given to me by the other kids. Does **peer pressure** *shape you to become your best* or to conform you to the crowd? I didn't become Thom until age 14 to 15, short for Thomas. *Humor:* I did not like too much the "as" at the end of my name. I wore thick glasses starting at age 4, as I was, and, of course, still am very far-sighted. Have you had or still have liabilities? Handicaps?

HANDICAPS ARE STEPPING STONES

Mom told me to identify with Tom Terrific who was a cartoon character on the Captain Kangaroo show. She told me constantly from a very young age, "Tom, YOU ARE TERRIFIC! You can do anything that those other kids can do, if not better!" Mothers never lie, do they? Sales managers, affirm your salespeople.

BELIEVE IN YOURSELF!

To *Become #1 in Selling* you **must believe in yourself.** And it really helps to have others believe in us, doesn't it? Every great person experiences numerous set backs, but what is the difference? P E R S E V E R A N C E!

I think about a man I know in San Diego whose company I have served recently as a business management consultant. I helped him Become #1 in his product market niche, however, his **partner** did so much more.

This guy has a wife (no children) who knows how to build him up. She **helps him** believe in himself after he deals with *rejection, criticism, discouragement, and disappointment all day long.* Regardless of age, we all need a great *encourager*!

Over the past twenty years, I have observed this is often the case with men who *Become #1 in Selling!*

And, YES, "All the world is selling!" (Robert Louis Stevenson)

How about women? For women to Become #1 in Selling, if married, they must also have a very understanding and supportive partner. *Set a goal to be your best for others*, and trust people are and will be their best for you.

Become 🐻 **in** *Selling!*

VALUE ADDED SERVICES

Scott MacLeod, Branch Manager at Eureka, asked me to drive a Dodge van, and to meet him at the warehouse office every morning at 7 to 7:30 a.m. to load it. I didn't resist for long. He helped me with a more focused and disciplined itinerary. What a great mentor!

He proved to me that if I took care of our dealers, our customers, "they would take care of me!"

"Set up each dealer on a minimum/maximum inventory control program. With each sales call, take an inventory and bring them back up to the **maximum** level in each product they stock, one to show and X to go (in their backroom)."

The Dodge van gave me a *distinct advantage over the competition.* I challenge you to look for and/or develop unique personal, outstanding company product and/or service ideas and advantages to beat your competition.

If a dealer only needed 3 or 4 items, I could go to the van and deliver the items on the spot! This may not seem like a **unique idea** to you today, but in late 1969, it was **revolutionary** in this type business. My research indicates unique *value added services* propel any business to attract and retain customers.

I was trained to invest 75% of my time serving, selling, and training existing dealers and 25% attempting to set up new dealers. **Acquire new customers!**

The first few months I was doing quite poorly until they wisely gave me the Dodge van to drive.

I still was unsure of my future when I attended a Divisional Sales Meeting in Cincinnati, Ohio, "The Queen City."

TURNING POINT...THE RED STORY

This would prove to be a major turning point in my young sales career. If you have been selling for long, you will be able to **identify** with this, or if you cannot, I hope a Red Connell comes into your life. We all have many key turning points or crossroads in our careers. If you are a veteran, use this book to help your salespeople grow.

"Red" Connell was the "top dog" of the then 300-person-sales organization. His superior **reputation** proceeded him, just as your reputation can help you in the market place.

I met Red at a Cincinnati convention center, not far from where now sits Riverfront Stadium, home to the Reds and Bengals.

At a cocktail party after business meetings, I approached Mr. Connell, and introduced myself for the first time. I said, "Mr. Connell, I'd like to **introduce** myself. I am Thom Lisk" . . . like he was supposed to be impressed with me! And, of course, he was not! (In my live seminars, we sometimes teach people how to introduce themselves properly through a role play exercise. Can you improve your introduction?)

He said, "Hello, son." I thought "why is he calling me son?" I almost tuned him out at that point, but I luckily decided to proceed.

"Mr. Connell," I said, "can we sit down and visit for a few minutes? I need to ask you a few questions?" I figured he was the **"sales doctor"** with the most answers and if I wanted to succeed (and I did), he is the best person to ask.

He said, "Sure, son, sit down here with me."

NON-VERBALS FOR SUCCESS

I *lowered my voice, leaned forward, smiled, started nodding my head* in the affirmative, and *looked him in the eye*, (five good key non-verbals) as I said,

"I'm only 20 years old, I have a wife and a young son. I plan to finish my college education, but I think, **most importantly**, I need to learn how to be more of a success in selling and business from a leader like you. I just joined the company September 1, and I'm not doing too well yet. I have been inspired by what you have said today and the new product line. I am thankful for the **opportunity** I have, but I know I need a lot of help. Will you help me?" (You *must* be willing to ask for help!)

He lowered his voice, leaned forward, smiled, nodded his head, and looked me in the eye. He mirrored my behavior! (Or, was it the other way around?)

"Of course," he said, "how can I help?"

I went on, "Sir, I am very ambitious, maybe too much at times. (ADMIT TO A WEAKNESS ONLY TO TRUE FRIENDS) I want to *Become #1 in Selling* with Eureka. And quite frankly, I asserted, "I want your job some day!"

I later learned that statement is a good test to see if someone will commit to be your mentor. See how they respond to that statement. A great mentor will *not feel threatened.*

Red was 61 and I had just turned 20. He could have been my grandfather! People really want to help you Become #1 in Selling, if asked correctly. And, *if their position and economic security are not threatened. Help others understand why you want what you want. Help them to see how *helping you make the sale, or reach your goal will help them* get what they want.

Red laughed, his red ruddy complexion lit up. He said, "Son, what makes you think you can get my job someday?"

I exclaimed, "Sir, I am willing to do whatever it takes to get there, please help me." GOOD ATTITUDE!

Some of the most **valuable success principles** you will learn in this book are that we must be willing to:

✓ **FIND** help . . .
✓ **ASK** for help . . .
✓ **ACCEPT** help . . . and most importantly,
✓ **GIVE** help . . .

Who can you find help from today? _____
How will you ask for help? _____
Are you **ready** to accept help? _____
Who can you give help to? _____

Some people are really hard to help. That's OK. There are always others who will **respond**.

Here is what this wise *seasoned* executive (who had been a sales leader among leaders for many years, even before he led Eureka to *prominence*) said, "Son (this was a term of *endearment* to him), there are two *master keys to success.* They are:

1. *Develop a thirst for knowledge*, the right kind of knowledge.
2. *Have a great opportunity.* **Then persevere.**"

I soaked this in for a minute, then said, "Sir, can you please elaborate?"

He brought further illumination by saying "Thom, FIRST, set aside as many hours as possible each day learning all you can about how to be a success. It's not what some people really think.

Read the psychology, self-help and success books, the Horatio Alger stories for inspiration, attend seminars led by the leading experts, learn from the best, buy the new-fangled tape cassettes, and listen to them in your auto. Turn wasted time into time to learn and to improve.

BECOME A LIFER

Become as they say in the military 'a lifer'. Give your life to learning about success. As you learn, you will naturally want to **apply what you learn** and eventually it will *pay off.*"

He also remarked, "YOU CAN BECOME A GREAT ONE IN SELLING."

"Thanks, Mr. Connell!" I said gratefully, "and what about #2, the great opportunity?"

"You are fortunate, Thom. Not only do you already exhibit some of the right attitudes at age 20, a willingness to WORK HARD, but you also seem to have some of the other characteristics needed for success. Your Branch Sales Manager Scott is the only person in the (now 85-year) history of this great company to have Become #1 in Selling two years in a row!"

"Scott's Columbus, Ohio Branch has been #1 twice, in spite of high quotas, stiff competition, etc."

"No wonder Scott had his first heart attack just before I joined his sales team at age 50," I thought. I had to *get rid of some* **negative thinking**.

"Thom," Red caringly said, "If Scott can do it, so can you Become #1 in Selling."

That's really all I needed to hear. Red believed I could do it! So I believed I could! YOU MUST BELIEVE!

He went on to say,

(A) *Humble yourself. FIND* (Scott's) help.

(B) *ASK* for help with every need, problem, prospect or account. Your boss can't be with you on each sales call, but, begin calling him at night (with his permission) with unanswered questions or concerns when you meet with him, do what he tells you, or how he tells you to do it. He does not have the answer to every "WHY" question.

(C) *ACCEPT* his help. Be willing to change if you need to, I've gotten all that money could buy, I suppose, but I learn **something new each day**, and so must you.

(D) Do what Scott tells you. **Do more of it than anyone else.** I guarantee you, because **you have been willing to allow a great mentor to help you,** you, too, can and will *Become #1 in Selling."*

"In other words," Red said, "*GIVE* away the help he gives you. *Make more of the right sales calls on more of the right people. Say more of the right things.* I am now giving away this help in this book by handing you blueprints on Becoming #1 in Selling."

25 YEARS OF RESEARCH FOR YOU

I began to take this advice. The balance of this book progressively will share with you what I have learned in more than 25 years from my personal sales career and from some of America's #1 salespeople. My **research** is *every bit as complete* as any Ph.D. in any field. In 1970 I more than doubled my income, thanks to mentors, and I learned a lot about how to Become #1 in Selling! That same year Eureka was rated for the first time #1 in Consumer Report. We *must also have a good product to sell.* In those days, Eureka was always the underdog to Hoover. Know the feeling?

UNDERDOGS CAN BECOME TOP DOGS!

In 18 months, I was 3rd in America (at age 21) in this international sales organization; thanks to my marvelous mentor, who gave me the how-to's, a great product line, some wonderful customers, **hard work** and **positive expectant serving attitudes. Two years later, my sales branch was #1 in the U.S.A.**

I traded the Dodge van for a new Ford van. This began to change my self-image and the **image portrayed in the market** place. You do need to be careful to portray a positive **professional** image. I was again becoming Thom Terrific. I was popular with all my customers. My wife was proud of me. My two-year-old son Todd had what he needed. Get motivated!

MOTIVATION! I was enthused and it showed. I loved my work and I gave it 100%. When you can **love your job** and **your associates,** *you can love your customers and succeed.*

HUMOR: In selling we must never feel we have arrived. One sales person had "LEGEND" on his Cross pen. He is a legend in his own mind! You *can give* legendary service, too.

Become 🏃 *in Selling!*

SUCCESS IS A JOURNEY NOT A DESTINATION!

A doctor is always learning and getting better. So do great salespeople.

Those interested in the status quo will not take me so seriously. These average people can keep you from becoming all God has **designed** and willed you to become. *He designed you for greatness!* The negative nells and neds of life would have you believe otherwise.

Life is a process, a journey, not a destination, and so is selling. We **dare not rest** on our laurels or the past.

The title of this book is not *Became* #1 in Selling! You'll learn that I did Become #1 in Selling, but I want to do it again, again, and again. And so must you!

Selling is fun, selling is challenging. Selling is WORK! Selling is putting others first always.

Selling is a great career!

Let us learn how to be our best through selling and prosper.

Love to sell! Love to serve! **Live to give!**

Make a lifelong study of selling. You will come to understand others and yourself. With enough courage, perseverance, ethics, integrity, and improvement you can *Become #1 in Selling!*

YOU CAN BECOME THE PERSON YOU WANT TO BE!

You have **gold within you**! You can choose to get *a better how-to input* so you can get a better output. Not only that, you can be **conditioned for more success**. I offer that to you, too. You can soar like an eagle over every challenge of life.

Mining For Gold!

The title of Roger Dawson's book says it: *"YOU CAN GET ANYTHING YOU WANT (BUT YOU HAVE TO DO MORE THAN ASK)."*

If you purchase a used computer and you might have to **deprogram** the hard drive before you can use it. That's *the reason* why this book is written as it is. I am hoping that as I *reflect* on my career, you will, too! You, thereby, will **determine** where you went wrong, and deprogram these negatives from **your subconscious minds**. Program new outcomes, better outcomes, with a *more motivated focused behavior*. We can offer programmed learning exercises in our seminars that guarantee assimilation and application.

My psychologist friends tell me "95% of what we do or say is controlled by our subconscious minds (that vast storehouse)." I intend to **deposit more gold** into you, with God's help, so you can glow, make better decisions and have more gold.

You want to give your best, too. Please help me to help you! That is what many people are thinking subconsciously when you meet with them, "Can he (or she) help?"

Remember, our minds are like **parachutes**, they must be **open** before we can learn, grow and improve.

Commit to never letting your gold mine go bust! This book is designed to feed your mind.

GOLD! To keep producing gold in your sales career, you need on-going input. WHAT WILL YOUR CUSTOMERS NEED AND WHY WILL THEY NEED IT? You need to know. The **foundation** of selling success is to know your customer. The **foundation** of personal success in selling is to know God and yourself so you can improve properly. I plan to answer these and more of *your* needs and questions as we proceed.

Become 🐻 *in **Selling!***

REVIEW & APPLICATION

Dear Reader:

At the **end of each chapter**, I suggest you detail the most important things you have learned and what you will do about it. Set some **goals**. Also, on the following page are a few review questions. These can be answered by you, or **in a group** setting, if you are using this book as a study guide. *Sales managers or company owners* could have **sales meetings** using a chapter each week. Purchase 12 books if you have 12 salespeople. Simply have all read the chapters in advance of the meeting then discuss how the principles apply in your situation. Then set goals for implementation. Encourage each other! You *will* get **better results.** Guaranteed! Write us with questions or testimonials of your success, please.

In friendship and for your success,

Thomas (Thom) A. Lisk, LHD

CHAPTER ONE

REVIEW QUESTIONS

1. Why is listening very important for your success in selling?

2. What are four things salespeople sell?

3. Can you sell these better?

4. Why is *thankfulness* a prerequisite for success in selling?

5. Can you conceive of yourself doubling, tripling or quadrupling your sales and income? If not, why not?

6. How can you interrupt the pattern or routine of your life so you can get better results?

7. How can you appreciate your customers, clients or patients better now?

8. Why must we always be honest?

9. What other characteristics or attributes are at the heart of a sales (or any other) career?

10. What distinct advantages can you develop over your competition? Or, do you now have them that you can emphasize more?

11. Did you fill in the blanks in the chapter? If not, please go back and do so now. And do so in future chapters.

12. What are the four HELPS? And what can you apply *now* from this chapter to sell more?

Become *in Selling!*

NOTES/IDEAS

Writing helps to crystalize thoughts. You do not know it unless you can write it down.

CHAPTER 2

Another Mentor Is Born!

WIN WITH THE RIGHT PEOPLE!

The Ohio State Buckeyes ended the season rated #1 in the College Football poll the year I graduated from school. Some of you will remember that 1968 season. Woody Hayes, author of "*3 Yards and a Cloud of Dust*," and the book "*Win with People*" was the Ohio State coach.

You have heard about my friend, Archie Griffin (he's everyone's friend in Columbus, Ohio). He is the only 2 time Heisman Trophy winner! Just like Scott MacLeod, he did it twice! Me, too. (You, too?!) What is the "secret?"

I'll never forget the OSU-Purdue game in the fall of 1968. I was sitting on the first row in the bleachers just outside the end zone. How could I predict a touchdown in the pivotal game of the season would be scored by bruising Jack Tatum right in front of me on an interception? Purdue *had been* rated #1. A great victory!

What excitement!! What a thrill! To be in the middle of the celebration and to touch the players who won the championship! To be a part of it all!! To chant . . . **"We are #1. We are #1!!"**

Any sports fan can identify with the thrill when his (or her) team wins the championship game. There's nothing like it, is there?

The same is true for those who Become #1 in Selling! Some act like they're a middle linebacker during their pursuit. Don't dare get in their way! Focus and eliminate distractions!

Do you have that kind of fervor? Not now? Not yet? You will by the time you have finished this book. But, "Thom!" you say, "Is this kind of dedication really necessary? I'm not sure I'm willing to pay the price!"

Become in *Selling!*

Zig Ziglar says: "YOU must ENJOY the price paid for success." Then you can go **"Beyond Success to Significance"** to quote the title of my keynote speech.

CHAMPIONSHIPS ARE BUILT ON COMMITMENT

In this chapter, I will deal further with the significance of a great mentor or coach in one's life, and I hope to birth in you the desire to be a great mentor. Find a terrific mentor first!

Also, in 1968, Mark Spitz won his first Olympic Gold Medal. Mark is my age. What did Mark teach me...what can Mark teach YOU about how to Become #1 in Selling! . . . ?

Mark got a taste of gold in 1968. However, it wasn't until 1972 when he won 7 gold medals and set 7 world records that he became a household word. He made a comeback in 1992 for the Olympic team, 20 years later. He still competes! His self-esteem improves due to daily victories, and so can yours.

Sometimes we must get back in the swim again, just like Mark, to prove to ourselves that we are **champions!** It is never too late to Become #1. What motivates YOU?

Mark probably doesn't need the money. Or, the fame. He thrives on the challenge. The recognition. The sense of accomplishment. It improves his self-image and self-esteem.

You, my friend, can Become #1 in Selling through: a daily plan of building your self-esteem, great attitudes, better actions, and the right choice of words. YOU ARE THE RIGHT PERSON. YOU CAN BECOME MUCH MORE. GOD BELIEVES IN YOU... AND SO DO I.

Did you see the movie RUDY? The boy who fulfills his dream by playing football for Notre Dame, overcomes every odd against him, and finally plays one play at the end of the season. In the process, however, he wins a college degree, and esteem, not only personally, but also the esteem of his family, community, and teammates. His team became #1, he never did, other than in practice. However, his contribution was critically important! His teammates made him #1 in their hearts.

RULES

Most great athletes had or have great coaches. Some few go on to become great coaches themselves. Those that do can follow the rules. They were great followers, so they became great leaders!

This is seldom true in the world of selling. Few #1 salespeople have the patience and empathy to teach others how-to. Or, maybe those who aspire to learn from the #1 saleperson can't stand the hectic pace. Or, they have a difficult time with the needed sacrifices, or cannot follow the rules to become #1. There is no short cut! And, in the late 90's, some of the rules are changing.

National Cash Register did a study years ago. They hired clinical psychologists paying the team over $100,000 to study their top Branch Sales Mangers. They thought . . . "If we can only package what and how these guys do what they do, then transfer it to all others . . . or hire people in their profile . . . then . . . WOW look at what we could accomplish."

N.C.R. was the epitome of professional selling, as one of my mentors would prove to me! What did these "shrinks" find?

The synopsis of their study or research? The conclusion . . .

The superstars did what they were told and didn't question it! They did *more of the right things each day*, and as a result, they became #1. Some earned $99,999.99 in the 50's! They wouldn't let them earn $100,000 because that is what the President of the company earned. However, they earned more than middle management.

Many of the players under Woody Hayes in 1968 were playing pro ball in 1971-1973. I will share some sales lessons I learned during those years that still apply and can help you Become #1 in Selling in the 90's. You can be more professional.

YOU WANT MORE MONEY?

Is that what you want? More money? Why do you want it? If you had an extra $10,000, and you had it right now, all stacked up in neat stacks of $5 or $10 bills on a table in front of you, what would you do with it?

What do you see? A new home? A boat? A new car? A family vacation? A college education for your children? A secure financial future or retirement? Extra money for the special church fund? A sabbatical? Or, do you want or need goals first like: integrity, faithfulness, a sense of accomplishment, family harmony, respect, discipline, focus, empowerment.

What do you smell. . .taste. . .touch. . .hear. . .**see?**

WALT DISNEY ON SUCCESS

Four keys and "C's" to success given by a great dreamer, Walt Disney, were. . . .

1) CURIOSITY
2) CONFIDENCE
3) COURAGE
4) CONSTANCY

Curiosity does not kill you, like it did the cat! Confidence is a choice. Do you believe in your intellect and wisdom, your instincts, and your intuition? Courage to make a decision and take action. Constancy to stay focused on your goals, especially your long-range vision. Don't go from one job or career opportunity to another. Constantly build upon your base. Thank God for opportunities to learn from great salespeople and mentors like Walt Disney.

FAILURE AND SUCCESS

Recently, I drove along the coast of Southern California. What a beautiful sight! Some waves fail to produce much surf. And the surf must go out before it can come in.

You must send out some seeds if you are to reap a harvest. However, many seeds never germinate. Why?

When I was first promoted with Eureka, I never imagined that I'd experience so many good things in this life. And so many "failures" or learning experiences, too.

God has been very good to me . . . and so has selling! The best **selling power** comes from God.

I am thankful! Thus, one primary motivation for writing this book to you. I write this almost like a letter with many special emphasis because I want you to know I care. How else can I motivate you to learn, listen, and apply? Do your customers, clients or patients know you really care? I also must be an example of excellence for you, just as you increasingly need to be for others.

I was driven to Youngstown, Ohio, at age 21, by Walt Maerke (not Walt Disney) in his long shiny new white Cadillac. He took me 3-1/2 hours away from Columbus to explain the sales and management opportunity that could be mine. I was beginning to understand that Walt was not only a fierce competitor, but also a great strategist.

He explained that the prior person had lived in Akron. He had failed to make many in roads in the 8 counties I would acquire as the new Branch Sales Manager. One's failure became my open door to success. I persisted in planting positive seeds and nurturing these seeds so they would grow into prosperous new accounts.

STRATEGY

Legendary coaches like Woody Hayes and Bear Bryant were strategists like Walt Maerke, Divisional Sales Manager (1/4 of USA) . . . I could understand this mentality!

Become 🧍 in Selling!

 You see, I had cut my teeth, so to speak, following every detail of the career of the New York Yankees, and specifically Mickey Mantle. He *had* a strategy.

Mickey was a great sails man. He could sail the ball out of the ballpark faster than almost anyone, ever. Mickey's strategy grew out of what he learned from his father and grandfather. His dad made him hit 100 balls right handed every night and his granddad 100 balls left handed, so he would develop the reflexes and all else needed to become a super star!

I remember a game in 5th grade where I pitched a no hitter and hit three home runs, and I thought for sure I would be in Yankee Stadium someday in center field. That is where Mickey played! And Lou Gehrig. And Babe Ruth! *It was only a dream, not a goal.*

In selling to Become #1, one must be willing to strike out a lot if one is to sell a lot, especially when you first begin. Later, when you learn more, your **closing ratios** will improve, or you will make more presentations to more of the right people.

At age 21, I didn't know everything some of my readers now know, but I knew I wanted to: Become #1 in Selling! How badly do you want it? Enough to *change*?

The "great opportunity" came when Walt proposed that we move to Youngstown, Ohio, to begin a new Branch Profit Center. I was to become Branch Sales Manager, and the only salesperson, at least initially.

Walt explained it this way. . . "Red (sales **tactic** appeals to a higher authority) is not pleased with the numbers the other man has been delivering as the Akron, Ohio, Branch Manager in this area. He has too much territory. So, here is our strategy: we have decided to take eight counties from him . . . 4 in North East Ohio, and 4 in North West Pennsylvania." Sounds familiar to some of you?

I really thought that this made sense. Mr. Bryson could concentrate on a smaller area so he could produce more sales, see more people each day, travel less, and have less overall pressure.

Walt exclaimed . . . "Yes, Thom, this new Branch will be quite a challenge. There really are only a few accounts, however, there is a great opportunity, **great potential!**

The area already has a couple of Bellcow or Tiffany type (big volume potential) accounts who do little with us because no one *cultivates* them, like you have your accounts in Central Ohio the last 2 years. "Thom," he built me up. . . "You've done a helluva job the past 1-1/2 years, and you are third in the USA right now. You are very young (21); Red has had his eye on you, and likes your numbers. WE want to promote you, Thom, to the **big leagues!** Are you ready? We will need you to move to Youngstown right away!"

A BAD TERRITORY?

I thought my wife was going to scream! Youngstown, Ohio is not the end of the world but, as someone once kidded, you can see the end of the world from Youngstown.

That's when Walt really began to sell! He knew my wife liked the nice things this life has to offer (don't we all). She had gotten a taste of the "good life" when we dined as guests of Scott & Ginny MacLeod, so she was susceptible to Walt's ideas.

"Lynda, Thom will have to work hard for a time, but once he gets it rolling you'll be able to afford a nice home and take care of Todd much better. You do want what's best for Thom, don't you?" "And besides," Walt enthusiastically sold, "Thom will be eligible for those beautiful trips, if he makes 100% of quota, trips like you've seen Scott & Ginny enjoy."

Talk about MOTIVATION! We had heard the stories and seen the *pictures* of the cruises and exotic trips that the **"winners"** had received.

Red Connell knew how to motivate salespeople. It's well documented. What **extra incentive** do you need?

Eureka grew 452% while the industry grew only 210%. Eureka made up almost all the industry growth during a ten-year period, and I would experience the very best of this growth with sales increases totaling over 1000%. Was I lucky? Was I just in the right place at the right time? You could say that. Check out Dennis Waitly's research in Nightingale Conants cassette tape program entitled *"The Psychology of Human Motivation"* for an explanation.

Call it God's providence and grace, which also can be cultivated. Have you read Max Gunther's well researched book, *"The Luck Factor"?*

Product positioning, advertising, sales promotion, public relations, marketing strategies, new account acquisition, major account development, merchandising, marketing research, product pricing, channels of distribution . . . some austere college classroom? I was learning on the firing line, and I was learning from America's best salespeople. What **fun** this was!

Actually, it came so easy, even though I worked very long hours, that I later would wonder how could anyone not become a success in America.

AMERICA! THE LAND OF OPPORTUNITY!

When we are young, we can take too much for granted. I sometimes wish I could go back and relive . . . savior those innocent first years in professional selling and business. ENJOY THE PROCESS! LEARN THE NEEDED LESSONS EARLY.

Why do immigrants often out perform native born Americans?

In recent years, I've had to relearn that no matter how sophisticated or **high tech** the product or industry, the basic principles herein still apply! And a periodic review is necessary! If this is true of me, I know it is true for thousands if not millions of others!

We are never too old to visit basic training. Some of this book would be considered ADVANCED TRAINING. Having known many millionaire company owners of America's best companies, I plan that they will want this book for all their managers and salespeople. POSITIONING!

As I progress, you will learn more subtle and elaborate principles and techniques, however, we must be certain, in a book like this, that we touch each essential step across the river rapids to become our best. YOU CAN WIN A CHAMPIONSHIP!

STEPPING STONES

Picture on each stepping stone a mentor to greet you as you firmly plant your feet. And, once planted, you are in a position to help another sojourner across sometimes troubled waters. Great mentors empower you to make your customers #1 with you.

Sculpting a sales career into a masterpiece takes time. A great work of art is beautiful to behold. Seldom, the painstaking years the artist invested to become skilled and able to produce a priceless piece of treasure, are considered. EACH WORD BECOMES A STEPPING STONE TO THE MASTER PIECE AND SUCCESS.

My sales mentors helped me to realize my life is valuable. . .a potential piece of art. . .a treasure that can go to the highest bidder.

There is no more secure a profession than that of selling. Yet no more volatile, full of problems to solve, changes to make.

HUMOR: Great salespeople, when faced with a recession in their industry, proclaim . . . "I have decided not to participate!" Each difficulty is a stepping stone to the promised land.

MOVING

My young family moved into a beautiful townhouse just south of the largest shopping mall in my eight counties. Never mind that I had 12 counties, based in Columbus. . .this now was mine! I was in charge! Who is the most important *person* to be in charge of first?

Most salespeople will find that they will one day need to move from one company to another, or maybe one city to another. These can be expanding growth experiences.

Become 🌸🤸 *in Selling!*

. It would be years before I would learn from Prentice Hall that **"90% of all the buying decisions,"** according to a survey of several thousand salespeople, "are emotional/psychological" not rational, or logical. That often includes the decision to move or not to move.

It's not what people want, but why they want it that motivates them to action.

☞ **What do you want?** ☜

☞ **Why do you want it?** ☜

Scott MacLeod taught me the importance of GOAL SETTING, lessons that I would need in my new assignment! These lessons apply to any person in any job anywhere. **Success principles** are universal. Pursuing excellence is a lifestyle, and is reflected in every decision.

Shortly, after the January meeting with Red Connell, Scott taught me his 4 PRINCIPLES FOR SUCCESS. They simply were, and are:

ALWAYS BE. . .

        1. SELF-CONFIDENT
        2. SELF-MOTIVATED (and self-disciplined)
        3. A POSITIVE PERSON
        4. GOAL DIRECTED

Always is a long time!

With "self" he never meant become self-centered. Scott was focused on *serving others*. . .better. Almost to a fault! At the point of your greatest strength, I have come to understand, is where you can be the weakest, or the most vulnerable. This is true of your customer, too.

Have you learned that all motivation comes from WITHIN? The definition of motivation is "that WITHIN the individual that INCITES or IMPELS to action."

I reviewed the list of my paid professional speeches, submitted in 1983 to the National Speakers Association (NSA) for their Certified Speaking Professional (CSP) Award, with a 22 year old recent college graduate. "What motivates you to pursue excellence...to pursue Becoming #1?" she asked.

WHY DO YOU DO IT?!

Some go for it to prove it to themselves. . . "I can do it!" Some go for it to prove it to others. . . "They told me I'd never do it!" Others go for it for the tangible rewards they can enjoy and acquire. Still others go for it because they cannot settle for 2nd place. Their upbringing/training insists on their attention to every detail in the pursuit of their best. My daughter once gave me a plaque that says "#1 DAD!" What parent can settle for 2nd place? SELF-ESTEEM!

All the principles for becoming #1 in all areas of life, God's way, as we sort through the various options of life can be found in the best selling book, the Holy Bible. A few, including this author, look at becoming #1 or their career as their "calling" and, therefore, they must do their best to please God and to be at peace.

SELF-CONFIDENT

We salespeople must deal with rejection day in and day out... and like it! Learn how to **reject rejection and learn from it.**

Confidence comes from knowing what to do and how to do it! What to say, and how to say it! The best confidence comes when we know the answers to the why questions.

I will teach you those things in this book. Be patient. Be a. . .

POSITIVE PERSON

From our new home in Youngstown, Ohio, I was positive I would succeed. I was *expectant.* I knew I could succeed because I had before. I knew what Scott had taught me to do with the Central Ohio customers would work elsewhere. See your point?

I was actually surprised that so few had had much contact from the company. Brand X (Hoover) had saturated the market! The resistance was high. I actually know salespeople who refuse to verbalize their competitors' name!

I was *trained to overcome every objection.* Even though Hoovers corporate headquarters and factory were only 90 minutes away in North Canton, Ohio, that did not matter.

I was taught how to present the features and buyer benefits of our wonderful products. Buying HABITS can be changed. . .like all other habits, if. . .you have enough persistence. *YOU GOTTA HAVE THE WANTO!* (The title of one of my speeches)

Many prospects had been selling only Brand X products (Hoover) for 10-20 years, or more, and never considered stocking and displaying one Eureka, until. . . . .

I appeared in my Ford Econoline Van.

The day I went to pick Chuck Breckheimer up at his hotel was the first day I would make sales calls in counties in north western Pennsylvania. When I knocked on his hotel door, all he could do was stare with his mouth hanging open. I wore a wide lapel, bright blue suit. . .my best one! (Actually one of my few.)

He said, "Thom, you can't make sales calls on the conservative people in Pennsylvania dressed like that! You go back to your new apartment and change into your most conservative suit or sports coat." This is part of knowing your customers.

Years later I would read Malloy's book (and research) entitled *"DRESS FOR SUCCESS"* and again be grateful for some of these early lessons by the masters.

I spoke to a large group at a major university on *"Keys to Selling Yourself."* Just before me, an insurance executive (male) and a sophisticated human resources executive (female) would give their views on how to dress for a successful interview. I thought, "where were they when I needed them way back when?"

Today **(age of specialization)**, many of us have personal tailors or favorite salespeople at certain shops or boutiques who Become #1 in Selling! They build a clientele who look to them for their advice on how to "Dress for Success."

How does one keep a positive expectant attitude in spite of all the twists and turns in ones sales career? Have a thankful, grateful mentality, and express it! Always!

I worked very long hours to build an account base from our new Branch Profit Center. The first month, Youngstown was dead last in sales versus quota out of nearly 100 Branch operations. That was a slap of reality! I actually took a significant cut in pay to accept this "wonderful opportunity".

I then remembered what Scott taught me about. . .

GOAL SETTING

After my "chat" with the "old man" (Red Connell), I had a heart to heart, almost father to son chat with "Dr." (of Sales Methodology) Scott MacLeod. He asked me. . . "Thom, what is your goal for this year?" "Goal!" I remarked, "you refer to that sales quota of $120,000?"

INCOME OBJECTIVES MOTIVATE

I said, "I can't live on that!" "Well," he went on. . . "I will help you, if you will listen, will you?" WILL YOU!? PLEASE!

If you were as broke as I was, you would have listened, too! Maybe you are broke now. . .or might be someday. Or, just maybe you understand all these principles so well that you do them unconsciously each minute of each day.

A good reminder never hurt, did it?

Many things motivate the salesperson, both positive and negative. One of the things, and often not at the top of the list, is money. And, it is not the money that really motivates, it is the *goal of how to invest or spend the money*. And, the Victory!

Become in Selling!

Of the various levels of competency, it is the unconscious competent that accomplishes the most. . .they make it look easy to Become #1 in Selling! Just like a great surgeon who understands the objections the body can give when he begins his "performance".

Scott did some simple math. . . "Thom, with 12 months in the year you need only do $10,000 a month, or about $500 in sales a workday." That looked like a big mountain considering the same territory selling very much the same products had only produced $55,000 in sales the prior year.

They wanted more than a 100% increase in sales, and the boss thought that would be easy! Been there?

400% INCREASE IN SALES

He had set (and together we continued to) so many sales records that I'd be worse than a fool to not listen.

I have a step son, Marvin, who graduated **Summa Cum Laude** from Xavier University, and graduated recently from medical school at Ohio State University. He knows he needs to specialize and choose practicing physicians as mentors who are where he wants to be to accelerate his success, or who have knowledge, wisdom and understanding from which he can learn.

Some salespeople are only legends in their own minds. Scott really was a (humble) giant. Even in retirement he still **placed the customer #1**. The master key Scott really taught me?. . .OTHERS MUST BE #1! This attitude was more caught then taught.

I didn't have to wait until Tom Peters wrote his book about "excellence" to learn how-to. I worked directly with the epitome of the "swim with the sharks without being eaten" philosophy. Can you too?

ACCOUNTABILITY

Scott said, "Thom, I want you to make a commitment to me." "Not another one!" I thought to myself. "Every day allow me, for 30 days. . .1 month. . .to help you schedule who you will see that

42

day. Then in the evening. . .I don't care how late it is. . .phone me and let us discuss your success and failures of the day."

"I'll commit, if you do, to counsel you, and offer you: suggestions and corrective sales methods, time management ideas, account management ideas and success principles, so you can develop the habits you will need to exceed your daily, weekly, monthly, and yearly goals! OK?" OK!

I read *Psychology Today Magazine*, along with *Sales & Marketing Digest*, and read that "it takes 21 days (one average work month) to break any old bad habit or develop a new better habit." What habits *must* you have?

Because I learned how to have a *sense of urgency* about the use of my time to reach my daily goals, I would do over $220,000 in sales 400% of the prior year's totals. Three years later, as a Regional Sales Manager, I was responsible for over 5 million in sales at age 24. This is shared not to impress you, but to impress upon you as what is possible. Get rid of your limitations . . . and your bad habits!

It was logical to shift back into a goal's mentality when building a new sales area. . .my own Branch Profit Center. What will you build this next year?

THE POWER OF BELIEF

How could Roger Maris have broken Babe Ruth's home run record of 60 with 61 home runs in 1961 without the belief that he could?

How could Roger Banister have broken the 4 minute mile barrier, something many others had strived to break, but no one had, without a belief that he could?

How could Carl Lewis break what was thought to be an unbeatable long jump record if it were not for BELIEF!?

Leaders give people something to believe in. In selling, it often starts with helping others believe in themselves. Great companies are built by visionary leaders.

. 3M is a company, like Eureka in my days with them, who is said to have an extraordinary commitment to *internal entrepreneurship.* Management believes that people can make the correct decisions if the incentive is there for the individual or the team. And, as my friend Ken Blanchard says, often all they need is one minute of praise (see The One Minute Manager).

In the 90's, markets are more crowded than in the 70's or 80's. Eureka has more competitors than it did in those days of fighting for market share. One more reason why *every salesperson* MUST be *equipped to compete better.* The years 2000-2020?!

Leon Royer, a 30 year 3M veteran, just like Scott and Walt for my alma mater, Eureka, says "It's the soft stuff that makes a win." (Life in the Trenches) Royer who heads the company's Surface Mount Supplies unit is a cheerleader who bear hugs, and energizes 3M teams to success over and over, no matter where he is assigned. His past victories include Post-it Notes and Scotchguard Carpet Protector. He puts his team on a **passionate mission** and they deliver. They believe!

Have dream stealers stolen your dream(s)!? A most successful **rags to riches** story comes to us from the skin care industry where Nu Skin International has grabbed market share. They have done this through their unique quality products, and **network** marketing program. Is your net working?

Blake M. Roney, founder of Nu Skin, says, "As we were creating Nu Skin, we were told by the 'cosmetic experts' that we would fail in a matter of months because we had too high of a goal. We wanted to create the first product line in the world containing only ingredients known to be good for your skin and not one thing known to be bad."

ALL THE GOOD AND NONE OF THE BAD!

None in the industry was taking this approach! He had less than $5000 start up capital, and without any corporate debt, built in 10 years a company that exceeds 1 billion in sales! Just as he says he knows "Nu Skin products are best for you, and we have felt from the beginning that **you** would want and need the best." I am taking this approach with the creation of this product. The book must be the best because you want the best!

One of the things that causes stress and not delivering our best is worry and regrets. I want to help you "GO FOR IT!" Stress has reached epidemic proportions and has become a killer! Almost all stress is self-induced!

OVERCOME & CONQUER STRESS!

Eliminate:

√ Disorganization   √ Disorderliness   √ Uncertainty

√ Frustration   √ Indecision   √ Apprehension

In business, or other vocations, how could numerous innovators have developed new products or new technologies, without a belief that they could? Then one can develop the plan, and then, work the plan. Planning and doing the MOST important things FIRST overcomes stress!

Along the highways of life have you noticed many people try to discourage you? Or side track you from your goals? View all as learning experiences. You *CAN!*

Abe Lincoln said:

"THE WOOD CUTTER WHO STOPS TO SHARPEN HIS AXE WILL CUT MORE WOOD."

Become 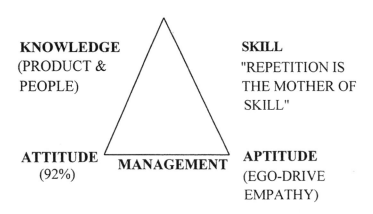 *in Selling!*

The Learning Triangle

KNOWLEDGE
(PRODUCT &
PEOPLE)

SKILL
"REPETITION IS
THE MOTHER OF
SKILL"

ATTITUDE
(92%)

MANAGEMENT

APTITUDE
(EGO-DRIVE
EMPATHY)

Do you have the success profile to be successful in selling? Not all do, right now. Can you trace over the large triangle above?

For several years, I utilized Dr. Herbert Greenburg's Caliper personality evaluation with my clients. However, 1971 through mid year '73, I knew I did not have all the answers to the why questions, but I did know what I was learning, then doing, was working!

Like you possibly, in recent years, I have taken and scored extremely high on a number of other evaluations. The Wonderlick evaluation is given by many colleges (and the NFL!) to test students reasoning skills. When I received a 27, and was told most students score below the required 17 for entrance, I knew I was writing this book at the right level. You see the average persons reading skills are at the 7th-8th grade level!

This is a skill that many need to improve. Know your customer.

Greenburg defines EGO DRIVE as the inner need to WIN. When we win someone to our way of thinking or feeling, how we feel about ourselves **(self-esteem)** is enhanced. How we see ourselves **(self-image)** is enhanced! So, we are *driven from within* to feel better. . .to see ourselves as WINNERS. So we are driven to persuade others successfully for these reasons.

.Again, the **money gained** for the salesperson who becomes #1 in selling is not at the top of the items that motivate.

And besides it's not the money any of us want, it is what we can do with the money. Not what we want, but why we want it!

EMPATHY, along with Ego Drive in the proper balance, brings someone to the *proper psychological profile to Become #1 in Selling!* And this balance is often different in different industries or sales situations. We can "test" for this.

Set a goal: YOU MUST BE...BEFORE YOU CAN DO...YOU MUST DO...BEFORE YOU CAN HAVE. (Change the you to I and we have a worthwhile affirmation.)

Many must be more driven from within. A Christian believes it is God within driving when he is allowed to be in the driver's seat. Others must be more empathetic. Who will your positive role models with these attributes become?_____.

A man recently asked me a lot of personal questions. He tried to empathize with me when he asked me about my son, Todd. That felt good. At the end of the interaction, his unhealthy ego drive turned me off as he strove to get the upper hand or positioning on me. He was not trying to solve a problem or be a friend. He was out for what was in it for him, not for me. (WIIFM) Maybe he simply needed to learn how-to **negotiate win/win relationships**.

Those who Become #1 in Selling are sincerely interested in what is best for the other person. They *refuse to sell* a product, service, idea, or themselves *to someone who does not need it.* This is at the heart of empathy in selling. If I would buy it, then I can sell it to you.

And, in many sales situations, we must have **team work** or partner with those in our companies, or with our customer, to Become #1.

HUMAN RELATION SKILLS ARE LEARNED

It is true some have, more so than others, the proper balance of drive and empathy from day #1 in Selling. Was this modeled for

Become 🐿 *in* *Selling!*

them as children? There is much documentation from the field of behavioral psychology that backs this up. For those of us who are adults, it is not too late.

I became a good mentor when I hired my first salesperson, Jerry. Scott MacLeod had modeled properly for me the correct behavior (in most cases), as he supervised me.

Attitude is so very important to success in selling. . .to Become #1 in Selling, one must exhibit or live out more of the *positive expectant attitudes* than his counterparts.

A University of Chicago study reports "92% of how successful anyone is in anything is predetermined by their attitude."

Personality attitudes in action, include: enthusiasm, decisiveness, courage, optimism, cheerfulness, consideration, friendliness, courteousness, sincerity, warmth and relaxation. More on these in Chapter 3.

My first full year as a Branch Profit Center Sales Manager for Eureka I had the attitude that I could and should sell every potential account. To build the Branch, Jerry and I had to constantly prospect to open new accounts. Between us we opened two new accounts each week. What are your new account goals?

You will note in the prior paragraph I used the word "should". I have worked, notice I did not say "tried," to heap condemnation on yourself and others. In most cases, I now prefer the word could or must. "Stop shoulding all over yourself and others!" Great advice from mentor Rita Davenport.

ENCOURAGE EACH OTHER

Jerry worked for Brand X for several years much like his father before him. His attitude suffered when his employer treated him unfairly, THUS MAKING him a more susceptible **recruit** for me.

I am pleased today to say that as I craft this book in the 90's, Jerry worked for The Eureka Company for nearly 20 years! He was a sales leader in the company since I promoted him to the Branch Manager's job, and even before that as a salesperson!

Great salespeople, like Jerry, bounce back quickly from adversity. They do not take rejection personally!

Most of all, those who Become #1 in Selling **love others!**

I'm not talking just about that Philadelphia type love. . .brotherly love. . .or that lustful erotic love. I'm talking about giving, sacrificial love. Agape is the word the Greeks used to describe the kind of love prescribed. Jerry had it for his customers.

Great salespeople *always put their customers' needs #1.* They give great service because they love. . .they go the extra mile because they want to. . .because it is the right thing to do. . .not always because it is what they feel like doing. Napoleon Hill wrote a little book that is a must reading entitled. . . .

"Going the Extra Mile"

What person would like to get his or her brand new suit dirty or rip it while putting together a vacuum cleaner on a retail selling floor, before giving advice and training on how to sell it to an accounts retail salespeople!? That's what Scott insisted we do! So that is what I did! And that's what I taught Jerry, too!

My attitude could have been "Let's just ship them the merchandise!" We wanted their landed cost to be as low as possible to *give* our accounts *wider profit margins.* And more incentive to sell our products, versus. . . . .

COMPETITION!

Many of the #1 salespeople I have met and evaluated over the years thrive on competition. Especially competing with their prior best. Encourage each other to do better or yourself.

It's always the little extras that make the big difference. *Do the little things better.* And, do them more consistently.

KNOWLEDGE AND SKILL

Socrates said, "Knowledge is Power" I was taught as a young salesperson that not only did I need to be expert with our product or technical knowledge, I also must know all about my competitors' products. At first, I didn't understand the **obsession** with this. As time went on, I was pleased that I was taught our product line inside out.

Not only must we know every feature and benefit, but also we can know how these benefits make our product and service better than our competitors! What are all the applications?

Almost without exception the person who Becomes #1 in Selling knows more about the product than all others. This adds to the confidence level.

As a consultant in recent years, I am constantly amazed at how short-sighted some companies and managers are when training their salespeople. You must keep training and learning!

There are two kinds of knowledge each salesperson must have. To reduce it to the simplest terms: PRODUCT (or SERVICE) knowledge and PEOPLE knowledge.

Equal emphasis MUST be taught in helping salespeople to acquire the people knowledge. I learned this lesson early, actually from my mother, father and relatives. How about you?

Yes, as Woody Hayes said we do "Win with People" knowledge.

Human behavior is a fascinating subject! This book is dedicated to *GOD*, and to helping *you understand others* and yourself. Only then can you cause people to act differently.

Selling successfully long-term is like engineering a new, *more precise* mechanical system.

SELLING IS A LEARNED SKILL

Selling success can be designed just as a great architect designs a magnificent award winning building.

Unfortunately, many salespeople have learned too many of the wrong methods. So some have to unlearn, before they can relearn. In other words, we have to *displace the old*, before the *new can be ours*, for good. Repetition is the mother of learning. The new input can overcome the old and generate better *RESULTS!* It is best to erase a cassette tape with a message on it before recording a new message. Why not say to yourself: *CANCEL!! CANCEL!!* when a negative happening comes your way? Do not allow the bad experience to give root and grow in your subconscious! Immediately look for the seeds of benefit from any situation, record them if possible, then *GO ON!*

That is largely why this book is structured the way it is. Some of the veteran salespeople may be bored by now and may have skipped ahead or stopped reading, because I may be too basic so far, or have used the word "I" too much to suit them. That is understandable, but unavoidable because I write this *step by step for anyone* who really wants to Become #1 in Selling!

Some need to develop and maintain sales ability through acquiring better mentors or role models. Some need to examine and change attitudes. Some need to set goals to develop more product or people knowledge or both. And all of us can . . . BUILD A BETTER YOU!, as mentor Joel Weldon exclaims.

Some have few skills for success in selling. Although I can write about the skills, I can only tell you how to develop them. Reading about a skill will not make it yours! I do suggest you highlight as you read, write in the margins, or in an accompanying notebook as you proceed.

In 1973, I had to apply *all* that I was taught to Become #1 in Selling! Our Akron Ohio Branch was #1 in AMERICA.

I had to see more of the best DECISION MAKERS each day, and get the salespeople who worked for me to do the same. I had to *say more of the right things in the right way.* You too?

Let's imagine we go to a golf clinic taught by Jack Nicklaus, recognized as the greatest golfer who has ever played the game.

Become in *Selling!*

Jack imparts all his knowledge of the game to us at hundreds of dollars per hour. Then we go to the golf course or driving range to APPLY the knowledge.

HOW SUCCESSFUL CAN YOU BE?

We must apply the knowledge AND we must execute in a near perfect way. Without the teaching pro to spot the weakness' in our swing and to offer correction, we could develop a bad habit the first day we begin playing golf. Then the longer we approach a certain shot the wrong way, the more difficult the habit is to break! Is this true in the various steps in any sales process? YES!

SEE THE POINT?

I became a mentor because I was willing to *allow others to correct* me. I sought out, and continue to, the corrective advice of others. Because of this teachable spirit, I became a good teacher. That does not mean, however, that I will yoke myself to just anyone.

To be a great leader, AGAIN, you first must be a good follower at times. And great leaders do not push. They set the vision. They inspire. They *pull out of people* their best and GUIDE AND INSPIRE us to the top.

MANAGEMENT

Those who learn to manage themselves can Become #1 in Selling! It takes discipline. It takes sacrifice. It takes honesty and integrity. It takes developing the best habits of thought and action possible. And we must manage our emotions.

Once this book is published, I may write and publish a book about Leadership and Sales Management.

Seldom does the #1 salesperson become a #1 manager. But, he or she can if they can *win by helping others win.*

Great salespeople manage themselves in some very interesting ways. Some have lots of self-talk. Some thrive on record keeping and knowing their batting average, so to speak. Others become sticklers on time management. Still others just out work or out serve all others. . .*out perform* or *out execute* the competition.

And, your customers must give you 100% trust. This is **partnering**. It is a *covenant relationship* and hard to *earn*.

WIN TODAY!

Success was manifested in 1972 when we purchased our first home, just a few miles from The Hoover Company's corporate headquarters, in North Canton, Ohio. I was only 22. I could look out the bedroom window each morning, shake my fists (in my mind) at the competitors smoke stacks and say to myself. . . "I am going to get you today!" "I will beat you today!" Fairly, and ethically, of course.

"I will win today!" (A GREAT AFFIRMATION)
"I will Become #1 in Selling! TODAY!

Do your very best today and tomorrow will take care of itself!

This attitude will propel you over the rough roads ahead! You must want to "Become #1 in Selling!" so badly that you do not settle for 2nd place. If you **shoot for the moon** and miss, you will end up in the stars!

MUCH BETTER OFF!

As one great salesperson once said, "I never saw anyone I wanted to be #2 to." And even when not #1, the great ones are satisfied with how they finish the race because they know they gave it their best. And isn't that *reward enough*? To know you did all you could?

Become in **Selling!**

May that be our prayer for each other as we proceed, "Help me do my best today. . .and if I Become #1 in Selling, I will know that you, God, have allowed it, because no matter what I do or how I do it, I cannot control everyone or everything. Nor can I always persuade or partner with all whom I desire . . . but I can *give 100% today* and, give God 100% credit. Help me to always do that, God!" Positive prayer is my *best weapon!*

You are **one step closer**, so you soon can Become. . . #1 in Selling!

In concluding this chapter, please, let us consider who our mentors will be. Or, possibly you prefer to think of them as role models. As an example, Patrick M. Morley, author of *THE MAN IN THE MIRROR*, is not a man I have met or expect to meet. However, I can model much of what he teaches. Please fill in the blanks *NOW*.

My mentors will be: Date: _____

1) _____

2) _____

3) _____

REMEMBER YOU MAY OUT GROW THE NEED FOR CERTAIN MENTORS AND HAVE A DIFFERENT LIST LATER.

Make decisions and plans on how you will ask for and accept their help: _____

_____

And, who are three people "I can mentor" in some way?:

1) _____

2) _____

3) _____

ONE IS NEVER TOO OLD OR SEASONED TO MENTOR OR BE MENTORED.

Plato's rings of influence speaks to the magnetic force a great mentor exudes. Many believe Jesus was more than the "mentor sent by God". His model is a great one. He taught 12 people up close over a three-year period to "sell" his message. Of course, Christians believe He sent a helper, the Holy Spirit, to empower them.

Today we hear a lot about *empowering people.* Great mentors equip those they lead and influence to *make decisions* and be *accountable* for those decisions.

Salespeople need all the correct empowerment they can get! One great sales idea, again, is the "I have to talk it over with a **higher authority**" tactic. Then they can receive more empowerment to meet the customers' demands, needs or questions. Briefly, leave the prospect to consult with another.

Mentors equip us to overcome all handicaps, obstacles and *persevere.* They admit their own mistakes first. A good example.

LASTING IMPACT!

Mentors can make a *lasting impact* in the lives of those they influence, and SO CAN SALESPEOPLE. It is an awesome responsibility! Years later we still pay homage to those who helped us. You and I would do well to have that kind of lasting impact, wouldn't we!?

If that is *what* you want, *why* do you want it? Once you understand, you will have more motivation to do your very best. . . . . TODAY . . . . Never forget:

YOU ARE THE RIGHT PERSON! YOU CAN BE A WINNER! A CHAMPION. BUILD UPON SMALL VICTORIES EACH DAY. *YOU* ARE #1! (You are my customer)

Become in ***Selling!***

AND REMEMBER, IT IS NICE TO BE IMPORTANT. . .
IT IS MORE IMPORTANT TO BE NICE

"To be what we are, to become what we are capable of becoming, is the only end in (this) life."

. . . Robert Lewis Stevenson

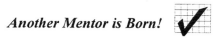

REVIEW QUESTIONS

1. Do you have a favorite athlete or person with whom you can identify, and who can motivate you? Who is it? What characteristics does this person consistently exhibit that you can practice more?

2. How much more income would you like to earn in the next 12 months?

3. What Bellcow or Tiffany-type accounts do you have now? And which ones do you plan to acquire?

4. How much time did you invest in front of customers or prospects last week and month?

5. How does "The Power of Belief" apply to your sales career?

6. How does one become trustworthy and build trust?

7. How can you acquire more Drive and Empathy, or the correct balance?

8. What can you do to encourage others and yourself more?

9. Are you a good follower? And following the best model you can? Or being the best leader possible? If not, what do you intend to do about it?

10. Did you complete the blanks on who your mentors are or will be? If not, please DO IT NOW!

11. What can you do to EMPOWER yourself or others better?

CHAPTER 3

Attitude Is Everything!

IF IT IS TO BE,
IT IS UP TO ME!

You have been given a number of the characteristics, attitudes and a few of the habits that can make you #1 in Selling! We have focused on how to become #1, and what to do, what not to do and what not to become. It is up to you!

In a sales presentation it is wise to: TELL THEM WHAT YOU WILL TELL THEM; THEN TELL THEM; THEN SUMMARIZE WHAT YOU TOLD THEM.

It has been proven that the person who expects success will get success. And just the opposite is true! You will love this chapter!

There are three great positive attitude activators . . . FAITH, HOPE and LOVE. The opposites are FEAR, DOUBT and HATE. You know that negatives like a lack of truthfulness or integrity can damage a sales career. Stealing will ruin you, whether it is minutes from your company or customers, or magazines from your client's lobby.

BORROWING **great ideas**, however, have propelled people, companies, and nations (I was in Japan recently) to the top in many markets. EMPLOY great ideas! Employ great attitudes!

The Big Three (not Ford, Chrysler or GM) of **Faith, Hope and Love** generate seven core attitudes that you must have to Become #1 in Selling!

Think about great people you admire who have the following seven keys to success and significance.

Become **in Selling!**

Prayerfully, incorporate more:

- **Anticipation**
- **Belief**
- **Confidence**
- **Expectations**
- **Humility**
- **Patience**
- **Understanding**

I have never met someone who Became #1 in Selling that did not have each of these attributes. Will Rogers said, "I never met a man I did not like." Because of his attitude!

Two thousand years ago a great persuader commented about what he called the fruit of the Spirit by writing that love generates joy, peace, long-suffering, gentleness, goodness, faith, meekness and temperance. He wrote to a new group of people who called themselves Christians in a town called Galatia. They changed and shaped the history of the world!

Before I get into sales tactics, techniques and methods in later chapters, we will now explore the seven (7) *core attitudes* needed for success in selling.

ANTICIPATION

My grandmother, Myrtle Bynner, was a great salesperson all her life. When she turned 100, she was interviewed by the local newspaper. Because of her heritage (her gene pool), she *anticipated* a long life and certain things out of this life.

"I met Claud (her husband of 73 years and my grandfather) in a Flinch game," Bynner said. The article reads, "I was visiting his cousin's house at the time. We were married in 1912. He died at age 94 in 1984."

How is it that a young lady *sells* the young man that she is the #1 girl for him? As a man, I also know that we men do all we can to Become #1 with a special lady.

What young man does not anticipate or hope for that good night kiss at the end of the date?

"Claud always rode the horse to the store because of the mud. The general store was about one mile from the farm. Children always got their feet muddy when they walked to school. I think that is why they called the area Mudsock," explained Grandma Bynner.

Did you have a class pet in your class in elementary school? I had a friend's wife who recently remarked that she "hated 4th grade." When asked why, she said, "I was the teacher's pet in 1st through 3rd grade, but couldn't sell myself to the 4th grade teacher!"

In other words, she could not Become #1 in Selling that year. Well, none of us can win them all. Sometimes our sales style does not match up with the buying style of the customer, try as we will, we have a hard time selling them all. Unless . . .

WE BECOME PROBLEM SOLVERS

"I once traced my roots as far as Otis James, who signed the Declaration of Independence," Grandma Bynner went on.

What an example of salesmanship and anticipation! We have all read about the war with the Red Coats (the British) that led to the formation of the 13 United States of America and our Declaration of Independence from British Rule.

The families and men who fought in that war had to have had tremendous anticipation . . . united vision . . . and *team goals . . . to persevere.* And **George Washington** who became our first president certainly was #1 in selling himself. History shows George as a man of faith, hope, love and honesty. I have a friend, another professional speaker, who does a wonderful George Washington characterization in full attire.

Become 🌸🎋 *in Selling!*

REMEMBER THE CHERRY TREE?

Grandma Bynner said that her mother was named after her great uncle, Giles Smith Morgan, a Civil War general. In recent times, we have seen how generals SELL, haven't we?

Abe Lincoln *anticipated* victory, how else could he have stood by and seen so many men killed in what was the bloodiest war the USA has ever seen? A great salesperson *anticipates* the sale mentally, emotionally and physically when with a customer or prospect.

Abe was someone who really understood what was needed to Become #1 in Selling. What a SENSE OF HUMOR he DEVELOPED. His attitude was remarkable!

And talk about rejection! Old Abe lost many more elections than he won including one in 1858, just two years before he was elected to the highest office in the nation . . .

PRESIDENT!

Almost every company has at its helm someone who understands how to Become #1 in Selling. If not, watch out! And many C.E.O.'s were #1 in selling early in their careers. Lee Iacocca of Chrysler (the man voted most respected American executive recently) was a prime example.

Can you imagine what it takes to become a general in the Navy, Army, Air Force or Marines? Lots of salesmanship! They sell their directives every day.

When Chuck Breckheimer retired from Eureka as a Regional Manager, I really did not anticipate consciously that I would be offered his job. Not so soon anyway! I was still 23 and all the men I would supervise, with the exception of two, would be old enough to be my father.

But, remember, when I had met Red Connell 3-1/2 years earlier, I told him "I want your job someday!" My anticipation was helping to bring it about.

Attitude is Everything!

Recently, I mailed 300 letters to 12 target markets, or 25 letters to each market segment. One list was the Top 25 "Highest-Paid Executives" in San Diego County, California. Enclosed was a capabilities' brochure, a return post card for their response and a *Free* offer! One would not do such a mailing if one did not anticipate a response.

The list reported as Kim Fletcher, Chairman and C.E.O. of Home Fed Corporation, to be #1 in the area for public companies with an income of $1,173,327.00!

It's interesting that of the Top 25, 12 were not on the list the prior year. How did they get there this year?

If I were a betting man, I'd wager that they *anticipated pay increases* and sold their way up the income ladder. They Became #1 in Selling in their company! In this case, they sold the stockholders or Board of Directors on their worthiness or may have created a more lucrative compensation package. They negotiated a better "deal." And, they undoubtedly led their company into a more profitable year! Can you **focus on creating more profits for your company or others**? Have *faith* . . . you will be rewarded.

PROFITABILITY THROUGH COST CONTROLS AND INCREASED SALES: The name of my recent speech at the national convention in Washington D.C. for the National Vacuum Dealers Association. Every size company needs selling lessons!

BELIEF

To be paid better than all others, you must first believe you are worth it. Few might realize it right now. You may need to acquire more knowledge, ideas, and develop more skills, and apply them.

In the last chapter, I wrote about "The Power of Belief." I mention it here again because repetition adds to learning. Remember how we were taught the multiplication tables? Repetition is so valuable to success in selling.

Early on I was taught that I MUST **remember names and faces**. I was given a formula for doing so:

Become ☙🏃 in Selling!

- ☞ RECOGNITION
- ☞ REPETITION
- ☞ ASSOCIATION

YOU can benefit by my sharing more about Grandma Myrtle Bynner. Grandmas sell too! Bynner rhymes with dinner.

Bynner became a one room school teacher in West Jefferson at the age of 15. She taught school by day and studied her own school lessons in the evenings to receive her diploma. She left teaching after marriage. Married women were not allowed to teach then!

Things have changed! You still cannot get a diploma in selling at a major university. A recent study points out that 80% of the marketing graduates get into selling in the first five years out of school. And, as a later mentor of mine often said, "*Not only don't they know anything, they do not even suspect anything about selling!*"

Change? Women, married or single, not only teach today, buy many women Become #1 in Selling! Some are almost "naturals!" They often have more empathy than us men.

In 1973, I had about 30 total salespeople reporting upwards to me . . . all men. Things have really changed! And for the better.

One study concluded: "4 out of 5 salespeople tested should not be in selling based on their current profile!" (Dr. H. Greenburg) Shocking? Or "they should be selling other type products or services!" Maybe, rather than require a one call close "they could be in a servicing sales capacity with repeat calls on the same prospect" if they are to Become #1 in Selling. Do you know any round pegs in square holes?

SELLING IS A TRANSFERENCE OF BELIEF!

Those who Become #1 in Selling always believe they have the best product, service, ideas, company, and/or solutions to the prospects or clients' problems. They convey these beliefs. And, they KNOW, you must first . . .

SELL YOURSELF!

BELIEF generates certain attitudes in action. And action is what counts in selling. Action that gets **RESULTS!** Associate your improved action with fulfilled goals so your subconscious will propel you upward. You must *manage beliefs* and feelings that associate some action with pain, or you will not consistently do what is needed at the right time.

Here are eleven personality traits that the seven (7) core attitudes generate:

☺	**Cheerfulness**	☺	**Friendliness**
☺	**Consideration**	☺	**Optimism**
☺	**Courage**	☺	**Relaxation**
☺	**Courteousness**	☺	**Sincerity**
☺	**Decisiveness**	☺	**Warmth**
☺	**Enthusiasm**		

The Generator System for Success was developed by a great mentor. I'll tell you about that methodology later; however, I will say, now, that with any methodology we cannot Become #1 in Selling unless we have and maintain these personality attitudes in action.

Remember, the original activators are *faith, hope* and *love*. These bring: anticipation, belief, expectations, confidence, humility, patience and understanding.

When someone says business is bad, decisively tell him or her cheerfully, "I have decided not to participate, my business is terrific." It soon will be!

Love is an act of the will. To Become #1 in Selling, you must will to love those who reject you, and keep going back to them until your. . .

EXPECTATIONS

. . . bring the desired results! Reject rejection! 60% of the sales are received after the 6th request!

"My grandfather went to Washington when they started the Republican party," Grandma Bynner said.

"Henry Wales Smith helped found the party and was present at Ford Theater when President Lincoln was shot", she exclaimed.

He was my great great grandfather!

Did he expect the Republican Party then to become the powerful party that it is today? I would say, "I doubt it!"...but that...doubt... activates all kinds of negative attitudes. Remember the opposite of faith, hope and love is...

FEAR, DOUBT & HATE!

Notice I used the word "but" in the prior sentence? That often is not a good choice of a word. I could have said, "however." Many negatives and excuses follow the word "but" in day to day dialogues. A fellow trainer and speaker in the Beauty Salon and Hair Care industry (one of the many markets we know a great deal about), Dr. Lou, who serves Redkin internationally, says "We must stop sitting on our buts!"

How could I at age 23 have taken a Region approaching 10 million in sales yearly from 9th in the USA out of 13 regions to 2nd in 6 months, as I did, with fear or doubt or hate? Impossible!

My expectation level was very high!!

For some it seems the farther removed we get from the innocent days of childhood, the more difficult to have the expectation level that will propel us to Become #1 in Selling! IT NEED NOT BE SO! With God on your side, you CAN be #1 regardless of age, sex, nationality or skin color. "With God all things are possible!" Ohio Motto.

CONFIDENCE

Confidence comes from knowing what to do and how to do it. In selling, we must also know what to say and how to say it.

One overly confident salesperson was described as a legend in his own mind. I actually met a man who was in one of my seminars for Fred Astaire Dance Studios who had a cross pen with the words "legend" inscribed on it! Fred Astaire may be a legend, however, is this man a legend as well? Maybe it is a goal! That's OK, however, let us guard against thinking we can do no wrong. We can all improve! And we must improve!

HUMOR: One person's confidence was manifested as egotism. Egotism is a disease that makes everyone sick except the person who has it!

Jim was confident but not very knowledgeable about how to make an effective sales presentation. So he failed and his self-confidence was damaged, not realizing it because he missed some of the steps in the presentation. Fortunately, he found a mentor who cared enough to teach him the how-to's.

Paul admitted he often did not do what he knew to do, thus bringing about failures. He turned his sales career around when he admitted he needed some objective help. A mentor helped him with a personal assessment and setting new goals. These goals brought about a new improved SELF-MOTIVATION and realistic confidence--through a written plan. His mentor kept him ACCOUNTABLE to fulfill the plan.

HUMILITY ... ACTION PLAN

Ben Franklin developed a list of attributes he desired as a young man. When a friend looked at his list of 12 characteristics sought, he said to Ben, "You need humility on that list." This became his lucky #13. He affirmed each three times a day for a week, then repeated this process for 13 weeks. There is a popular hymn which says: "Let the weak say I am strong. Give thanks with a grateful heart. Let the poor say I am rich because of what the Lord has done for me."

Humility is not the opposite of self-confidence. Because one can have a true confidence, knowing that one's life is a gift from God.

Prayer is an act of humility. It is true that the family who prays together stays together. It takes humility to acknowledge the need for a Higher Power. All those who stay #1 in selling or repeat as champions have a faith in God, I have found.

I heard former President Ronald Reagan, who committed his life to God, say that the purpose of life is to glorify God. This takes humility because our natural inclination is to want to glorify ourselves . . . to bring honor to ourselves.

Increasingly, we read and hear where those of great achievement give credit for their accomplishments to God. And to other great mentors. This takes humility. Can you do this?

THIRD PARTY APPROACH

To Become #1 in Selling use third parties to impress your prospects. That is, quote people's opinions or experience with your products, services, ideas and/or company. People are more impressed with satisfied customers' opinions than they are with your opinion. This is smart. This takes humility. A lack of humility is often manifested in thinking "I am right" (and, therefore, others are wrong). Leaders build consensus and humbly listen to opinions.

PATIENCE

Early in my sales career, I sometimes lacked patience. As a baby boomer, I grew up in the instant gratification generation. You were exposed to instant everything.

Attitude is Everything!

Since 95% of what we do or say is controlled by our subconscious, it is common sense to understand that this instant gratification can get manifested as a haste with customers and prospects.

We *cannot afford to be hasty* with our customers, prospects, family members, strangers, acquaintances, bosses, employees, leaders or anyone.

KEY TO SUCCESS:

Being a competitive person can force mistakes if one does not patiently set up an organizational systems which dictates and controls behavior.

As a Branch Manager and Regional Sales Manager with Eureka, I felt I had to become #1 today, tomorrow, or at least this year. Give your trip to becoming #1 the proper amount of time. Don't break the speed limit!

Do not take short cuts that will have negative consequences tomorrow so you can become #1 today.

TIMING

The Butler Company hired me to speak at their annual convention. They sell veterinarian supplies direct to Vets throughout the USA on a highly concentrated focused basis through more than 96 field sales representatives. They are #1 in their niche.

It has taken patience to gain the knowledge, skill, and experience needed to position myself so that large companies would hire me as the speaker at their conventions.

It took patience to assure that their National Sales Manager reviewed my information. Then, once he phoned, I set an appointment to meet with him and the Vice President of Marketing to identify their needs, before making a verbal proposal. In this case, the proposal was accepted on the spot. Good timing! It takes wisdom and patience.

I scheduled to meet with Jerry Linkhorn of The Butler Company again in a few days to finalize the details and to present a written agreement which we signed. He asked to meet over breakfast a few days before my speech and seminar to insure I further understood their needs. This employee of this 30-year old company is a thorough and patient professional. Are breakfast (or lunch) meetings appropriate in your sales career? If so, how many will you have next month?

GOAL: _____

Giving a good speech is a matter of timing. A great opening and closing are important and the meat must be tasty. Just like in a sales presentation, one must patiently prepare. To be humorous, motivating and educational all in the same forty-five minute speech, and have it custom-tailored for the client, is a real challenge.

Tremendous **energy** is needed and given as in any salesperson's quest to Become #1 in Selling! What did you do today to insure you will have the energy you need tomorrow? What can you do?. . .

FIND A NEED AND FILL IT!

The Butler Company has had some of America's top professional speakers at their conventions. Dave Yoho . . . Ed Foreman . . . Dr. Buck Matthews . . . all with messages to meet their needs.

I was introduced as a **"Young Zig Ziglar."** (I'd rather be the best Thom Lisk I can be.)

That got their attention! Creative marketing is needed by many salespeople. I now have demonstration video and audio tapes of presentations like this to give or loan to prospects. We live in a high tech society in the late 90's. A VCR in nearly every home and business. A CD in cars and homes. What are you doing creatively in your sales and marketing effort? Can you think of something new now? The internet? Fax on demand?

IDEA: _____

Are you always selling to a NEED? Of course, you can create the need. Identifying needs that your prospects do not know exist, can create more sales.

Some people offer to speak to the local Rotary Club, Kiwanis, Sertoma or other community or civic groups to create visibility. Offer service, network, gain sales and creditability. Recently, I "booked" a speaker who ran for the US House of Representatives for my Rotary Club.

If politicians can do it, so can you!

THE LIMITING STEP PRINCIPLE

Look at your work in a day by day or even hour to hour basis and ask "What is the limiting step that may keep me from reaching my goal(s)?"

I did that as a Branch and Regional Sales Manager with Eureka, anticipating what the future impact of my decisions and actions could be. As we mature, please realize your judgment will become better. When young, as I was then, it is even more important to be willing to listen to the best advice of others. Develop good habits early.

In preparing for the aforementioned Sunday night highly motivational humorous speech, and the sales seminar on Tuesday, I asked myself "What would or could prevent me from being well received, receiving ongoing work, and marketing them 100 cassette tape programs?" If it is to be, it is up to me!

And, if it is worth doing, it is worth doing right!!

A critical part of setting and maintaining priorities is to gain a greater . . .

UNDERSTANDING

.Faith, hope and love will cause you to want to understand. Understand others and you can then understand yourself.

What is it you can do better than all others? What is it others can do better than you?

Doing more of what you do very well and less of what you do not do well will give you *better results.*

That's how people who attend our seminars in the 90's have large increases in their sales. However, it always starts with "be happy" ☺ positive attitudes.

Andy attended a February open Blueprints for Success Seminar/Workshop facilitated by yours truly. In these programs, we have people from all walks of life unlike our customized industry programs. I saw Andy 2-1/2 weeks later when I spoke to an agency meeting. He reported to all present that he sold more life insurance the first week after our seminar than in the prior quarter or 13 weeks. That sounds like a **1300% increase!**

Jack Evan wrote me a letter one July saying the first full month (May) in his new sales career in the Mortgage Banking industry he out sold all the other 20 salespeople in his company. He attended my seminar April 28. He had never been in selling!

Understanding *how-to* and not getting bogged down in low payoff priorities can help you Become #1 in Selling.

In a later chapter, I ask you to complete some assessments to help you understand yourself better so you can understand others and sell more.

Understanding, anticipation, expectation, confidence, patience, humility and belief create a better personality.

PERSONALITY

Attitudes in Action are known as your *personality.* Because of the attributes described in your life, you can be more:

Attitude is Everything!

- ✓ **Enthusiastic**
- ✓ **Decisive**
- ✓ **Courageous**
- ✓ **Optimistic**
- ✓ **Cheerful**
- ✓ **Considerate**
- ✓ **Friendly**
- ✓ **Courteous**
- ✓ **Sincere**
- ✓ **Warm**
- ✓ **Relaxed**

Can you see the benefits of these personality characteristics in greater abundance in your life?

Now, we could discuss each in great depth, couldn't we? Notice all the questions I ask? I am modeling the desired behavior.

The key is for you to decide which of these you need more of, then set a written goal to prayerfully have them implanted into your life. Success with happiness is an inside job!

Circle or check those attributes on the prior list you desire to develop.

You have observed those who have an abundance of each attribute. These people are: _____

(name people)

Next, AFFIRM:

I am _____

I can _____

I will _____

"With God's help, all things are possible."
(Fill in the blanks with the words from the lists)
And affirm the above statements for 21 - 30 days.

If you have faith, hope and love, more of these attitudes and attributes can "show up" in your life.

W. Clement Stone, a multimillionaire business magnate and publisher, reports that Napoleon Hill, author of *"Think and Grow Rich,"* was a mentor to him. Together they wrote a book . . .

SUCCESS THROUGH A POSITIVE MENTAL ATTITUDE

Their "collaboration" and research of successful and happy peoples lives pinpointed 17 keys. This helped me (even though there is more recent research), so please let's share this finding with you. The Think and Grow Rich Newsletter expounds on these 17 necessary ideas, giving fresh perspectives. These are:

1. Develop a Positive Mental Attitude
2. Define your Major Purpose
3. Go the Extra Mile
4. Think more Accurately
5. Master Self-Discipline
6. Use the Master Mind Principle
7. Employ Applied Faith
8. Develop a Pleasing Personality
9. Discover Personal Initiative
10. Acquire Enthusiasm
11. Control your Attention
12. Build on Teamwork
13. Learn from Defeat
14. Cultivate Creative Vision
15. Budget your Time and Money
16. Maintain Sound Physical and Mental Health
17. Develop Good Habits

Maybe you could write a chapter on each. I think I now could, however, that was not the case in my early to mid 20's. And, reading does not put the attitude into action, does it?

WHAT GOALS WILL YOU ESTABLISH NOW?

_____

_____

RESULTS

Attitude is Everything!

In 1974, I may have earned $100,000 had I stayed with the company as a Regional Sales Manager the entire year. *Recently,* at Butler Company, I was told that several of the field salespeople I would speak to earned **over $100,000 a year.** Invariably, it is these superstars who study this material more so and listen more intently than others. They are determined to sustain their success and get more results. They do the 17 above!

How about you?

The personality *attitudes in action bring:*

- ► Success
- ► Inner Peace
- ► Security
- ► Energy
- ► Achievement
- ► Happiness
- ► Service Orientation
- ► Recognition
- ► Love (More!)
- ► Friendship
- ► Health
- ► Adventure
- ► Growth

Love is a result as well as an attitude activator.

Let's major on majors, not minors! *Values and actions that are in sync bring about peak performance.* A major league performance day in and day out.

Some of the people employed with the Eureka Co. years ago, in my personal experience, did not always place *personal integrity ahead of success* in their career as we must. As a result, some sacrificed their health or family to their career and financial goals. Prioritize correctly!

VALUES

Every company has a set of values just as each individual has. Responsibilities need to be consistent with your current set of values. You can have a great company, great products and great people, but if your family is young, value to discontinue traveling 4 nights a week, as I did, so you do not lose your family.

You must have *courage* to follow your values And courage to change and improve where and when needed. This will *pay off* in the long run and you will maintain a clear conscience.

The value at one client company which is #1 in their local market niche is: *Quality over Quantity.*

They will not pursue or accept work or jobs that they cannot perform with quality, make a profit and feel good about.

Wilson Floors has been at it since 1900. Chuck Wilson is a good example of many of the principles taught in this book. Even though his name is Wilson, he was not born into the family, but after many years of faithful service, he negotiated the purchase of the company.

Nepotism is a real problem in some companies. It may prevent some from Becoming #1 in Selling in some companies. But do what is right. And, you will be rewarded. *Do more of what is right everyday than everyone else.* This is the **Become #1 habit.** Believe you will be rewarded for faithfully doing what is right.

The Eureka Company with Red Connell at the helm as Vice President of Sales had Jim Connell (son) as a Divisional Sales Manager. To the best of my knowledge, no other relative was allowed. Jim may have been equally gifted, but it would often be thought that he had his job because of the "old man." I think this was harder on Jim than all others.

When at the banquet for The Butler Company, I sat next to Jerry Linkhorn and across the table from his son who was one of the 96 salespeople. Since Jerry is not an owner, the son would have to be on his own and Become #1 himself before earning future promotions, most likely.

HUMOR: You have heard of the s.o.b.? The son of the boss! This young man had a distinct advantage with Jerry as his Dad and business mentor.

MORE HUMOR: A young man was overheard by an attorney saying: "I am going to sue my employer for passing me over for the promotion, and for his promoting his less experienced nephew."

The attorney piped in, "Young man, you may need a good attorney. Here is my card . . . call me!"

With that the attorney walked off. You can imagine the young man's reaction when he saw the name of the law firm! Walker, Walker & Walker, & Sons, Inc.

Doing business with the next generation in a privately or closely held company can be challenging, can't it? Sometimes the values of the son or daughter are much different from the parent(s). One General Contractor client told me of a CEO of a well-known company who has awarded him nearly 14 million dollars in work and now that the sons are taking over, he will get $0 more! Even though he did all he knew how to build trust with the "boys" (they are about 40 years old), they want their people, not Dad's.

The right attitudes help you to anticipate these possibilities and prepare accordingly. Do not rely too heavily on any one account, if at all possible.

Of course, with all the mergers taking place these days, along with down sizing, new management or competition can knock you out of an old account when you least expect it. The solution?

Keep locating, developing and nurturing new accounts or new customers. I will develop how-to's for this later. However, for now, let us *know* that POSITIVE ATTITUDES and responses to changes in the market, a growing account base, and prospecting, are often important KEYS to success.

MASLOW'S THEORY

Maslow's Hierarchy of Needs theory explains that one of our highest needs is for self-actualization. The desire to "live on" once retired or gone! People want to be remembered for their contribution. I have met many great sales leaders that reach this level of need in life. *Understanding the needs of others and appealing to them properly is paramount for your success.* One does not have much success talking about a product that helps the prospect be remembered forever, when the prospect's basic needs of food, shelter and clothing are not first met. Know people.

Yes, *if it is to be it is up to me!* **Ten simple two letter words,** that you would be wise to memorize!

Give yourself an *advantage* by finding mentors who have the attitudes described in this chapter *and* are at the top of the pyramid of human need. If you are late in your sales career, I *challenge you* to help others Become #1 in Selling! The rewards may be long remembered!

Really *work* at **listening** with the attitudes described in this chapter so you can and will understand the needs of others and respond correctly. Then I can say YOU WILL BECOME #1 IN SELLING! Or at least, a much better and happier person.

What additionally do customers (and *employers*) want and need? They all want:

LOYALTY

Remember the following rules. This was given to me at an Ohio League of Credit Unions meeting where I was hired to speak at a President's night recognition banquet.

"If You Work For A Man, In Heaven's Name, Work For Him. If He Pays You Wages Which Supply You Bread And Butter Work For Him; Speak Well Of Him; Stand By Him And The Institution He Represents. If Put To A Pinch, An Ounce Of Loyalty Is Worth A Pound Of Cleverness. If You Must Vilify, Condemn And Eternally Disparge--Resign Your Position, And When You Are Outside, Damn To Your Heart's Content. But As Long As You Are Part Of The Institution, Do Not Condemn It. If You Do That, You Are Loosening The Tendrils That Are Holding You To The Institution, And At The First High Wind That Comes Along, You Will Be Uprooted And Blown Away, And Probably Never Know The Reason."

. . . Elbert Hubbard

Summary

You can write your *attitude development goals* further. This will improve your self-image and self-esteem and help you sell more through developing and maintaining positive relationships. You must become before you can do, and do before you can have. We need a reminder to stay focused. Focus on the attitude activators of FAITH, HOPE and LOVE.

What will you *become more of* in the next day? The next week? The next month? Is it a goal? It must be written down! Do it here and now! *Please.* Thank you!

_____

_____

_____

_____

_____

_____

_____

_____

_____

"Attitude is Everything" . . . Jeff Keller

CHAPTER THREE

REVIEW QUESTIONS

1. What are the three greatest attitude activators?

2. Does the best mentor feel threatened by you if you want his or her job some day?

3. What must you always believe to BECOME #1 IN SELLING?

4. What are the attitudes in action that you need most?

5. Share one thing you will do to incorporate some of these attitudes and change for the better.

6. Why will an organizational system for a competitive person dictate, control and focus behavior? *AND IMPROVE SALES!*

7. What new marketing or sales idea did you write down or get from this chapter?

8. What personality attitudes do you most admire in others? Why?

9. What top three result producing attitudes do you want to acquire?

10. What values or habits are most important to you for your company to become #1? If you are to Become #1 (or stay #1)?

CHAPTER 4

Qualities of Successful Salespeople

THE CUSTOMER IS KING OR QUEEN!

In many respects, selling professionally is more of an art than a vocational category. Doctors make their rounds in their respective hospitals, much like outside salespeople make their rounds each day. Both have clients, customers, or patients.

Dr. Adolfo Millan, my wife's brother, is a neurologist and a Filipino-American who came to the U.S.A. as a young medical school graduate. His education was costly. How much have you invested in your **sales education**?

So many people choose one education, however, end up in a totally different vocation, once they have options, and determine their TRUE APTITUDES. The point? It is not too late for YOU!

My beautiful wife is a chemical engineer by training with a masters degree in chemistry. You would not catch her employed as a chemist at this point in her life. Her outgoing personality makes her a "natural" salesperson. She is an investment and a financial analyst and very involved in religious ministry. She also is an award winning artist. So what? She has purposefully developed her best qualities. So can you!

THE BEST INVESTMENT? INVEST IN YOURSELF!

Personal Selling Power, the Professional Journal of Sales and Marketing Executives International, reported that in one year salespeople *invested* more than $100 million on sales development materials. And much more!

Professionals want to get better each year so they invest in themselves and their professional **proficiencies**.

Some people enter the field of selling because they did not have the formal education that equipped them for something else. Something better? Some became salespeople or sales managers to learn selling so they can better themselves financially. Some are told "You have a gift for gab . . . you should be in sales!" Some salespeople are highly educated. Some great ones have little formal university education.

In art there are principles that **guide** the artist. One can paint abstract, portraits, landscapes or bowls of fruit. The list and type of colors are nearly endless. I know! Lorna, my charming wife, is also an award winning artist. She took art classes as an adult. *Exercise your many talents* so they improve. Most salespeople need ongoing classes to become a master.

In selling, there are also guiding principles and there are many options. In selling, one can be outside or inside; wholesale or retail. This list of options is endless. And, *everyone* does some selling nearly everyday.

Whatever your *reasons* for wanting to learn how to sell better, I remind you that there is no totally comprehensive book or course of study that, when finished, will issue you into the ranks of the professional. It is our goal to give you many sales and personal success principles. How many have you **internalized**?

MASTERY

The Art of Mastery was the theme of Al Walker, CSP, CPAE, President of the National Speakers Association, as he led 3000 of the world's top professional speakers (and salespeople). To some the *ultimate challenge* for a professional salesperson is to give a presentation to a large group, command a high fee, and receive a standing ovation. It is a *refinement* of the art we speak about in this book. The mastery of selling or speaking can take many years. Are you *totally dedicated*, like a Doctor?

PREDETERMINE

Salespeople are looking for something and someone to help them become more successful. A body of knowledge, I thought, is needed for salespeople to pursue their goals . . . a reasonable approach based on an organized body of information.

What makes one salesperson more successful than another? I thought I had learned this while with Eureka. I was taught . . .

> "A successful salesperson is one who is achieving what one predetermined he or she wanted to achieve."

I read where one of America's largest companies (NCR) facilitated a survey and found this . . .

"The successful person is willing to do the things the unsuccessful person will not do!"

APTITUDE

Dr. Herbert Greenburg whose Caliper personality evaluation is widely accepted in the 90's to PREDETERMINE sales aptitude was little known when I took one of his "tests" in late 1974. Based on the positive results, Carl Stevens (consultant, sales educator/ mentor, and professional speaker), recommended I join his client, Kurfees Coatings, Inc., January 1, 1975.

Does your company use someone or something to *objectively predetermine* the *success potential* of an individual before making hiring decisions? The personality or psychological profile is the **most important**.

Dr. Greenburg found I had high levels of . . .

DRIVE

&

EMPATHY

These are the two key characteristics this clinical psychologist researched and has proven to be the keys to success in selling. Drive is the *desire to succeed.* Love is a drive, too, that propels you.

When we win someone to our way of thinking or they acquire our products or services, our self-image and/or our self-confidence is *enhanced.*

Some types of selling require more drive and less empathy. Others, vice versa. Can you guess which?

One call closers must have higher levels of this drive than those generating repeat business or in customer service.

The way to ACQUIRE MORE of this drive is through behavioral modification techniques. You must *associate with or model behavior* after those who have more of this key characteristic.

You have the *potential aptitude* to Become #1 in Selling in SOME SALES ENVIRONMENT MORE SO THAN OTHERS. You may lack some of the aptitudes and attitudes for this level of success, right now, however. So what will YOU do about it? Here is one example of what I did at a cross roads earlier in my career for your benefit.

CARL STEVENS

Carl Stevens was a man with high levels of drive when I first met him. He was a good model for me, as I had taken a short sabbatical after leaving Eureka.

Coach Stevens, as many would call this great man, had been a Dale Carnegie instructor supreme and a full-time investment banker for years in San Antonio, Texas.

His long time friend, Byron Carter, was the President of Management Horizons, an international management, marketing and retail intelligence consulting firm (and now a division of Price Waterhouse) based in Columbus, Ohio. Byron and Carl became acquainted when Byron was Branch Manager for America's most prestigious sales organization of that era, NCR (National Cash Register). That was a tough sell!

Carl was DRIVEN to regain the dollars he had lost, just before moving to Columbus to join MH. Many times *adversity* is just what *is needed* to *birth* a *new success.* Be thankful during the tough times! I met Carl when he moved to Columbus, Ohio. He became a great mentor to me. It is *true* that "God causes all things to work together for good . . . " (Romans 8:28)

Carl offered his sales seminars BLUEPRINT FOR PROFESSIONAL SELLING from Columbus for several years. Do you have all the blueprints you need for success?

I attended his 2-1/2 day seminar in January just after joining Kurfees Coatings, Inc. I determined: "I will master all what Carl Stevens taught and use him as a personal coach, role model, and mentor. I will become his *star pupil* in this, his client company. I will Become #1 in Selling again, and then I will join this mentor and become a professional speaker like Carl." WILL POWER!

All this, and more, came true! Your dreams and goals are more likely to come true in selling if you develop the best characteristics. And, the best way to do that is to *know which you need more of,* then **model behavior** after those who have what you need!

The following was in the *Wall Street Journal*:

"You've failed many times although you may not remember. You fell down the first time you tried to walk. You almost drowned the first time you tried to swim, didn't you? Did you hit the ball the first time you swung a bat? Heavy hitters, the ones who hit the most home runs, also strike out a lot. R.H. Macy failed seven times before his store in New York caught on. English novelist John Creasey got 753 rejection slips before he published 564 books. Babe Ruth struck out 1,330 times, but also hit 714 home runs. Although you want to minimize failure, don't worry about it if it occurs. Worry about the chances you miss when you don't try."

Have you ever met a salesperson whose empathy bordered on sympathy, when attempting the sale?

Sympathetic salespeople cry with the customer or prospect who says, "I can't afford it" . . . or . . . "Your price is too high!" They buy the objection.

The empathetic salesperson may asserts in response to a similar objection . . .

"You can't afford not to buy, and here is why . . . " Or. . . . .

"I understand you FEEL the price is too high. Others have initially FELT that same way, however, once they FOUND all the advantages to this product, they were willing to invest more. Allow me to explain all the benefits."

FEEL . . . FELT . . . FOUND

Anyone has the aptitude to overcome with a technique similar to the one just described, if they have enough drive to implement, *enough empathy to relate.*

Whom do you know with more drive than yourself? Someone whom you admire? Write their names below . . .

_____

_____

_____

Now, resolve to analyze the characteristics that bring them success and model their behavior.

And how about those with empathy? What do they do better and differently? Write their names here:

_____   _____

_____   _____

And, again, set goals to acquire more of their positive characteristics.

Modeling others' positive attitudes or behavior is what I have had to do periodically. It works for others - it will work for you!

ATTITUDES AGAIN

In Chapter #3, we analyzed the attitudes needed to Become #1 in Selling **Affirm** . . .

"I must be, before I can do . . . I must do before I can have."

The attitudes of other less self-motivated salespeople can derail you. Be careful!

CASE STUDY

Steve was a fun loving guy who liked to party. He was outgoing and a back slapping type salesperson. He was people oriented in style. He yielded some influence. He was just the type of guy that could be the catalyst for peer pressure to cause one to abandon one's goals or values.

He almost did me in, in early 1975, during three weeks of basic training with my new employer, Kurfees Coatings, Inc. I wanted to learn all I could, but my roommate was a party mogul. Fortunately, I said "No" often enough to get a good start in selling with this company.

Within one year, Steve *left the company*, as do many each year who are *not truly dedicated* to professionalism in selling. I earned the respect of Don Kurfees, now retired President of this 100-year old company.

You are *writing your future* with your habits of thought and action today. God gives us the will and ability to choose. Can you make better choices?

PRODUCT EXPERT

If I work for your company in sales, I think I would *first choose* to become a product expert. Product knowledge builds self-confidence.

Recently, I spoke with a sales manager of a Porsche dealership. He said his people could not attend our Blueprints for Success seminar now because of priorities to acquire new product knowledge first.

I had to remind him that unless these salespeople had the people knowledge they could miss many sales by pushing the product rather than understanding people who have needs and problems. Luxury automobile owners are near the top of Maslow's Hierarchy of needs . . . they want to self-actualize. Can you relate?

There is such a shortage of professional salespeople. This means that a pro who believes and does what I teach can be in high demand!

SKILL ANALOGY

Don Kurfees, grandson of the founder of Kurfees Coatings, Inc., was a skillful salesperson, manager and leader. He, as President, inspired skill development. I'll never forget making sales calls around Ohio in *his airplane*. He has been an instrument rated pilot for over 40 years, and President of the National Paint Manufacturers Associations.

Talk about *using time between calls wisely*! He did. He also got there faster than any other salesperson (certainly the *company President MUST be the most committed and best salesperson!*). Don had all the answers, and much more!

Knowledge is not enough. One could read all the books on golfing and have an awful game until the APPLICATION is made. Knowledge is knowing what to do, whereas, skill is specifically HOW TO DO IT.

The starting points of professional selling that must be improved before one can Become #1 in Selling will always revolve around...

👍 Attitudes/Self-Esteem/Self-Image

Qualities of Successful Salepeople

    👍 Focused goals

    👍 Time and activity planning

    👍 Knowledge AND skill **development**

Yes, we *must* learn many skills. America's greatest sales trainers agree on the basics, most of which are given in this book. Advanced selling techniques, technologies, methods, strategies are all stair-stepped from the foundations taught.

Most of these so called *advanced methods* either revolve around the use of computer technology or further behavioral applications. When working in-house with companies, we can help with these strategies. Sometimes I work as a personal trainer or coach one-on-one with salespeople, much like someone would work with you in an athletic club, or give you piano lessons. Someone to eyeball and *immediately critique performance*. This is what millions of sales people need most!

You can attend our open seminars. I am always researching advances in selling and psychology so as to serve our clients best. Sometimes I have been known to take *10 pages of notes* while with a new client before beginning our services, whether a one-time tailored speech or an in-house ongoing consult. We, artfully, will CREATE NEW IDEAS TO BENEFIT CLIENTS. You, too, must take written notes to be as effective as possible.

One must master certain skills before one can fully appreciate and apply newer technologies. Remember that in this book, I am detailing what made me (and others) Become #1 in Selling in the 60's, 70's and 80's . . . and still is serving me well in the 90's. When I receive my Ph.D. equivalency in selling; even the Ph.D. or M.D., however, has continuing education requirements. Let us *keep growing*.

DISCIPLINES TO SERVE!

.We must manage ourselves better if we are to become #1 . . . again . . . and again. We need not move into management. However, we must *manage ourselves!* DISCIPLINE is a master key. Serving others best, is THE master key.

I hear repeatedly from sales leaders and successful people I interview everywhere. . .

Discipline and good management includes learning how to say... "NO!" . . . to self and others, when, and as needed. Do you agree? Let me explain.

Sacrifice is not uncommon to the person who manages a successful sales career. Continually ask **"what am I willing to give up to get what I want? And . . . "Is it worth it?"**

Master the learning triangle!

Blast off!

We all have transition periods in our lives. I had a big transition. I can empathize with you. The college student needs that summer or Easter break. Some time away can bring one back with new DETERMINATION and PERSPECTIVE!

Just after finishing the edits on this book, as an example, I went to San Diego for a hiatus. Of course, I worked there with clients, but at a different pace than I had the prior year. You see, I plan to live to be 105 like my grandmother whom I told you about earlier. RENEWAL! RETREAT TO ADVANCE!

To Become #1 in Selling become #1 with your customers! Discipline yourself to make them KING or QUEEN!

Don Kurfees structured regional distribution centers so as to get the products delivered the next day. "Operate from our inventory," we told the customer. Just like a company has 5-9 major benefits to offer, so does a salesperson. They are:

☞   Aptitude

☞   Attitude

☞   Knowledge (Product/People)

Qualities of Successful Salepeople

☞   Skill

☞   Management

My older brother, Rodger, has an electrical engineering degree. What do you think of when you hear the word . . . PROFESSION! What vocation? Write it here:

_____

Did you write doctor, dentist, engineer, architect, or _____ Salesperson?

As I write this I start two new consulting projects. First, for a sizable consulting engineering company, and a two-office architectural company. You may wonder "What can you do for them?" I have developed many skills, in addition to selling and sales training skills, and most likely you must, too, one day. Let's remember that professionals have three things in common. They are:

☛   An accumulated body of knowledge

☞   A generic language

☛   Structured procedures

Things you need to become a professional salesperson and Become #1 in Selling,

Doctors go to school for an accumulated body of knowledge. And, this takes 8 years before they enter their residency for another three years. Twelve years of preparation! They DO NOT NEED to REINVENT anything. Improve? YES!

Red Connell had said as much when he gave me his condensation of 40 years of professional selling. LESSONS FROM THE TOP. I recommit myself to learn from the "experts." How about you?

Become #1 *in Selling!*

It took me more than 12 years to become an expert. How can we reasonably expect to be paid like one earlier? I did earn "BIG BUCKS" only because of my mentors, and I have found this is the case with most people who do very well very young.

You would not want a surgeon operating on you by trial and error. Salespeople say "Well, I'll try this and if that does not work, then I'll try that." "There are a lot of ways to get the job done."

This is maybe true, however, there generally is one (#1) best way. You are receiving those **best methods** in this book, "Become #1 in Selling!" You must *continually remind your customers of the benefits of your product.*

HUMOR: Henry Ford said "The worst way to learn anything is by **trial and error.** The only thing wrong with the school of experience is that by the time you graduate, you are either too old, too tired, or too poor to enjoy it.

O.P.E. . . . **Other People's Experience** is one of the *best instructors.* Other people who are where you want to be! I first heard it put this way by the beloved CAVETT ROBERT, CSP, CPAE, Chairman Emeritus (and founder) of the National Speakers Association. His letters to me "Dear Protégé" are treasured keepsakes for the rest of my life!

I began to dream of Becoming a *Professional* Speaker and Sales Trainer (later a Consultant), because I had a VISION OF THE FUTURE.

I chose to master the generic language of selling which Carl Stevens was teaching.

I challenge you to do the same, and more! Decide to master the structured procedures, principles, et. all.

Anyone can *acquire* the knowledge and *convert* it into skill, then discipline themselves and manage themselves to the top. Anyone? Yes, anyone!

However, few will. It takes a lot of hard work. We must change HABITS. Some habits more than others. Which habits for you?

FIVE P'S

HUMOR: *P*rofessional   *p*roficiency   *p*resupposes   *p*rofessional *p*reparation. Say that 5 times fast!

Preparation for the Salesperson equals better role models and more input or training, starting always with how to be, then on to what to do.

The preparation before a sales call begins with a PLAN! And, a check list to make certain you have everything with you.

"Luck is when preparation meets opportunity."

The church marquee I saw one day in between sales calls read "Luck is God's preordained coincidences, or appointments." This infers, if one knows God better he will also become luckier. I proved to myself that this is true. I know "HE causes all things to work together for GOOD . . ."! (Romans 8:28)

"80% of the business is done by 20% of the salesmen." (Paredo principle)

Kurfees Coatings had about 20 salespeople or branch sales managers. I was the first to sell both the Kurfees product line and Jewel Paints, a new subsidiary company. Because of this I had two color systems to learn, and unique products in both lines.

Twenty percent of these 20 people (4 people) acquired 80% of the new accounts. Why?

I found (as it had been at Eureka) that the top 20% of the top 20%, or in this case, *one person* did more than everyone else. I was determined to be that person. It took me two years to become #1.

SUCCESS DOCUMENTATION

It took Jack Evans only one month to become #1.   His incredible story is told in the letter I received from him. It begins:

Dear Thom:

"Your seminar *BECOME #1 IN SELLING!* really provides people BLUEPRINTS OF SUCCESS so they can have success through service, as you stated in your promotion. I am proof! I attended your April 28 seminar in the morning at the Hyatt Regency Convention Center and found it so ENLIGHTENING that I attended AGAIN when you repeated it that evening. Both times I invited others to attend and they benefited and were very pleased. I was #1 in sales out of 20 + salespeople or loan originators/officers in May. What makes this amazing is that this was my FIRST month with this company after a career change from being an electrical contractor for many years. I "bought" all of what you said and applied them. Thank you! You are a terrific mentor, Thom. I recommend your seminar!"

For your success,
Jack Evans, Loan Officer

Thomas Edison said, "There is a way to do it better . . . find it." You CAN, can't you?

He was a scientist, an inventor, and a great salesperson who had to sell his artful inventions.

Is it possible to make a *scientific approach* to the Art of Selling? I discovered one and have assimilated it for you. You will, however, receive more EMPOWERING in one of my "live" or video taped seminars, than in a book.

ANATOMY

What is the ANATOMY of most sales? **Very Important!**

A. 30% of your time must be invested to determine the problem and the solution.

B. 60% of your time often needs to be invested in motivating the prospect or customer to want what you are selling. And, it is best to present that as part of the solution.

C. 10% of your time invested in closing the sale.

You will see, over all, that this book is written based on these ratios. Each chapter isolates some problems and presents workable solutions. And much of each chapter is invested to motivate you to not only want the solution, but to want to implement the solution. I am working to model the procedure for you. **Please stick with it**.

You do notice that I utilize closing the sale methods throughout, don't you?

You know the alternate of choice close, don't you?

If you were given the choice between wealth and poverty which would you choose? Wealth! Then why self-destruct, or sabotage your chances for more success and happiness? Get rid of any negative self-fulfilling prophecies! Don't be like . . .

ELVIS PRESLEY

. . . who died at the same age that his mother did because he held a subconscious belief that he would!

When I spoke before the military officers of the Philippine Military Academy (the West Point in the Philippines) who were taking business graduate courses, I told them "PMA does not stand for the Philippine Military Academy." Where I come from, it stands for POSITIVE MENTAL ATTITUDE." Elvis had PMA except for his attitude towards life expectancy.

Stick with this book, and improve your success plan. Maybe I will help you surface some attitudes and expectations you did not know you had. I can help you get rid of destructive behaviors.

Will you do what is needed to improve? Or will you point the finger at someone else? ELIMINATE DISTRACTIONS!

Point your finger at others (or make excuses) and many people will think you are pointing three fingers back at yourself. Take **responsibility**! Remember the root word of responsibility is RESPONSE. Respond positively!

A short pencil beats a short memory. *Writing and repetition crystallize thought.*

MEMORIES

A problem is . . . memories are mighty short!

Tests conducted by Walter Dill Scott, President emeritus of Northwestern University, conclude that the memory of man is mighty short. As an example, if a salesperson hands a copy of an advertisement of some sales promotion literature extolling the merits of his wares or services to 1,000 people . . .

☺   1 day later 25% would have forgotten

☺   2 days later 50% would have forgotten

☺   4 days later 85% would have forgotten

☹   7 days later 97% would not recall

How artful are you at getting others to remember you and your products? Remember this:

THE SALESMAN
by John Wolfe

When labor toils and factories hum
and out plant doors the products come,
The payment for it all comes from
THE SALESMAN

In any business office, where
White collar workers earn their share,
They all should thank in grateful prayer
THE SALESMAN

When banks and institution lend
The funds on which the firms depend

For Finance, they too, have a friend--
THE SALESMAN

And miles of gleaming railroad track
And roads and highways there and back
Could not exist without his knack--
THE SALESMAN

So 'cross the land, behind each door,
Are worlds of wealth and goods galore.
They'd ne'er be there--were it not for
THE SALESMAN

Yes, others may salute their trade,
The contributions they have made;
But it's for him that I'll parade--
THE SALESMAN

For it is sales that keeps us free,
That fuel our great democracy,
And that is why I'm proud to be
A SALESMAN

Be proud to be a salesperson! And let's sell correctly!

HUMOR: A lady walked into an appliance store and asked to see some toasters. A high-pressure salesperson decided instead to sell her an expensive freezer. "Madam," he said, "believe me when I tell you this freezer will pay for itself in no time at all." "Fine," said the lady. "As soon as it does, send it over."

An example of incorrect selling.

FOCUS

Now, before we proceed, let's do this number exercise. Follow these directions:

Time yourself or have someone do so. In one minute, circle as many numbers consecutively as you can on the next page. Number one is circled . . . find and circle #2, then #3, #4, etc. Circle as many numbers as possible in consecutive order.

READY? GO!!

ONCE COMPLETE . . . READ THIS . . .

How did you do? Now, complete the same exercise on the 2nd page. This time please note that #1 is in the upper left hand quadrant, #2 is in the upper right hand quadrant, #3 is in the lower left hand quadrant, and #4 is in the lower right hand quadrant. See the pattern?

This pattern maintains itself throughout the exercise. Take one minute again. Work with a sense of urgency. Expect to circle two or three times as many numbers in the same time frame, now that you are more focused (organized)!

How did you do? Write some comments to yourself about what you learned from this exercise.

What am I selling you in this book? Solutions to your problems! Take a few minutes and write out what your major problems really are. . . personal or career. Once you have done so, one by one, search out all the possible solutions, then decide to act and focus on the ONE BEST solution.

Write your major personal and career problems or challenges and opportunities. Write all possible solutions for above problems. Circle the best solution and decide to act on it. You CAN solve your problems and reach your goals!

More importantly, you CAN *help others solve their problems* through selling more of your products, services or ideas, and yourself and your company.

① 61 13 42 74 14
41 9 81 70 18 22 46
17 45 86
21 34 2 30
89 49 38 50
37 5 69 78 6 90 10
85 29
25 82
33 65 54 26 58
53 57 66 62
73 77
76
15 79 39 32 16
40
31 3 71 8
47 83 80 24
27 85 28 56
7 52
67 72 4
51 75 11 12 88 60
36 20
19 23 43 48
87 44 64
35 59 63 68 84

(1) 61 13 41 9 81 45 17 21 89 49 37 5 69 85 29 25 33 65 53 57 73 77	42 74 14 70 18 22 86 46 34 2 30 38 50 78 6 90 10 82 54 26 58 66 62
15 79 39 71 31 3 47 83 55 27 7 67 51 75 11 19 23 43 81 35 59 63	76 16 32 40 8 80 24 28 56 52 72 4 12 88 60 36 20 48 44 64 68 84

Qualities of Successful Salepeople

.When new in sales and territory management for Kurfees Coatings, I could identify with a national survey report:

Salespeople's greatest needs are. . .

✓ How to overcome call reluctance
✓ How to build and maintain more self-confidence.

We have dealt with self-confidence in prior chapters and will continue to do this.

Call reluctance can be eliminated when you know what to do and how to do it, what to say and how to say it, in most situations. This reminder will stimulate you to learn the phrases that come later, and focus on the seven steps in a professional presentation. They are:

    ☑ **PREPARATION**
    ☑ **ATTENTION**
    ☑ **EXAMINATION**
    ☑ **PRESCRIPTION**
    ☑ **CONVICTION**
    ☑ **MOTIVATION**
    ☑ **COMPLETION**

It took me most of my first and second years to become prepared to Become #1 in Selling! Once you develop the right patterns, they can *serve* you well throughout your life.

I serviced accounts and managed the Ohio market. However, I did not yet have the confidence I needed in this new sales situation, even though I had been #1 in sales earlier with another company. I am certain it showed to my customers and prospects. However, I was dedicated!

Our mission was primarily to establish new accounts by persuading them that they must throw their existing paint line out of their store and put our full line in.

And, by doing so, they would have more satisfied customers, less problems, and more profits.

Initially, this seemed like mission impossible. However, I am a **possibility thinker**. *You must be, too!*

Some of these retailers, as you can imagine, were very set in their ways, some having carried their paint line for 20, 30 or 40 or more years.

We had to learn how to acquire the customer's ATTENTION, while asking various QUESTIONS on each visit, before scheduling a meeting to offer our prescriptions or proposal for their success (MORE SALES, CUSTOMER SATISFACTION, AND PROFITS). This strategy worked if one persistently and faithfully called on the prospect at least monthly for several months. Credibility had to be established and maintained with each contact.

The goal was convincing the owner (decision maker) that our product line would be the best *investment* for serving their customers while generating maximum profitability. These are the keys today in many sales situations!

This is critical as you use the proper four steps in a module of conviction, and the right wording.

CONVICTION

1. Present **ONE FACT OR FEATURE** at a time, then translate each, one by one into . . .
2. **BUYER BENEFITS**. While doing so, offer visual aids. . . (Key phrase: WHICH MEANS TO YOU . . .)
3. **EVIDENCE** . . . prove why the facts or features are important, before using a . . .
4. **WRAP-UP** question like . . . "Wouldn't you agree?"

EXAMPLE: 1. "This book will show you How to Become #1 in Selling."

2. "What *this means to you* is _____."

This statement helps you to properly translate the feature into a SPECIFIC benefit that is important to the buyer.

To motivate others you must understand others. They need to understand that we care about them benefiting. Communicate that you understand.

It was not just the *lure* of *increased profits* that helped me to acquire new customers . . . that was not always easy to prove. It was the *fact* they could tell I was (and still am) committed to help my customers reach *their* PERSONAL goals.

If it was more profits they wanted, I found out what they would do with more money if and WHEN they had it. This MOTIVATES. I helped them to dream, then *showed* them how we would help make those dreams come true.

If I offered you ONE MILLION DOLLARS and all your tangible dreams come true from learning and applying the principles in this book, would you do what I ask?

If so, initial here _____. Of course!

(P.S. I am <u>not</u> going to give you $1 million, you can earn it!)

How old are you? _____.

I plan on working successfully AND profitably until well past eighty. (I enjoy work and will work at a HEALTHY pace). If you are like me and have nearly 40 years to concern yourself with money matters, then, with me, divide 40 years into one million dollars. We arrive at $25,000. Would you like this much more per year?

Many of my readers can earn those extra dollars and more due to this book. Please write me with your progress.

I have had many seminar graduates who did double their sales and income the very next year. SOME THE NEXT MONTH! IT IS POSSIBLE! "All things are possible to him who believes!"

What would you do with an extra $25,000 if you had it *right now*? Write it down, please. Be specific.

_____

_____

.Now that you have this in focus, what will you do? Will you dedicate yourself to Become #1 in Selling? Or, at minimum, a 30 day effort to improve? Great!!!

I was determined to do what was needed to Become #1 . . . not for the trophy that collects dust, but for the self-satisfaction, and yes, for the money, and what I could do with the money. This year what will you be #1 in?

Current year: _____

PROFESSIONAL SALESPERSON'S CREED

I SELL BECAUSE SELLING IS MY LIVELIHOOD AND MY WAY OF LIFE AS WELL. AS A PROFESSIONAL, I WILL DEVOTE MY KNOWLEDGE AND SKILL TO THE SERVICE OF OTHERS, TO THE SATISFACTION OF THEIR PERSONAL AND MATERIAL NEEDS.

I RECOGNIZE MY OBLIGATION TO GROW, TO SEEK OUT NEW EXPERIENCES, TO WELCOME NEW IDEAS, TO EXPERIMENT WITH NEW METHODS AND TECHNIQUES, AND TO DEEPEN MY UNDERSTANDING OF THE HUMAN MIND.

I AM CONFIDENT IN MY KNOWLEDGE OF THE VALUE OF WHAT I SELL. MY BELIEF IN MYSELF IS THE SOURCE OF OTHERS' BELIEF IN ME.

I AM PROUD TO BE A MEMBER OF A PROFESSION IN WHICH MY SUCCESS DEPENDS ON MY INITIATIVE IN WHICH MY GREATEST REWARD IS IN MY ASSOCIATION WITH OTHERS.

Qualities of Successful Salepeople

I REALIZE FULLY THAT THE STANDARDS OF MY PROFESSION RISE CONTINUALLY, AND I EXULT IN MY HARD WON ABILITY TO LIVE UP TO ITS IDEALS.

... author unknown

Please initial here if you will pledge to this: _____

In a recent article in the newsletter BOTTOM LINE PERSONAL, Dr. Richard Restak from Georgestown University points out some interesting facts about the brain.

BRAIN POWER

He reminds us that "medical experts agree that no one uses 100% of the brain." Everyone starts out with about 100 billion nerve cells. The brain is a dynamic organ. The brain is not a computer, but it has certain computer like qualities.

And when you decide to do something new, it's almost like creating a program for that activity--which may, in time, be able to run on its own.

That is why certain activities are automatic for each of us. Take your watch off your wrist and put it on the other arm for 24 hours and you will only now be conscious of how often you look at your watch!

The same thing is true in any aspect of any procedure, including the unconscious verbal and non verbal procedures we use in selling! If we are not getting the desired RESULTS, we must be willing to create a new program. Some call this *neuro linguistic programming*. One of my brothers-in-law is a neurologist. Interesting!

Edit your existing program (sales presentation, methods for dialogue, etc.) to get BETTER RESULTS. Many times this takes time and a caring mentor.

Become 🏃 *in Selling!*

LIFE magazine had a fascinating cover article describing BRAIN EXERCISES. It has been shown that those who "exercise" their brain all their lives do live longer. I trust you are ready for the exercises that follow in this book, now. There are many others, some much more complex. I am deprogramming what I know is the average reader, so I can *reprogram* you *for success.*

In **summary**, let me remind you that many artists paint for the sheer JOY of it! Great salespeople **enjoy** their art and look constantly for ways to improve. This brings them great JOY, JUST AS MUCH AS MORE SALES and MORE SATISFIED, BETTER SERVED CUSTOMERS. And more income!

Quality artists love to show off their work, whether it ever sells or not. Are you so pleased with the QUALITY of your efforts that you would not object to showing your work off to anyone? If your answer now is YES, you are ready to . . .

PAINT A MASTERPIECE

AND

BECOME #1 IN SELLING!

"To be nobody but yourself (and your best self - Thom) in a world which is doing its best, night and day, to make you everybody else - means the hardest battle which any human being can fight and never stop fighting."

. . . E.E. Cummings

CHAPTER FOUR

REVIEW QUESTIONS

1. What role does failure play in selling?

2. Did you write names of driven and empathetic salespeople? _____. If not, do so now: _____.

3. Why is discipline to serve so important?

4. Do you agree with THE FIVE P'S? _____. What are they?:

5. Do you need to eliminate distractions to have more success in selling? _____. If so, what are they?

6. How can you focus to do twice as much work or make twice as many sales in the same time frame?

7. Do you agree with the ideas presented? _____. Do you admit you have these challenges sometimes? _____.

8. What are the 7 steps in our psychologically structured professional sales presentation?

9. What are the 4 steps of CONVICTION?

   Demonstrate, or role play, how to use these 4 steps. Convert the knowledge into a skill.

Understanding Buyers and Yourself

RUN WITH PURPOSE!

A cover of *Runners World Magazine* featured Rod Dixon who is a Master of the Mile and Marathon. Rod had just turned 40. As a runner in his 40's, I can relate to him. You can too!

The **purpose** of runners vary. Some run for the exercise, some run for social reasons, others because they have a positive addiction. Still others run due to doctor's orders. . . "get some exercise!" and some run for aerobic conditioning or to lose weight.

A few dedicated souls **run to win.** Winning is beating your previous best time, not necessarily winning the race or your age category. That could come later!

Selling is to be like this. If you *do better each day*, or at least *each year*, you can say you are winning. But how can you measure success?

In my twenty-five (plus) year sales career, my ideas of what success is has varied and *matured*. As an example, I have not always appreciated the total importance of positioning, typically a marketing concern to salespeople.

I visited a surgeon's office in beautiful and plush La Jolla, California. A framed sign on the wall said, "Success is doing the best you know how to do, then doing **better each time!**"

At one time, I thought the only definition of success for a salesperson was to Become #1 in Selling! My view began to change. I began to aim to be a better husband and father. . . to be #1 in these areas.

Can you sell your spouse that you will become #1 **(the best!)** as a spouse? Is this selling? And then do it

And sell your children that you are (or at least want to be #1 as a dad or mom). Is this also selling?

These would become the most *meaningful sales* of my life, the first more than the latter. I am thankful that no matter how long one has neglected (in my case due to so much work) his or her spouse and/or children, one can still change, and **lovingly serve** (and sell) his way back *into the hearts of others*. But, it can be difficult, and take time. Positive family relationships enhance your business.

Others must want to forgive and give you a second or third chance, if needed.

Prospects and customers (and bosses?) are not as **forgiving** as family members, usually, are they? Forget to *phone when you must miss an appointment* and you may be out for good!

FIRST IMPRESSIONS

When first meeting someone so many things are important to that great **first** impression.

Eye contact, the proper handshake, a smile, and an effective introduction are only a part of it. Since 60-90% of communication is **non-verbal**, how we get and maintain their attention is critical to building relationships and **closing sales**.

Many of my seminar attendees, as an example, have been taught to pause 1. . .2. . .3. . . between the saying of their first and last name when introducing oneself. Why? So that the new acquaintance **hears**, and has more of a tendency to remember, your name. That is what you want, isn't it!?

Some will meet me and say "Hello Thom. . .PAUSE TO THE COUNT OF 3 TO YOURSELF. . .Lisk." It is laughable when it happens, however, we both know that this person is working at remembering others' names. The *most important word in the English language* is YOUR NAME! Use the name often!

Before the start of each meeting or sales call, it is important to **establish** the purpose. Before each phone call, also, as an example, ask yourself, "what is the purpose of my call?"

In this chapter, as with each chapter, I have a central purpose, before beginning to write.

My purpose for chapter 5 is: **To teach sales styles and buyer styles**, primarily.

FRIENDS IN SELLING

Some of us need to learn how to be likable! I once had an owner of a company give me a *Reader's Digest* article. The essence of this condensed advice was how-to be a *great leader*. The troops must like us, respect us and want to follow us.

"A friend loves at all times." Can you **imagine** a salesperson saying to one of his customers who rejects one offer, "You must not like me anymore, I'm going elsewhere!" We know to get a friend we must first be a friend. Friendly salespeople *do not* always Become #1 in Selling!

However, friendly salespeople sustain their sales careers through the good times and bad times, better than others. **Relationship selling** implies we must **read** the buyer, **relate** properly, and **respond** correctly.

What is the *purpose of developing a friend* or relationship anyway? Your answer may be as good as mine.

_____

_____

Once in management, even though one wants to be likable and friendly, one *must* get work done through others.

As a salesperson who sells and services the same accounts week in and week out, it is critically important to be liked.

That was easy for me, but the transition to a higher level management position took more work. This book is not about management, so we won't get into that other than in an effort to encourage salespeople to have *more empathy* for those who supervise them, and to find and listen to great mentors. Some few will aspire to become a marvelous mentor themselves.

Become 🌸 *in Selling!*

I do believe selling of most types is **more fun** than management, simply because of the friendship factor. As managers, one must constantly sell his or her ideas and directives, and can have more success if people like them. These directives can be unpopular.

One sales mentor told me, "If you ain't having fun doin' it, it ain't for you or you are doin' it wrong!"

SALES STYLES

There are **five** basic sales styles.

First, we have the **PEOPLE ORIENTED** salesperson. They say . . . "I am or want to be the customer's friend. I want to understand him (or her) and respond to his feelings and interests so that he will like me. This personal bond leads the customer or prospect to *purchase or buy* from me."

DOMINANT STYLES

Every salesperson has a dominant and secondary sales style, whether they know it or not. It becomes easy after a while to *read* their sales style. And we must understand sales styles before we can understand how to adapt to the five customer or *buyer styles*.

Some would say we can "*read the buyer*".

After being promoted to Regional Sales Manager with Eureka, I had a distributor who **sold** our products in Altoona, PA, and another in Williamsport, PA.

The distributor in Altoona was a "good ole boy", if you know what I mean. To do business there you knew all the interests of all your customers.

Have you visited offices where it was so obvious that the guy was more interested in his hobbies than in his business? Certainly one needs to pick up on that and comment accordingly.

It takes desire, discipline and dedication--The Three D's--to develop **new habits** like *preferring to talk about others' interests more so than our own.*

Of course, it's great when we have mutual interests.

When traveling to some cities in my early sales years, I would take my golf clubs with me. However, I'd prefer to visit a ball game and take a customer.

We'd work at becoming friends with our buyers by taking them out to lunch, dinner, golf or a ball game.

"TAKE IT OR LEAVE IT" STYLE

How many people have you known who would say about **exercise**, running or walking. . . "I can take it or leave it!"

The fact is you better not leave it if you want to end up unable to sell at your best when you reach your later years in selling. When I run, the endorphins that go to my brain stimulate my creative thinking. I have more energy and oxygen to all areas of my body. The benefits for one's business life are obvious!

In high school I ran track three years. I lettered, but was not all league or world or anything like that. I played basketball and led our team and league in scoring as a senior. I played football through 10th grade and ran cross country as a junior, and lettered also. I know the *disciplines needed to excel*, and the overlapping benefits from one area of life to another. Do you?

I use a runner's training log to record mileage and times in the 90's. I have goals for total mileage each week. I have short- and long-range goals for physical fitness. **Keep score on yourself!!**

Take it or leave it type salespeople do not want to exert much effort. They seldom want to figure out: WHAT DO THEY WANT AND WHY DO THEY WANT IT?!

My Branch Sales Manager in Harrisburg, PA. . . Bill. . . was a "take it or leave it guy" in many respects.

Bill's attitude activators were not always faith, hope and love. Bill hated to be challenged to change. He had doubts about my ability to lead him and help him. And, like many, he had some fears that seemed to paralyze him. Over the years, I have met many like him, haven't you?

Now you will remember from the prior chapter that anything other than faith, hope and love as your positive attitude activators does not bring the best results in **daily living**. . . and selling!

Bill would seldom reduce his prices . . . he greedily, I thought, wanted to maintain a full margin on every item he sold, most of the time. As a result, he had the highest profit margins. But based on his **buying power** index (total units per 1000 people sold compared to all sold), Bill had one of the worst, if not the worst sales records, in the region.

He gave them the steak with no **sizzle**! "Here it is, you can take it, or leave it!" Have you ever had a cook take that approach with you? If you did you probably did not go back to that restaurant again!

How can you **add more** sizzle to your sales efforts? Sometimes marketing people add sex appeal as with the beer commercials or jean ads. *Pizzazz*! Be careful how you appeal though.

Even at McDonald's counter salespeople (what do you call them?) are asked to say, "Would you prefer a large or small order of fries with your sandwich?" *Build* the average ticket sale is one great **sales strategy**. You have to *do more* than just deliver the product or service!

Just how YOU want it!

When I met and visited with Dan Evans, CEO, of the very successful restaurant chain, Bob Evans Restaurants, I was reminded that many great restaurants think of their *servers* as salespeople. My help in documenting and training servers to improve their *sequence of customer service* has resulted in sales increases for many. **"TREAT THE CUSTOMER LIKE YOUR VIP GUEST!"**

There is nothing like Mom's good home cooking for many of us. When relatives would gather at our home, my dad would call our family dinners a "Bynner Eatery". Bynner being, of course, my mother's maiden name. The point?

Mom would ask you what you wanted to eat, then *fix it just the way you wanted it!* The only thing she never seemed to master was her biscuits. As Zig Ziglar says, "They often got cooked in the Squat!" Salespeople and biscuits must rise for each occasion.

With my mom's home cooking you could NOT take it or leave it! She knew how to *find a need and fill it!* And she still does, as evidenced by a phone call at my office with a dinner invitation one recent Monday morning. "Would 6:30 or 7:00 be better for you tonight, Thom?" (Alternate of choice close)

She loves to cook. She always hopes and expects the food to turn out well. She has faith that those who eat it will like it. It's no wonder that some have recommended to her that we turn the old home I grew up in, originally built in 1875, into a historic land mark and restaurant. Can you see the points and applications or analogies for you?

Discount retailers take this approach to selling, and some like Wal-Mart and K-Mart do it so well that they Become #1 in Selling in their market niche. When I visited K-Mart's corporate headquarters in 1985, then again in 1989, in Troy, Michigan, it became evident why they were so successful. They lost market shares to Wal-Mart because analysts say they did not keep up! **Change! Modernize! Redecorate! Improve technology!**

You must stay abreast of the changes in the markets you serve, *stay on top of trends.* Wal-Mart zoomed by everyone including Sears which dominated the American market for decades. Why? Their **customer is KING or QUEEN!**

Yes, it is hard to find much help at the discount store, even at K-Mart, but the great ones like the Wal-Marts and the K-Marts say: TAKE IT. . .IT IS THE BEST VALUE. . . THE BEST PRICE. . . GREAT QUALITY. . . or LEAVE IT.

Become 🐜 in Selling!

They *sell the sizzle* not just the steak, even if the steak is discounted! They *answer the prospects' possible objections in advance* and tell them what is in it for YOU!

One of my largest accounts years ago was quickly becoming K-Mart. Another national accounts salesperson **negotiated** and serviced that national contract. Our best local salespeople did not like just being *order takers* by visiting the stores only to fill in the basic stock. Do you? Most pro's want to be much MORE!

The winners always add more than "take it or leave it"!

On a national basis, companies like Eureka develop different colored units for **key accounts** like Montgomery Ward and K-Mart; some call this private brand merchandising. I do this today with custom audio and video tape programs, where appropriate. Or, we can tailor this book or our seminars more to your specific needs. How about you? What **better, unique and different things** do you do for your key accounts or customers?

Once 2000 units of Model 2010A rolled off the assembly line, the paint sprayers would simply change their spray paint guns from blue paint to green paint and paint the next 500 units green for K-Mart. And, even though it was the same unit in construction, it would be given a different model number and sell for $10 less than the blue unit. This is *good business* and a *wise use of time* and *human resources*, isn't it? Plus, they can *justify* the price difference better.

WHERE THERE IS A WILL . . . THERE IS A WAY!

Those who Become #1 in Selling look for ways to sell every possible prospect or account. It can be done in time, however, it really is not necessary.

As I write this book, I have dozens of practical examples, analogies and funny antidotes I could share to make these various points, so you can understand, apply and then Become #1 in Selling! Pray and work for a *Will to make better choices.*

For several years, I was on the faculty for the Ohio Association of Realtors. I facilitated two *custom tailored* seminars for their industry, as I have for some other industries. Some have CE credit today from the Ohio Division of Real Estate. How do you custom tailor?

The first, *Blueprints for Real Estate Sales*, was for salespeople and the other, *Blueprints for Real Estate Sales Management* was for the boss! 100-200% listing and sales increases were not uncommon from my graduates. *So what?*

Great Realtors can never say as they show the home, "Take it or leave it!" They must help the prospective home owner *visualize* themselves in the home. And, of course, they only show the homes that the person can **qualify** to buy. . . homes that have met the *criteria* of their needs analysis. Do you need to **qualify buyers** better? You can!

PAINT THE PICTURE

"Mary, can you see your living room furniture fitting in nicely here?" "This is a spacious kitchen, isn't it?" (positive tie down?)

"And, John, what do you think of the gas patio grill? And, I knew you'd like the work bench in the garage for all your tools!"

"I searched every listing to find this one to show you. Based on what you told me you wanted in your dream home, this is it!!"

PROBLEM SOLVING ORIENTED

Solving problems can be tiring mentally, physically and emotionally. Plus it can be costly. *ELIMINATE THE COST!* See it always as an *INVESTMENT!* And, more as an **opportunity, situation or challenge**.

I had the largest challenge of my adult life one July. My employer wanted us to move to Pittsburgh from our home of two years, in North Canton, Ohio. We had moved three times in three years! This was enough! Traveling four nights a week for a year! This is a concern with a young family.

I had little or no family life, no church, community or social involvement. There were problems brewing, yet I was driven to *make it to the top.*

Although I was playing some golf, I was not running, then, and was nearly burnt out.

When solving problems it's important to:

A. Clearly and objectively identify the problem (situation).

B. Make a list of all possible solutions.

C. Seek counsel, if need be (and it usually is advisable).

D. Pray (seek more insight and wisdom) and think positive!

E. Set a deadline for your decision.

F. Make the best choice possible, considering the implications on all involved.

G. Don't look back or second guess the decision.

It was painful (rewarding) for me to look back and do the laborious research to write this book, in many respects. There is no gain without a little pain. Although I have mostly positive experiences, stories, and training applications to share, I have had my share of "situations" (failures), too. Research proves to me that too much retrospection or looking back, apart from forwarding thinking goal orientation, does more harm than good, if you have a tendency to dwell on situations (not failures) which did not turn out how you wanted. Usually, they turned out how you needed for reasons you may not yet understand.

Someone said, "Show me a man who never succeeded and I'll show you a man who never tried. Show me a man who has never failed, and I'll show you a man who has never really tried."

We always *learn more through our failures than through our successes.* So. . . Listen! They are *not* failures!

For nearly five years with Eureka, all I did was strike gold. I worked as if there was gold with each swing of my sales ax. Eureka means literally **"I found it"**.

When reviewing options and "opportunities", even before I was formally taught the technique, I *weighed the ideas for versus the ideas against.* Yes, some call this the *Ben Franklin technique for closing sales.* It's equally effective for our own *decision making.*

IDEAS FOR VERSUS THE IDEAS AGAINST

On one side on a sheet of 8-1/2" by 11" paper, list the ideas for taking a particular action--on the other side the ideas against it.

Carl Stevens, "America's #1 Sales Architect", and marvelous mentor to me, would teach me we must have **2-1/2 times** the ideas *for* versus the ideas against to garner a "YES!?"

I concluded that I must either resign my HIGH PAYING job or RISK losing my family! I came within a few days of buying a condominium in Pittsburgh, while keeping our home in North Canton. What are the trade outs? Again, always ask: "What do I have to give up to get what I want?" and, "Is it worth it?"

The plan was that my wife would stay in North Canton, and I'd move to Pittsburgh, get settled, and she'd come over later, when Erin was older. In retrospect, I had wished that I had listened to my wife and never had taken the promotion because I'd still have my job as a Branch Sales Manager. I did not have this to go back to as I had located and hired my replacement in Akron earlier.

"What am I trying to say?" "What does this have to do with my Becoming #1 in Selling!?" you ask.

Study this definition of the *most successful salesperson.* The salesperson who is effective with every type behavior, every buyer is. . .

THE PROBLEM ORIENTED SALESPERSON

Become 🐛 in *Selling!*

He says,

> "I consult with my customer or prospect so I can be properly informed of all the needs in his (or her) *situation* that my product, service or ideas *can satisfy.* Together, we work toward a *sound purchase decision* which yields the benefits he or she expects."

Once married, we had better be properly informed of all the needs of our spouse. He or she is the first one that must be sold or your *career direction* can be sidetracked, delayed, or rerouted.

Sometimes that is just as it must be for you to learn the lessons you must to reach just where you fit best in this business world.

As I've said for years, now, "If you aren't having FUN doing it, it's either not for you, or you are doing it WRONG!" Commit to do it RIGHT!

Either way, you must *prioritize* better to Become #1!

My best problem solving oriented Branch Sales Manager was good old Tom Montgomery. He always operated by the golden rule. . .(not that he who has the most gold rules) or platinum rule (chapter one).

He was FAIR in his pricing, and helped people *feel good* about their purchase decisions. I probably learned more from Tom than he learned from me, although he was always saying, **"Thank you!"** and **"Yes Sir!"** and **"Please"** and **"May I?"**

Tom would *never* think of selling someone too many of any one item. He had lots of empathy, always making sure that his customer, and their customer got the expected benefits. . . or they would receive their money back!

It's no wonder everyone in the company *respected* Tom Montgomery. They might not have agreed with his *plodding methodology,* but they respected him.

And after all, our **reputation** is always *more important* than a few extra sales, or dollars.

In some sales organizations that are very. . .

SALES TECHNIQUE ORIENTED

The problem solving oriented person may not fit, or last for long. What's ironic is that the guy with the solutions always outsells the guy with all the techniques, if given *equal* opportunity and *enough* time. Some techniques, like those used on me when I leased a new auto recently, can back fire on you ! And some are necessary. Examples?

At each step in the negotiations, the salesperson said something like, "*If my sales manager approves this, will you go ahead and lease the car?*" When I said "yes" he actually wrote the proposal out on a legal pad, asked me to sign an informal agreement, and took it to the manager. Small closes lead to the sale. It worked. . .I liked the way he "was *going to bat*" for me!

The negative was that although the price was negotiated down before the lease was agreed to, when they took me to the finance man (another technique) by myself, he could not agree to some of the things I thought I would get, like the price in writing! Leases can be complicated, and to make money, they can side step all your objections, hoping you will forget the *small* (earlier) *demands*. Not me!

Many sales technique oriented salespeople come from a direct sales or one call close orientation. This will work less and less in the future.

These people are often the sprinter as opposed to the long distance runner. The sheer numbers of their presentations guarantee some results, generally *much better than average results*.

Not long ago, I received a letter from Tommy Hopkins, who some (including himself) call America's #1 sales trainer. He was very *technique oriented* and was America's #1 real estate salesperson at one time. He, like me, had a great mentor. His was J. Douglas Edwards, a true sales legend (just like some of my mentors). Tommy's techniques focus to solve problems.

At times we must all utilize the other sales styles. The guy or gal with the solutions, after asking all the **right questions, "wins" the most often**.

Become ❀ in Selling!

A key, then, is to be flexible to see enough prospects or customers. . . to make more presentations, if you are a problem solver.

Jerry Iwanejko was my sales technique oriented expert. His dad had been moving Hoovers for years and had *ingrained* this style into Jerry long before I met him.

Jerry was, and always is, very positive. When **"programmed"** with lots of sales techniques, and answers to every objection, one's *self-confidence increases*, and generally one becomes *less susceptible* to the negative influences of others. So, yes, let's all learn *more* sales techniques! However, there are many other higher principles which bring lasting success and happiness.

The Sales Technique Oriented salesperson exclaims:

> "I have a tried and true routine for getting a prospect or customer to buy. These techniques motivate him or her through my blended personality and product or service emphasis and explanation."

What some salespeople have not realized is that *"practice does not make perfect."* As Vince Lombardi said, **"Perfect practice makes perfect"** whether you are a salesperson, teacher, football player, executive, author, mom or dad.

Many salespeople practice the wrong verbiage or approach over and over again the wrong way until they have a bad habit that becomes *very difficult* to change! I also know one aspiring preacher like this. . . I pray for him. . . even he is too proud to ask for help. Objectivity is needed by everyone.

HUMOR: Henry Ford said, "The only thing wrong with the school of experience is by the time you graduate you are either too old, too poor, or too tired to enjoy it!"

He went on to say that **O.P.E** or "other people's (successful) experience is the best way to learn. FORD surrounded himself with and listened to people smarter than himself.

BE JOYFUL!

The Sales Technique Oriented person is usually half way between the people oriented and problem solving oriented types on a continuum.

Both the "take it or leave it" and "the people oriented" salesperson are *concerned* for the customer. . . one a great deal, and the other, hardly at all.

The problem solving oriented person is also very concerned and his methodology is **superior** to the other sales styles mentioned. You'll learn why as we proceed.

The sales technique oriented guy (or gal) on a scale of 1 to 10 being high, is in the middle on concern for his customer. He'd just as soon be done with it, and home with the family, or on the golf course. He may grow *impatient* with this book, because I have yet to get to the techniques that can make him more bucks, today. (He doesn't focus for long on the *long-term implications*.)

He relies a lot on his personality. I know.

When I was in high school I was voted most popular by my senior class. I wanted to be everyone's friend. It was very important to me to *know everyone's name*, and *have them know mine*. These are *keys* to becoming #1 in selling.

I was often misunderstood by my girlfriend, however, who took my friendliness for flirting. You see she was the. . .

PUSH THE PRODUCT ORIENTED

. . . type salesperson. This person says:

> "I take charge of the customer and hard sell him. I pile on all the pressure I can and get him to say. . . yes!"

Thank God **people can change!**

If you have a good thing, and you know it, it is very natural to want to "push" it on others. Take the story of the lady I once met at a ladies figure salon. I was there to make a sales call on their regional sales director. I hoped to enroll some of their people in our sales or management seminars.

Become 🐝 **in Selling!**

.While waiting, I made some **small talk** with the receptionist as most salespeople know to do. Some salespeople do this because they are naturally friendly and caring people, and others because they want to get data or *pre-approach information* about the business, or decision maker.

I asked the lady, "Do you *believe* in the product or service you offer?"

"Do I!" she exclaimed, "Why just look at this!" And with that statement, she pulled out her "before" pictures. She was at least 50 pounds over weight in the photos. I looked at her. I looked at the photos. Sold!

A PRODUCT OF THE PRODUCT!

This receptionist (sales lady) was a product of the product. She sort of pushed herself on me. She sold me!

But there was one problem. I was *not a prospect* for this ladies figure salon!

This is exactly the *down side* of the push the product oriented type salesperson. They often forget to *qualify* their prospects *properly*. And even when they are talking to a **legitimate buyer**, they are only somewhat effective with three out of five type buyers.

There have been many studies done by many reputable organizations on why one salesperson is more successful than another. In my own research and experience, it's often because *too few sales calls are made on too few of the right people*.

As many as 80% of the sales calls are made on someone other than the real decision maker. Certainly there are those who **influence the decision maker.** They may be consulted, so you had better *impress* them favorably.

"The Buck stops here!" as Harry Truman said.

In selling to homes, salespeople know they must appeal to *both* the husband and wife.

HUMOR: A man married 70 years was asked, "How is it that you have been married so long!?" He replied emphatically, "In my home, I have always made all the BIG decisions!" He then was asked, "In 70 years how many big decisions have there been?" He said, "There haven't been any yet, however, I am *ready* when they come!"

Of course *to NOT decide is to decide.* And, many more decisions than we often realize are made by *someone other* than who we think!

I received a letter recently, as an example, from the **WHITE HOUSE**. It reads: "Your continued interest in serving the Administration was recently brought to my attention. Thank you for sharing with us your concerns about the status of your candidacy for an appointment as the UNITED STATES AMBASSADOR to the Philippines: I've carefully noted your background and interests and forwarded your credentials to my *Associate* Director, Liz Montoya, who handles that appointment. Again, we appreciate your offer of service and your continued support."

> Sincerely,
> J. Veronica Biggins
> Assistant to the PRESIDENT and
> Director of Presidential Personnel

And you thought the President *actually* made all the "BIG" decisions! Who influences the President? Your prospects. . . your customers. . . your clients? Has the decision been **delegated?**

The person selling office equipment must influence the person using the machines or computers that "they have the *best* product." However, he or she can lose the sale if he hasn't met the needs of user. Often, the latter has the most influence. Are you **USER FRIENDLY**?

Those who simply push the product (or service) often lose sales and never know **why.**

The "Push the Product" Branch Sales Manager all star was Joe. Joe was a heavy set Jewish gentleman who always smoked cigars. Being that I was a contact lens wearer, this, of course, irritated me, as he would blow his cigar smoke in all directions without concern for my comfort. The customer's comfort was in jeopardy.

This was before the current craze and concern for non-smokers' rights and the Surgeon General's warning. . . "Smoking may be *dangerous* to your health." There are many **habits** that are dangerous for the well being of an aspiring sales superstar.

Joe knew the products inside and out and he wanted everyone to know he knew. You *know the type*. He'd talk right by the sale, and sell features and benefits a customer has no interest in, at times.

Overall he did a good job because the. . .

REPUTATION BUYER

. . .and the. . .

PUSHOVER BUYER

. . . were impressed with his smoke blowing razzle dazzle. Of course, almost anyone can sell to pushovers except the take it or leave it salesperson.

I wish I had time and space to share more stories about all the salespeople I know or have known that fit into the five sales categories. Some anecdotes about some I can share are quite humorous. *Please dialogue* with your associates about those you know who fit the categories. Then take the ideas given to adapt the best style to fit your buyers, hence, get more sales.

LAUGH AT YOURSELF!

It's a good idea to laugh at yourself! Not take yourself too seriously. I recently heard my beautiful sister, Sally, comment on three separate ministers from her Methodist church, over the years. She liked a certain minister the best because "he used relevant humor and still made his point". Sometimes the most effective humor can be to put yourself down! *Put others at ease*!

Those who Become #1 in Selling do take their work and the profession of selling seriously. These serious minded people are reading this book. . . not only reading it, but studying it. And determining how to apply the ideas, or needed improvements in their lives and sales careers.

The best humorists (and salespeople) really work at their *craft*. Their timing is impeccable. Their delivery is spotless!

Briefly let's review; here are five sales styles in order of total effectiveness:

1. **Problem Solver**
2. **Push the Product**
3. **Sales Technique Oriented**
4. **People Oriented**
5. **Take It or Leave It**

Once you understand these, and which style you fit into, if you really want to Become #1 in Selling, you may need a tune-up or adjustment into the style that best fits your customers to make them want to buy.

Who first said, "There is no gain without a little pain!"

I'm not one taken to a lot of trite clichés. I am interested in what people do and why they do it. And why we do not do what we know is best. The Bible explains this better than anyone can.

Is it true the fear of success is greater than the fear of failure in some cases?

A book on selling would not be **complete** without addressing the area of a person's *self-image* and *self-esteem*, would it? Correct the why and we correct the outcome. Evaluate the symptoms properly then we can offer the right prescription to heal the root problem.

Every problem solver knows that as they help others get more of not just what they want, but also why they want it, they sell more.

P.S. STANDS FOR PROBLEM SOLVER; then you are. . .

P.S. A PEOPLE SATISFIER; then you are a . . .

P.S. PROFESSIONAL SALESPERSON!

Only when you are a problem solver are you a people satisfier. And only then are you a **pro**, in my book.

Become 👤 in Selling!

Zig Ziglar says throughout his wonderful book, *See You at The Top*, "If you will help enough other people get what they want then you will get what you want!"

Selling is asking questions. Selling is sharing.

Selling is listening. Selling is caring. Selling is honorable... when done correctly and professionally.

HUMOR: My two ears and one mouth remind me I must be listening twice as much as speaking. Yes, it is true the good Lord gave us two ears and one mouth for a reason!

And *when speaking* 1) ask the *right questions.* . . or 2) paint *positive word pictures.*

I want you to finish this book and use the ideas. I need you to recommend me and the book to others, please.

To **earn** that, I must stay focused on helping you get what you want. You must do the same with your customers. Are you? And what's that want?

More income (most cases): And:_____

(please fill in the blank)

Yes, I realize you have *many* other **motivations**. And, priorities are different

HUMOR: And someone else analyzed "money won't allow you to buy happiness, but you can look for it (happiness) in some very interesting places!" And another, "It beats being poor!" I recommend your money is spent or invested in wholesome pursuits.

HUMOR: When "*The Waltons*" TV show was on TV and very popular several years ago, I was told, "We were so poor when we were growing up, we had to borrow from the Waltons." Another said, "We were so poor, we thought "slightly irregular" and "marked down" were brand names!"

In the *San Diego Tribune*, I read a *Forbes Magazine* summary of the wealthiest people in America. The Sam Waltons and Les Wexners were on the list, of course. However, many were widows of rich men.

"Behind every great man there is. . ." --you finish it. And many men manage the money of these *great women* once their husbands are dead! And *many great women earn big incomes* these days through selling.

It dawned on me early in life that being rich, but losing my family, was not a good definition of a purposeful life. However, marriage failures take place, as do premature deaths. Businesses fail (some merge). Sales attempts fail. Learn and move on! If you did your best, you *need not feel guilt* over your failures. Set **new goals! Commitment, long-term**, is critically important.

Because we understand selling (and buyers), we know we can succeed elsewhere. Selling is the most secure profession, but one where you can, and do wake up, unemployed one day. Whether on salary, draw against commission, percentage of profits, or straight commission, stop selling, and soon that *paycheck* stops!

Let us discuss the *5 buyer styles*, briefly.

PUSHOVER

This buyer's psychological profile says. . . "when a salesperson who likes me recommends something, it must be good. So I am likely to buy it. I buy more than I need, and many things don't suit me, or never get used!"

None of us want to be that kind of buyer, do we? However, just as each of us has some or all 5 sales styles potentially *operative* in our own lives, we also have *tendencies* or weakness' (and strengths) as each type buyer. Maybe, that's why each of us can *identify* with each, and *understand* the need to work properly with each type buyer.

I'm a pushover for buying books after I hear a speaker speak. In the last few months, I have heard some of America's most outstanding speakers, and bought numerous books and had them autographed. I treasure them like gold bullion. **Invest in yourself** with greater knowledge continually.

Even easier to sell is the. . .

Become  **in Selling!**

COULDN'T CARE LESS BUYER

This is, if you can get eyeball to eyeball with this buyer. And seldom is he or she the real decision maker. If you are selling by phone, good luck!

The couldn't care less buyers says. . .

> "I avoid salespeople, if I can. Seeing a salesperson is an inconvenience. If there is any risk of my being wrong, the boss (spouse?) or someone else had better okay the purchasing decision."

I once dealt with a man, Paul Paula, like this at a large department store in Akron, Ohio. I made the terrible mistake of calling this 50 year old (when I was a mature 22) "Paul". He quickly corrected me by saying, "Son, to you, I am **Mr.** Paula!

P. . .A. . .U. . .L. . .A! Got it?"

And, he was the housewares buyer!! What happens if your entire future with an account depends on selling a guy like this? He couldn't care less about us.

The word "thankfulness" actually comes from the word "thinkfulness." Thus on *Thanksgiving* we *think about* what we are thankful for.

This is one of dozens of needful habits to **cultivate** daily.

I was THANKFUL that I learned that the divisional merchandising manager (Mr. Paula's boss) made most of the "big" decisions. So, I carefully went about *ingratiating* myself to this man, by finding out what he saw as their problems, needs, and sales and profit margin objectives, for Mr. Paula's department.

This man was a. . .

REPUTATION BUYER

When I showed him Eureka had recently received the #1 rating in Consumer Reports for 2 or 3 models, I could see, non-verbally, that I really got his attention. Attention is critically important, isn't it? You can create interest!

126

Reputation buyers often give themselves away by the type of auto they drive, or brand name clothing they wear. A cross pen in every shirt pocket!

If this buyer thinks others will *think of him more favorably as a result* of this purchase from you. . .you need only ask for the order.

If, however, you offend his often *sensitive tastes*, he may give you two orders. . .

"GET OUT. . .and STAY OUT!!"

Who do you know is a reputation buyer?

Reputation buyers are more emotional than others.

Prentice Hall did a survey of several thousand salespeople, asking them this question:

"What percentage of your buyers' buying decisions are rational and what percentage are emotional?"

The synopsis was that 90% of all buying decisions are *emotional or psychological*, and only 10% are rational, or based on the facts alone!

Again, it's not what they want, but why they want it that motivates people to *action*. . . and the decision!

What I wanted was to be a good father to my son, Todd, (turning 5) and to my new daughter, Erin. I wanted to see my wife more. PRIORITIES! And someone's priority which causes them to say "NO" today, may change and they can and will say "YES" a few weeks, months or years later to the *same* offer.

What I wanted at age 24 was to find more PURPOSE for my life. I was running without real purpose. It wasn't enough any longer to Become #1 in Selling and to earn over $60,000 per year or more each year.

After all, why would *anyone* want to Become #1?

Why would I quit a great job that paid big money? Later, I'll discuss our DOMINANT BUYING URGE or the hot button.

Every buyer has one. . .or more of these buttons. . .and they always are emotional . . . or psychological.

Now, just in case you are the

Become 🐸 **in Selling!**

DEFENSIVE PURCHASER

. . .I'd better talk straighter!

"Remember, Thom, K.I.S.S.--Keep It Simple, Salesman!" "OK!" I retort.

You think I might be taking advantage of you, or wasting your time, or you don't need what I am offering. Or, you've been hurt too badly in the past. Why should you trust me? Why am I different? You are my buyer! KEY: Every buyer we come in contact with has a series of **unspoken questions** or objections that, if answered, can lead to the sale.

I know people who would never hire a consultant. They are too defensive for that. They must have (or think they have) control! Hiring a consultant (like me) who could do in 10 hours what an employee would take 40-120 hours to research and do, would be admitting "I can't solve this on my own." And, "I'd rather spend more money than admit I need help!" Is that smart?

Approach the defensive purchaser with **ideas** more so than solutions to problems. Some will *never admit* to a problem. All they have are *challenges or opportunities*.

Such is the defensive purchaser. I've sold to a lot of them. I know how they think and behave. In some sales situations they really are quite funny.

They must all have a little Missourian in them. "*Show* me" or "*Prove* it to me!" is what they really think.

However, on the surface they might think. . .

"No salesperson is going to take advantage of me! Instead, I will dominate the salesperson. If I buy, I will try to get as much as possible for every dime I spend!"

It's best to start with a high, high price with this guy or gal. And many defensive purchases *herd together*. Have you ever attempted a group presentation and lost the sale and not been able to figure out why?

Sometimes it is best to let these people think it is their idea. It might shatter their image if they thought they did not have a great buy.

I am reminded of my dad. He was a journalist by training. He was *trained* to look for ideas, be objective and to have a critical eye.

He was a great and selfless man in many respects. Just like my buyers, he could also be misunderstood. (Recently, the Harold Lisk Scholarship Fund in Journalism was awarded to a deserving senior from the fastest growing high school in Ohio (Hilliard) from which he graduated in 1934.)

The defensive purchasers can often times be sold to by the problem solving oriented salesperson. Why? Because you want to (and do) understand the guy or gal. Boy, does it take work, and maybe too much time. Be careful.

The Push the Product Oriented salespeople are only somewhat effective with this defensive purchaser.

A comparison will help you to determine how each style matches up with each buyer style.

Remember to love 'em all!

And lastly, the. . .

SOLUTION PURCHASER

I saved the best for last! This statement reminds me of the **Master Key to Success**. I will say this in many different ways in this book.

History records that a man by the name of Jesus lived and walked on this earth 2000 years ago. Some believe He was a great teacher. Some a lunatic. Some just another man. One third of the world population believes He is who He said He was. . . God. Historical facts proved this man Jesus lived for 33 years.

Many people know a little about Him. Some, a lot. Others want to. Others don't allow themselves to care.

THE solution

Become ✺ in Selling!

And, I know first hand that you can Become #1 in Selling without knowing much, if anything, about Jesus. When I worked for Eureka for 5 years, I never once went to a Protestant or Catholic church, or a Jewish Synagogue. I never once attended a Muslim, Islamic or any type service where religious faith was taught. I became #1 in selling due to hard, smart work, great mentors, knowing my product, having the right attitudes, caring about people, being dependable, loyal, trustworthy, disciplined, etc. The characteristics that Jesus taught! (I did attend church as a child.)

I knew I had a need, however, for more purpose in my life; a spiritual dimension. How did I know this? All my accomplishments left me unfulfilled. Satisfying myself, my wife, my children, and my employer was not enough, nor was a lot of money.

I found the solution for ultimate purpose and my self-fulfillment. I now attend church faithfully and read the Bible regularly.

Let me quote the Master Key *success principle* from the Master teacher. . .

MASTER KEY TO SUCCESS

"He who will be first (#1) will be last, and he who will be last will be first." Matthew 19:30

"Now," you ask, "what does this have to do with me and how to Become #1 in Selling!"

The Problem Solving Oriented Salesperson is first, and also is last. He or she is #1 (*most effective*) with all buyers, especially the solution purchaser. The problem solver is last because *he puts his own needs last*, as he (or she, of course) **SERVES** his customers collectively, and individually, better than all others. Because of this (the best service is hard work and demands long hours), his *customers buy so much* that he (or she) Becomes #1 in Selling! No wonder that some "burn out." A spiritual focus can prevent that possibility.

130

The solution purchaser thinks:

> "I have surveyed my general needs, and now I am looking for the specific product (or service) that will satisfy them best at the price I can afford."

The solution purchaser runs with a purpose. It's obvious! He wants to solve problems and *feels good* when someone helps in this process. The problem solving salesperson *believes the purpose is to bring solutions.*

Those who Become #1 are in demand. They **run** between customers who really appreciate their dedication to providing answers that work and service that is outstanding. Become part of the solution, never part of the problem!

SUMMARY

The Problem Solver sells the Solution Purchaser (and all others). The Push the Product person sometimes pushes the wrong product at the wrong price. The Sales Technique Oriented person can try to manipulate and lose the solution purchaser, forever. The People Oriented guy or gal can attempt to be buddies and our ideal buyer doesn't want that, they want the best solutions. Take it or Leave it? They may stumble into a sale or two.

Become #1 in Selling! **Become a problem solver!** *This is your solution! You will run with more purpose.*

> "Pride leads to arguments; be humble, take
> advice and become wise." Proverbs 13:10

REVIEW QUESTIONS

Name or list one buyer you know who fits each buyer style described in this chapter. Label the buyer.

1.
2.
3.
4.
5.

Name salespeople who fit each sales style (their dominant style).

1.
2.
3.
4.
5.

Please make a list of your top 10 buyers and your top 10 prospective buyers and label each. How many have the dominant style of a solution purchaser?

_____

_____

_____

Can you see how you have lost sales because you did not position yourself as a professional problem solver? What can you do to always be a problem solver?

_____

_____

_____

_____

RATE YOUR LISTENING ABILITIES

<u>ATTITUDES</u>	Almost Always	Usually	Occasionally	Seldom	Almost Never
1. Do you like to listen to other people talk?	5	4	3	2	1
2. Do you encourage other people to talk?	5	4	3	2	1
3. Do you listen even if you do not like the person who is talking?	5	4	3	2	1
4. Do you listen equally well whether the person talking is man or woman, young or old?	5	4	3	2	1
5. Do you listen equally well to friend, acquaintance, stranger?	5	4	3	2	1

<u>ACTION</u>

	Almost Always	Usually	Occasionally	Seldom	Almost Never
6. Do you put what you have been doing out of sight and out of mind?	5	4	3	2	1
7. Do you look at him?	5	4	3	2	1
8. Do you ignore the distractions about you?	5	4	3	2	1
9. Do you smile, nod your head, and otherwise encourage him to talk?	5	4	3	2	1
10. Do you think about what he is saying?	5	4	3	2	1
11. Do you try to figure out what he means?	5	4	3	2	1
12. Do you try to figure out why he is saying it?	5	4	3	2	1

Become 🏃 **in Selling!**

ACTION CONT.	Almost Always	Usually	Occasionally	Seldom	Almost Never
13. Do you let him finish what he is trying to say?	5	4	3	2	1
14. If he hesitates, do you encourage him to go on?	5	4	3	2	1
15. Do you re-state what he has said and ask him if you got it right?	5	4	3	2	1
16. Do you withhold judgment about his idea until he has finished?	5	4	3	2	1
17. Do you listen regardless of his manner of speaking and choice of words?	5	4	3	2	1
18. Do you listen even though you anticipate what he is going to say?	5	4	3	2	1
19. Do you question him in order to get him to explain his idea more fully?	5	4	3	2	1
20. Do you ask him what the words mean as he uses them?	5	4	3	2	1

Subtotal (Add each column) ___ __ __ __ __

Grand Total Score: _____

How id you do? A   B   C   D   F   (Circle one)

Set goals now to improve a listener.

CHAPTER 6

THE PROFESSIONAL SALES PRESENTATION

BLUEPRINTS FOR PROFESSIONAL SELLING!

Life truly is a process. You come and go just like the seasons. Like fine gold under the pressure of formation, you are being refined and perfected. And so are your sales presentations.

Repetition is the mother of skill. Many great salespeople practice a *perfect sales presentation* before they come face to face with a prospective buyer. They learn the steps and words. The track to run on. Then they are not so easily thrown off track by the prospect's objections. First, focus to become the kind of person people want to buy from, then learn what to do and say.

Have you ever competed with your peers, each giving his best sales presentation, with the group voting for a winner? Try it!

WHAT GOOD IDEAS CAN DO FOR YOU!

Tom Ryan attended my mentor Carl Stevens' 2-1/2 day seminar where he learned "How to make a professional sales presentation in the proper psychological sequence for maximum motivational impact." Mr. Ryan was admittedly not a salesperson by prior training or inclination and ready to quit his insurance sales career just before attending a Blueprint for Professional Selling seminar.

During the seminar he agreed that Carl Stevens knew what he was talking about. The research, stories, analogies, and principles given were compelling and persuasive.

Become 🐛 in Selling!

The third morning of this intensive seminar, which included numerous programmed learning exercises, was to be a competition using the procedure or BLUEPRINT taught in a role play.

Tom Ryan decided to go all out to WIN! He was motivated to stay up all night long organizing and learning his sales presentation.

Carl Stevens had learned his teaching mastery after years of service part time as a Dale Carnegie instructor, then instructor of the instructors while an investment banker in San Antonio, Texas. "Coach Stevens," as we students called him, became a master sales trainer. He had his own special mentors like Ray Busby, a homespun sales educator from the hills of Tennessee.

Carl mesmerized Tom Ryan! He sold him (and me, too!) that there was one best way to make a sales presentation. Tom figured that the $295 invested to attend this seminar must receive a return!

Consider that one can earn many thousands of dollars more each year through becoming better prepared. So, a small $300-$700 investment in oneself is easy to make.

Tom's Blueprint presentation was voted #1! Everyone watched and listened in awe as he used the key phrases in each of the seven steps just like the mentor, Carl Stevens, had taught.

HUMOR: One day recently I spoke to a large Rotary Club and asked, I thought rhetorically: "What is a mentor?" Before I could give the answer a man stood up and exclaimed: "Thom, a Mentor, that is a city on the lake near Cleveland!"

The **closing statement** . . . "That's what you really want, isn't it?!" "Let's go ahead with this now, ok?" . . . left everyone and the prospect with one choice then, . . . "OK!"

Sometimes, when a prospect is receiving three or more presentations, you would not want to go first, for obvious reasons. However, this day no one could match Tom's *precise* presentation. The price was never an issue. Nor need it be the #1 issue if you sell professionally.

He Became #1 in Selling!

His best effort motivated everyone else to do better. Great salespeople love and thrive on competition! Tom went on to be more successful in sales, and later opened his own company. The confidence he gained helped him earn more.

THE MUSICAL SCALE

Which one of us does not love and appreciate a beautiful piano recital? How Roger Williams, Liberace or the other great pianists generate so much variation from seven notes is beyond me . . . so much beauty!

Recently, we acquired a portable Yamaha piano/organ with synthesizing features (PSP 500M). It allows you to orchestrate 5 musical instruments electronically through one key board via one operator. It is simply amazing.

The music can sound like a beautiful orchestra with every note coordinated, once programmed, at the careful pushing of several buttons. You must KNOW which to push.

Some sales people can get so organized, just like a team of people, that beauty emanates from their lives. I recommend the Susan Silver's book, "Organized To Be Your BEST!"

Kurt is a Realtor who I first met in August 1977. In the mid 90's, he sometimes personally carries 80 listings, he reports. He outsells some companies with 10 or more people from his HER Realtors office on Cleveland Avenue in Columbus, Ohio. He has a system and a support staff that allows him to market a great many homes. People can tell through his advertising that he gets RESULTS!

When I first met Kurt when he attended our seminar, he did not remind me of a great orchestra, however, today he makes beautiful music! *P E R S E V E R A N C E!*

He is like the soloist that excels or the first violin in the best orchestra. His company is the largest in the area, and HER owner Harley E. Rouda was President of the National Association of Realtors. Success breeds success.

Become 🏃 ***in Selling!***

If one person in a 120 piece orchestra is playing a different tune than all others, do you think it will be noticed? Do you think the music will be perfect? Of course not! One salesperson in a company who does not play by the same good methods as the others can and will hurt all others.

7 STEPS

Just as there are only seven notes in the musical scale so are there seven steps in the professional sales presentation. I learned when I missed one step that the music. . . the presentation. . .may not result in a sale.

In Chapter 4, I introduced you to the seven steps of a professional sales presentation. Each note in the musical scale is not always played in the same order. Sometime a presentation might be outlined as follows:

Preparation . . . . . gather preapproach information
Attention . . . . introduction . . .
    Interest. . . . . . . .ask for action; take action
Examination . . . . a few qualifying questions
Prescription . . . . initial analysis/feedback
    Examination . . . more questions
Conviction . . . . . . convince with the facts and benefits
Motivation . . . . . . now and throughout discussion
Completion . . . . . a final close; use trial closes throughout the
                    presentation

MORE THAN A PROCESS!

Professional sales presentations are more than a process, actually, as the title of this chapter infers. They *must* be designed as a blueprint to:

- 👍 Build relationships . . . *WIN/WIN* . . . *GIVE/GIVE*
- 👍 Communicate value
- 👍 Transfer belief
- 👍 Serve the customer
- 👍 Demonstrate quality
- 👍 Solve the problem . . . overcome objections
- 👍 Close the sale

QUALIFYING QUESTIONS

Which of the above is most important to you now?
(This is a qualifying question)
Can you add to the list?   Or, write out some qualifying questions?

☞ 1.

☞ 2.

☞ 3.

☞ 4.

How effective have you been at qualifying the prospect? What further can you do to improve? Some say they have developed an intuition and they trust their gut instinct. Maybe so, however, that comes from years of asking the right questions and learning what is right.

The steps in a sales presentation are typically *designed to close a sale*, whether for the acquisition of the product or service, or to close for the next open door meeting or dialogue.

Become 🐸 in Selling!

Creativity is needed by many salespeople as they rearrange the steps needed to reach their goal to enter into agreement with 100% of the best prospects.

Of course, we know no one bats 100%. In major league baseball we learn of people who make the Hall of Fame who bat .300 or acquire 3 hits out of 10. They do so, however, consistently and persistently for years.

A new presentation by a new person to the same prospect (who earlier rejected the company) offering the same product or service CAN CREATE a sale. Or, the same presentation by the new person can translate into a sale where one cannot accomplish before. Why

HUMAN BEHAVIOR

A friend of mine once shared that "The difference between the right word and the wrong word in a sales presentation is the same as the difference between 'get,' and 'get out.'"

Understanding human behavior can translate into more sales than probably any other factor.

Maslow's hierarchy of needs begins with the need for food, shelter and clothing, (security) and climaxes with self-actualization, as mentioned earlier.

LARRY

Larry G. Calhoon C.F.P. is an interesting case study. A complex and caring man who once was a missionary and pastor, he now works as CFP, CERTIFIED FINANCIAL PLANNER. When at his best, he is one of the best salespersons one could know. His record may not be like Joe Gondolfo, who personally sold over 1 billion in life insurance in one year, however, his clients respond to his strategies and recommendations.

Why? Because he is a *PROBLEM SOLVER*. He is knowledgeable and experienced and he targets only the well off, for his estate planning and other services, because they are the ones knowledgeable and profitable enough to appreciate and act on his solutions.

To Become #1 in Selling, one must understand his/her own needs and wants and put them aside to *focus* 100% on the needs and wants of others which your product or service will satisfy. This sounds very obvious and basic. I can't tell you how many veteran salespeople I know who forget this. Larry and other pros keep *upgrading their product or service* offering to serve a more and more sophisticated buyer. How about you and your company?

PLAN TO IMPROVE

The greatest athletes and those who are the highest paid have a time of basic training *every year*. Why doesn't every salesperson?

Company owners can attend seminars like our Synergism for Personal and Company Growth program where we can facilitate issues of business management. Everyone's selling tools become dulled due to non-use or through association with the unskilled, uncommitted, or uncaring.

This book will *sharpen your tools*. It can be reviewed or thoroughly read every year.

When I attended a three-week training school in January, 1975 for my employer, basics were drilled into my head before I made a sales call. I not only learned sales presentations, I also learned our products inside out and outside in. Have you been through this, too?

They wanted us equipped to answer most questions or objections. They realized that this built for us confidence in our products, company and ourselves. Do you have a plan to learn your products and services and company mission better?

Become in **Selling!**

THE CHAUFFEUR

Have you heard the story about the famous lecturer who had a chauffeur who drove him from town to town? His speeches often received standing ovations, and rave reviews in the papers.

The chauffeur heard the speech so often he had it memorized. A salesperson can do much the same by listening to his perfect sales presentation or the presentation of another on cassette tape over and over again.

One day the chauffeur remarked to the renowned speaker, "Boss, I've heard your speech so many times, I believe I can give it every bit as well as you . . . if not better!"

The wise teacher remarked, "Young man, ok, I'll give you a chance to demonstrate your belief tonight. The community in which I am scheduled to speak this evening has had no advanced publicity photo of myself. Let us change clothing. You wear my suit and I, your uniform, and you deliver my speech!"

"Great," the chauffeur exclaimed, not wanting to back down and loose face.

"You're on!"

That night the chauffeur's speech was wildly applauded and everyone laughed at the appointed times. However, he made one grave mistake at the end when he asked (as the wise doctor often did), "Are there any questions?"

A polite gentleman in the front row rattled off a complex series of inquiries, to which the chauffeur showed stunned silence. Quick on his feet, however, he recovered by saying, "Bud, that has got to be one of the stupidest questions I have ever heard. So much so, that I will let my chauffeur (who, of course, was the famous lecturer) in the back of the room answer that and all remaining questions, as I am weary now."

*ANOTHER **WISE** PERSON*

A young person was said to have visited a wise old sage. The prophet was told the young whip wanted success very badly. The mentor took the protégé to the lake and said "Follow me!" He walked into the deep water and then proceeded to dunk the student until he struggled to escape and surface. The young adult, grasping for breath, said, "Sir, why did you do that?" The smiling elderly guru said, "Son, when you want success as badly as you wanted that breath of air, THEN you WILL have it."

To Become #1 in Selling you must, in most cases, want it very badly. Never want it so badly, however, that you sacrifice ethics in the process. You must remember that there are never any stupid questions asked by any customer or prospect . . . or by any young man or woman to a wise mentor.

And, furthermore, more salespeople get off track because they think themselves knowing it all, and thereby, ease off in the depth of their probing qualifying or diagnostic questions.

UNDERSTAND

Keep asking questions! When all else has failed you can usually *reapproach* prospects with a . . . "I must be a poor salesperson, because we believe we have the best products (or service) to meet your needs and you have said 'No.' Can you help me to understand where I went wrong, so I can improve, and do better with others next time? I'd really appreciate your help. *Can you help me?*"

LOST SALES SURVEY

Critiquing sales approaches and presentations after lost sales helped me to Become #1 in Selling. AND, this helps me help others become #1 in the '90's! Speeches and seminars are also improved through critical evaluation.

When I recently leased a new auto, one of the salespeople whom I spoke with followed up professionally. John of a Mercedes dealership phoned to ask about my decision making progress. Since he had sold my wife an auto, he was hopeful. However, I leased a new car from another dealership. He was curious as to why. Not only did this ingratiate him to me, the feedback will help him to better understand buyers in the future, thus increasing his service and success potential.

On election day, we always have a WINNER☺ and a loser☹. In life and in selling you are never a loser if you are learning.☺

God does not sponsor junk! He is for your success! He wants us, however, to always do things right.

You are special! You are *created in the image of God.* You must believe in yourself even when the big fish escapes your best bait. **Keep fishing. Keep knocking**.

Keep going up to bat! And sharpen your presentation with all these ideas and new revelations.

Abe Lincoln said: "The woodcutter who stops to sharpen his axe will cut more wood." He was not talking about actual wood.

In life, one can never be prepared enough, whether in assuming the responsibilities of becoming a husband, a wife, a father, a mother or a salesperson. That's just it . . . we ASSUME.

HUMOR: Break Assume into t h r e e syllables and you have . . . Ass . . . U . . . Me. Let's not do that to each other.

A MASTER

Tony is a successful consultant who owns a company offering contractor licensing services in California. Although people come to him for advice, he still must sell his advice. While I was at his home for dinner one night, he received a phone call from Guam.

I couldn't help but be in awe by the skill of his questioning. His preapproach information was complete as he anticipated the telephone ringing and the client's needs. Years of preparation and experience helped him to deal with some very sticky legal issues. He then sold his advice.

It is always a delight to see a master ply his craft, isn't it?

ANOTHER TOM TERRIFIC

Past president of The National Speakers Association, Tom Winninger, CSP, CPAE, reports he has several pages of computer printouts about any company before he goes to meet with a prospective client. In marketing, we call it marketing research.

Salespeople often call it *"gathering all the preapproach information" or "qualifying the buyer up front."*

At the end of this chapter, you will find a generic **preparation planning sheet**. In our seminars in the 90's, we help companies help their salespeople customize these and an entire sales system for their unique needs, their unique situation.

"How can I **accelerate** my gathering **preapproach information?"** Ask yourself that question, now. Fill in the blank after reviewing the work sheet at the end of this chapter, please. How can I be more prepared:

_____

_____

_____

ATTENTION

Life equals = "The study of getting attention!"

What gets your attention?

"Breaker . . . breaker . . . 10:4 Good Buddy, come in, this is the Paint Man, do you read me?"

This was the verbiage someone on a CB radio used to attempt communication with another. CB radios, once the rave, are now nearly obsolete. What insures your products, services, company, or you that you do not become obsolete?

Become 🐸 in Selling!

We know there is no total communication until the picture in your mind's eye (the sender) is the same as the picture in the mind of the receiver. The best communicator asks a lot of questions to keep attention and also paints word pictures through effective word choice. Good communicators use visual aids and effective word choices.

Good communicators use visual aids and positive nonverbals. Smile!☺

My father was the Bureau Chief for International News Service, an employee for 22 years. Then he became Public Relations Director for the Ohio Chamber of Commerce and later Vice President for a PR/Advertising Agency. He knew the art of getting others' attention! Here are a few methods he and others have recommended to me, and now, I to you!

S . . . Samples of free gifts create a favorable atmosphere

U . . . Use or drop big names . . . other customers, friends, etc.

C . . . Curiosity . . . appeal to this . . . arouse and capture attention

C . . . Compliment the prospect sincerely or someone close to him/her

E . . . Exciting News . . . that you know he will find interesting

S . . . Startling statements break preoccupation

S . . . Service that benefits him opens minds and doors

SUCCESS . . . I WANT MORE! Affirm and apply!

I . . . . Include him in your circle of friends

W . . . Waive savings in front of the prospect

A . . . Ask provocative questions

N . . . Nice . . . be nicer than everyone else

T . . . Testimonials . . . use reference letters

M . . . Money . . . give an incentive to act NOW

O . . . Orchestrate or organize a team effort

The Professional Sales Presentation

R . . . Reward the prospect for results
E . . . Eureka . . . I found it! Be enthusiastic!

The key to break preoccupation is to remember that every 7-8 minutes we *must regain attention.* How many words or pages can you read in 7-8 minutes? Have I maintained your attention in this book to this point? It gets better as you proceed!

At the end of this chapter, I have an attention-getting work sheet for you to *plan your unique attention maintainers.*

We only have *one chance* to make a good **first impression.** It can take as many as 16 new impressions to make up for one bad first impression. Thus, we must be prepared to make a positive impact from the start.

I hope I have you in a seminar some day when we discuss 1.) shaking hands 2.) making eye contact (and maintaining it) 3.) lowering your voice at the appropriate time 4.) smiling 5.) leaning forward to show your interest 6.) and nodding reassuringly. Be prepared as a conscientious competent person with all the **appropriate nonverbals.**

The Vice President of Manufacturing for Kurfees Coatings, Inc. (now a Division of Service Star of America) made some sales calls with me one day. He said, "You are always so upbeat; *your customers seem so glad to see you.* Why are you so happy?"

Abe Lincoln said, "Most people are about as **happy** as they make up their minds to be." I told him that daily, in the early morning, I dedicate my day and myself to God, and then I can decide to be very happy.

We realize that 87% of the mental impact comes from the visual, and that it is best to "show and tell to sell more." Unless we are *happy and positive,* we will repel rather than *attract and retain people.* That's why we invested so much time in earlier chapters on attitudes, foundational knowledge and becoming.

In January 1976, I had an attention-getting event that *changed my life for the better.* Have you ever met a salesperson that has done that for you? Would you like to be remembered 25 years from now by everyone you meet today? Maybe, you only want to be remembered for one week. Or, simply, you want to keep the attention through a one shot presentation. Then be prepared with better attention getters.

Today I am a Christian because of that January event. Christianity is often misunderstood.

Selling is often misunderstood, too, and given a bad rap by those who refuse to understand or accept the tenets of professionalism that is advanced herein. Let us all alleviate misconceptions about our products or services and about professional selling.

Socrates said *"Knowledge is power."* And, knowledge does bring wisdom to help you serve your customers and reach your goals. Do not reject knowledge because it does not line up with your prior acceptance.

Over the years, I have seen how religions of all types have gotten and maintained the attention of their followers. Some sales people reject church because they think they are being sold or controlled, when what really happens at the Christian Church, when one has the right personal relationship with God, is an **EMPOWERING**.

A *spiritual dimension* is important to develop if you want to be a well rounded individual who does not burn out. Weekly renewal and refocus through a fine church is very valuable. The benefits are eternal. The changes affected in us are needed

EXAMINATION

If you answered **"Yes!"** to the question about being remembered, then let's determine how to have others think well of us when they remember us. Study and apply this material.

I can recall giving blood many years ago. I can see in my *mind's eye* the nurse asking me key questions before drawing blood. The needle got my attention!

Employers or supervisors have lots of questions prepared before the vital **interview**. They want to draw key information from you.

A child asks constantly, "Why mommy? Why daddy?" And, generally a response like "Because I told you so!" . . . is seldom good enough.

What couples do not quiz one another endlessly before the marriage date is set?

Asking questions is a big part of developing any meaningful relationship.

Handing something to someone is an attention getter as is showing something with a pointing of your pen.

We ask questions about God. And the answers we find determine our *perspective* on who God is. Right or wrong.

The same is true with your perspective of yourself, and your prospects' perspective of you. If the right questions do not get asked and answered properly, *faulty conclusions* or beliefs can be attained. The same could be true of your products, your services, your ideas or your company. Since **SELLING IS A TRANSFERENCE OF BELIEF**, do you understand what you believe? And why?

You want people to see you in the best positive light. It can take years to perfect your "act." Of course, prospects need not know that you are still perfecting.

If Act 2 of your life is now complete in your 5-Act life drama, what script will you write for Acts 3, 4, 5? Write prayerfully, thoughtfully and carefully a *positive self-fulfilling prophecy*!

Act 3:
Age _____ to age _____

Act 4:
Age _____ to age _____
Act 5:
Age _____ to age _____

Probe deeper when needed. Who? What? When? How? Where? And get to what I call the **dominant buying motive** with the "Why?" questions. Ask yourself why you want what you wrote or thought about above. Your prospects and customers have similar wants.

Some call the *answer to the why* question the "**Hot Button.**" These sales people are sales technique oriented, usually. Do not hammer with too many why questions and always be sensitive to confidentiality.

DIAGNOSIS

The consultative situation (problem) solver is diagnostic. He uses an upgraded language suitable for one that intends to "Become #1 in Selling."

I have customized fact finders for salespeople within specific companies that can be suitable for entire industries. These questions *dig progressively deeper* much like a geologist would on an archaeological dig. Sometimes we must **keep searching.** The why questions are often the last ones you ask.

PRESCRIPTION

A.) "Based on what you have told me so far . . ."

is the beginning of what I call a *prescriptive phrase*. This statement positions us to begin playing back to those we have just examined their key needs, concerns or problems, before assuring them we have or will locate the solution.

How many problems could we have avoided in the past had we listened to others completely, then *clarified what we heard by rephrasing and restating it!?*

This is called **ACTIVE LISTENING.** I call it *the #1 need* of all people who want to communicate better.

HUMOR: To Become #1 in Selling, we must remember that "the good Lord gave us two ears and one mouth!"

Listen twice as much as you speak in a sales presentation, or on any sales call . . . or for that matter, when communicating with anyone at anytime.

B.) "And what you would really like to do is . . ." is a great follow-up phrase to introduce your solution to the problem.

PEOPLE DO NOT CARE HOW MUCH WE KNOW UNTIL THEY KNOW HOW MUCH WE CARE!

Remember to adopt this philosophy to insure you exhibit caring.

When I first was exposed to this verbal methodology, it was very unnatural for me. However, I was convinced it was the right way to proceed verbally, so I began practicing in the mirror, talking aloud to myself to practice. And, I worked at improving the method.

Role playing can help, too, if we have a great coach. I became Carl Stevens' star pupil. No wonder he wanted to recruit me to join him marketing his services, speeches and seminars. *Become the star pupil of your bosses' philosophy or methods and you'll be headed for success, too, of course.*

C.) "That is why I am here!" What a great statement this makes to nail down your prospects' assurance that you are the means to his ends. This logically follows the prior step in the prescription step, doesn't it?

D.) "It might be *presumptuous* of me to tell you . . ." is an effective transition statement to introduce a third party success story.

PRESIDENT'S AWARDS

I developed more new full line dealers for Kurfees Coating than any other salesperson/branch sales manager. This is one reason I won the company's President's Award on the second year of my employment.

Again, the *second time* in a huge company, I became #1 in Selling (both by age 27). You can do it, too!

Become in Selling!

It is not presumptuous of me to *share* (rather than tell) you how to become #1, is it? Yet you might prefer to have me use a word other than "I." You may prefer I gave **story after story** about *other salespeople* who have Become #1 in Selling, sharing their principles for success. Become a story teller.

Talking about others and how they successfully used your products and services, rather than we ourselves, is *more palatable* in most cases.

If I point out 200-400% sales increases for others using these ideas, then it is not presumptuous, is it?

See the point? It is not presumptuous *IF* you are sharing as a solution something that the prospect can relate to that has worked for someone else.

"It might seem presumptuous of me to say my product will permanently solve your problems you described, however, that is exactly what my other customers have told me. Their problem was solved once and for all!"

E.) A great wrap up or tie down question is: "It wouldn't have to be that good to be worth investigating further, would it?"

And, I love this kind of statement just before getting ready to CONVINCE someone. . . !

F.) "Would you like to know exactly how Mr. (Miss) _____ told me (us) he was able to achieve these results or get these benefits, step by step by step?"

With a question like this, we **pause for agreement.** The prospect will be saying, "Tell me more!" You've just asked for permission to sell him/her, and they will give it!

That is what you want, isn't it? Yes!

The Prescription step arouses interest by helping your prospect understand fully that you understand his problem and have a solution to it.

What patient goes to the doctor and does not take the prescription? You are the expert.

Of course, *you can create a sale* where there was no perceived need. In those cases some of this step can be used *up front* if third

152

parties are used skillfully, and if it is in the best interest of the prospect.

CONVICTION

When in a college town one day, I remarked to a younger man, "It is going to be a terrific day today!" He replied "No it ain't; it has started out bad for me!"

You might want to respond to people when asked, "How are you?" . . . **TERRIFIC . . . HOWEVER, I WILL GET BETTER!** This is a conviction I hope you will adopt.

Remembering that <u>we get what we expect</u>. We can learn how to better convince others.

An office I once visited had this statement in large bold letters in a frame on the wall . . .

"In business you do not get what you deserve, you get what you negotiate!"

To Become #1 in Selling, we must understand how to *negotiate*. Although I may not use the word "negotiate" often in this book, I do believe it is at the heart of Becoming #1 in Selling in many cases.

One reason I left Kurfees Coating, Inc. was I could only negotiate with my employer. My incentive plan was small. The Comptroller would not allow the other officers to negotiate a better incentive program for me or anyone else. Although income is only one criteria for a *satisfying job*, many sales people are very money motivated. Why? Family and personal needs and wants!

The primary reason I changed, however, was that, much like a pastor feels "called" into the ministry, I knew (and felt) I was "called" to teach others how to sell and serve better; how to succeed. Later I would expand that to help business people understand many aspects of business and human resource development. Expand your capabilities and services, if needed, and if possible. Focus your fastballs on your best customers or prospects.

Carl Stevens "convicted" me, so to speak, and recruited me to join him to market his sales and sales management seminars and motivational speeches, as an independent contractor. I was to apprentice with the master for 18 months before I chose to establish my own business.

Find some new . . .

1.) **FACTS!** Many sales trainers only talk about features and benefits. There must be more!

People want facts and then . . .

2. **EVIDENCE!** Never present a Fact or feature without giving evidence, if at all possible. Preferably visual evidence. If you can give a demonstration, that helps. Show pictures. Document your claims, then add a . . .

3. **RELATED BUYER BENEFIT!** Facts and features can be irrelevant unless related to the specific need of the prospective buyer. Memorize . . .

"WHICH MEANS TO YOU . . . . "

This is the key phrase. Now, use a wrap-up close or question.

4. "That is important to you, isn't it!? Or, some other kind of tie down or **wrap up questions** assures they agree. Get agreement before you go on. "That about does it, doesn't it?" "Let's go ahead today, OK?"

IMPORTANT ADVICE

When presenting facts and features about any product or service, you can do so in the examination step simply by *turning the feature into a question.* Here is an example: "Mrs. Prospect, would the fact this car has the safest radial tires available be important to you?"

Her response played back to her later, when ready to convince and motivate, before closing, brings you back to what *she said* was important.

HUMOR: This method helps guard you from falling into the trap of saying things like: "This hum dinger will give you 40 miles per gallon!" when the buyer couldn't care less!

"Where do we go from here?" is a great question for use when you are not quite sure where the prospect is in his or her thinking.

#1 FROM SERVING OTHERS BETTER

How did I Become #1 in Selling! in 1973 with The Eureka Company and in 1976 with Kurfees Coatings, Inc.? I fertilized and nurtured my customers and prospects better than everyone else. I also outworked and outsmarted everyone. In 1976, it seemed God miraculously led me to the decision makers who could say . . . "YES!" God and my mentors empowered me!

Since then I am so thankful for the opportunity to help many others become #1! Remember your attitude of gratitude!

Think about the following please.

"Until one is committed, there is hesitancy, the chance to draw back, always ineffectiveness, concerning all acts of initiative (and creation). There is one elementary truth the ignorance of which kills countless ideas and splendid plans: that the moment one *definitely commits oneself*, then ***Providence moves*** too. All sorts of things occur to help one that would never otherwise have occurred. A whole stream of events issues from the decision, raising in one's favor all manner of unforeseen incidents and meetings and material assistance which no man could have dreamed would have come his way. Whatever you can do or dream **you can**, begin it. Boldness has genius, power and magic in it. *Begin it now.*"

. . . Johann Wolfgang Von Goethe

1. **F** . . . . FACTS
2. **E** . . . . EVIDENCE
3. **R** . . . . Related Buyer Benefits
4. **T** . . . . Tie down/wrap up questions

CONVICT . . . PERSUADE . . . QUICKEN AGREEMENT TO YOUR Solution! *The Right Solution!*

Become 🧩 in Selling!

Carl Stevens rode to Columbus, Ohio with me in a blinding snow storm from Louisville, Kentucky, one Saturday in January 1976, because his plane had been cancelled. Mr. Stevens, an internationally known Sales Trainer and Speaker, really impressed me. His clients were many of the Fortune 500. . .DOW CHEMICAL, CLAIROL, JOHN DEERE . . . you name it!

Someone once said his best advice was to "take wealthy successful people to lunch or breakfast and pick their brains."

How would you like to be providentially sequestered in a blinding snowstorm in your auto traveling 30 MPH for 7 hours with the "World's Greatest Sales Trainer"? Do you want to know what he said was the *most important thing* for any salesperson to know? Carl gave me this "**GOOD NEWS**" . . .

FACT #1 . . . "The Bible tells you that you can know for sure that you have eternal life. Carl gave evidence: "These things I have written to you . . . that you may know that you HAVE eternal life." (John 5:13)

FACT #2 . . . "Heaven is a **FREE** gift!" Evidence: "The gift of God is eternal life in Christ Jesus our Lord." (Romans 6:23b)

FACT #3 . . . "Heaven is not earned or deserved!" Prove it! Evidence: "By grace you have been saved through faith, and that not of yourselves: it is the gift of God, not of works, least any man should boast." (Ephesians 2:8,9) "Do good works" Carl said, "to please and obey God." In doing this, you earn His favor, of course." Can you earn a free gift?

Carl began convincing me further just like any salesperson would sell any product. My mind and heart were fertile. Is your prospect open to your message? Some of you do not want to hear these facts from God or about eternal life. It's needed!

We all have been to funerals where we have heard scripture quoted. Don't worry, I'm only presenting the . . . FACTS . . . With EVIDENCE . . . then Related Buyer Benefits.

FACT #4 . . . Carl said, "Man is a sinner! I am; are you, Thom?" "Yes," I had to admit I knew I was. Carl said, "Sin is transgressing the law, falling short of the goal of perfection."

Every salesperson knows he must perfect his sales presentation. Carl Stevens inferred no matter what I learned or how hard I worked, I could never have the *wisdom* I would like or need to stay successful in selling without God's grace (unmerited favor).

FACTS 5, 6, 7 . . .

"Man cannot save himself (or herself). God is merciful and therefore, forgives sin." He gave me more evidence from the bible, and as is the focus of Lent (40 days before Easter), he showed me I must repent, and decide to change, turn from all sin.

I had not read what he called the "Manufacturer's Handbook" since I was a young teenager. Carl related all this to me while sharing applications for my life.

FACTS 8 & 9 . . . "*Jesus Christ,*" the Bible says, "is the infinite God-Man." "Jesus Christ came to earth and lived a sinless life, but while on earth, He died on the cross to pay the penalty for our sins and rose from the grave to purchase a place for us in heaven."

"Come on, Carl," I said, "you really don't believe all that stuff, do you?"

"Sure I do," he said "and I'll prove it to you, if you will have an *open mind!*"

"OK," I said, "My life is *lacking purpose* . . . what do I have to loose . . . plus I'm like everyone, I'd like the assurance of eternal life, so just in case your are right, go ahead, I'll listen."

FACT #10 . . . "Faith . . . Saving Faith is the key that opens the door to heaven. You must trust in Jesus alone for salvation. It is not enough to have mere intellectual assent, or mere temporal faith." Carl said, "Jesus says, 'Behold I stand at the door and knock (at the door of your life). If anyone hears my voice and opens the door, *I will* come *into* him.' Revelation 3:20."

"What does this mean, Carl?" I asked.

He replied, as our ride concluded . . .

"This means that you can pray a prayer and accept Christ <u>into</u> your life, into your heart, and have peace and assurance of eternal life!" Carl began Step #3 in CONVICTION.

Then he *closed,* "**That's what you really want, isn't it?**"

Become 🐾 in Selling!

"Yes!" . . . How could anyone say no to the **most important offer** anyone can ever make, I thought . . . and still do today?

"So, by faith, *pray* now to accept the person of Jesus Christ into your heart and he will give you eternal life and more purpose and power for this life."

I made an agreement with God! "Lord, Jesus, forgive me of my sins. Come into the center of my life now, and please always stay there! I commit my life to you and I will follow you the rest of my life. AMEN!"

I will give you more examples of how to CONVINCE others to purchase a tangible or intangible product. When selling always remember this sequence. . .

    A.   Facts
    B.   Evidence
    C.   Related Buyer Benefit
    D.   Tie down or wrap up question

MOTIVATION

Webster defines motivation as "something *within* the individual that incites or impels him to action."

Each of us has hopes, dreams and goals that, when stimulated, can "incite" us to action. And the superstar becomes passionate and successful because of the inner motivations. What really drives you?

Change your hopes . . . change your dreams . . . change your goals . . . change your focus . . . change your priorities . . . change your heart . . . and you change your M O T I V A T I O N.

When I saw a salesperson receive the President's trophy at a banquet after Don Kurfees' speech, I became motivated to work towards this goal for the next year. Visualize yourself winning a *big reward a year from today!* Or, see your bank account with a 7 times increase.

KEY: The best way to motivate anyone at anytime is to *project the person into the future as a satisfied customer.* Here are some steps for causing your prospect to want what you are selling . . .

S . . . Solution Review
A . . . Answer . . . "This is it!"
P . . . Project to a specific time
P . . . Paint a word picture

Yes, become a S . . A . . P . . P . . . ONCE YOU SEE YOUR GOALS CLEARLY!! THEN HELP OTHERS MAKE INTELLIGENT DECISIONS BY ACQUIRING YOUR PRODUCTS OR SERVICES, SO THEREBY, THEY WILL REACH THEIR GOALS.

Books longer than this are written on how to *close the sale,* aren't they?

Where do I begin?
You begin closing, the minute you begin selling!

COMPLETION

Completion of the sale *begins* with a positive expectant attitude and positioning yourself as a problem solver. A determined, never give up, attitude! Here is an acrostic to assist you:

C . . . Confess you can *better* close customers . . . put their needs #1
O . . . Organize your closing strategies
M . . . Memorize phrases, tie downs, wrap ups, techniques
P . . . Practice until you are convincing . . . and convinced!
L . . . Laugh at yourself. You will never be perfect
E . . . Enthusiasm helps prepare others for closure.
Be always enthusiastic!
T . . . Treat people respectfully . . . treasure relationships

Become 🕺 in Selling!

I . . . Integrity must be correct
O . . . Only say what is needed
N . . . Never give up

You are unique. Customize this to your situation. Or, phone **THE THOM LISK GROUP** ☎ (614) 841-1776 to assist. There is more on completion of sales in Chapter 15.

These ideas and the information can and will help you . . .
Become #1 in Selling!

PLAN IT

Now, using the ideas presented earlier in this chapter, will you please customize your own preparation sheet and attention-getting ideas for a specific prospect?

How do you plan to get your prospect's immediate and favorable attention? Your challenge is to get him (or her or them) to *switch* from his thought track to yours! If you both are not on the same thought line, how can there be a *meeting of minds* and consummation of business? Seldom are others ready and eager to talk about what you want to talk about! I LOVE TO LISTEN TO OTHERS may be the affirmation and prescription you now need.

Is your handshake an asset or a liability when you meet for the first time? Thumb joints need to come together firmly avoiding the possibility of a "dead fish" or "bone crusher" handshake. Remember that you may be judged by your handshake. Basic but true!

And remember the diplomats secret! SMILE!☺

HUMOR: There is an old Chinese proverb which says "He who cannot smile should not be shopkeeper." And a friend of mine asserts, "Smile, people will wonder what you have been up to!"☺☺

Prepare properly

You will not be in darkness
Then execute!

"I am the light of the world: he that followeth me shall not walk in darkness but shall have the light of life," Jesus said in John 8:12.

Become  *in Selling!*

PREPARATION

Planning sheet for: _____

My prospect's name: _____

His/her title is: _____

The exact company name: _____

Address: _____

Home Office? Branch? _____

Comments: _____

Phone numbers: _____ Fax: _____

I am sure she/he is the person who can say "YES!" because:

_____

The problem is: _____

Is this person aware of the problem? _____

Comment: _____

What info do I need from the prospect to sell? _____

_____

Information needed from other sources, who and which are:

_____

My specific recommendations to answer problem: _____

_____

Exactly how will it benefit him and how best can I communicate

this? _____

_____

What does he really want? _____

_____

Why does he want it? Real reason(s)? His dominant buying motive. What he lacks, wants or needs:

_____

_____

My most important preapproach info is: _____

_____

I believe the thing my prospect wants more than anything else in the world is:

_____

What else do I need to know to make an effective presentation and close the sale?

_____

Become ![bear logo] ***in Selling!***

I CAN BE BETTER PREPARED TO SELL THIS PROSPECT FROM CONVERSATION WITH: (CHECK, THEN FIND THE PERSON'S NAME)

☐ His accountant   ☐ Attorney   ☐ Customers   ☐ Banker
☐ Friends   ☐ Our other Customers   ☐ Other salespeople
☐ People within his company   They are:

FROM OBSERVATION:

☐ His awards in office   ☐ General environment   ☐ Literature
☐ Pictures   ☐ Annual report   ☐ Reading trade journals   ☐ Other

Do I know anyone else whose opinion he values who can lay some groundwork for me? Or whom must I quote during our meeting?

_____

Have I prepared my presentation? Do I have everything I might need with me? What visual aids will I use? If I have competition preparing a proposal for this same business, what will I offer that will be uniquely better? Do I need to offer special prices? If so, why? (The list could go on and on. As a consultant, I customize this further for clients.)

_____

_____

Some managers require their salespeople to add:

_____
Signature

ATTENTION

ATTENTION PLANNING SHEET FOR: _____

Now, will you please use the ideas given earlier and plan several methods to get this prospect's attention. These same ideas customized can be used at various times during the presentation and with other prospects. Once you understand these procedures and learn the products or services, you can sell successfully for anyone and to anyone. If you really want to!

_____

_____

_____

_____

_____

YOUR PROFESSIONAL SALES PRESENTATION CAN MAKE YOU #1!

MAKE GREAT CLOSING PRESENTATIONS TO MORE OF THE RIGHT QUALIFIED BUYERS AND YOU CAN DOUBLE YOUR INCOME.

REMEMBER: SELLING IS AN ART AND PRECISE PROCEDURES APPLY. AFFIRM: I CAN MASTER SALES PRESENTATIONS AND PAINT A MASTERPIECE. I WILL HAVE A MAGNIFICENT FUTURE!

CHAPTER SIX

REVIEW QUESTIONS

1. What are professional sales presentations designed to do?

2. Do you want selling success enough to Become #1?

3. How can you gather all the facts better?

   Will it result in better presentations and more sales?

4. What is preoccupation?

   How does it prevent your success?

5. Did you write some thoughts for act 3, 4 and 5?
   If not, please do so now.

6. What does FERT stand for?

7. What is motivation?

8. Complete, duplicate and use the preparation and attention-getting work sheets daily for 21 - 30 days!

9. How can you improve as a listener?

CHAPTER 7

YOUR MISSION AND VISION STATEMENT

A LIFE PURPOSE

"Compete against yourself!" was the best advice I could give a president of a small business recently when he described his almost insatiable need to compete and win. His emphasis was on winning and his company mission reflected it. I do not believe you have to crush others, or hurt others to fulfill your company mission or purpose in life. One must not want to Become #1 for self-aggrandizement or to prove to others "I am better than you!" The best salesperson realizes that if he or she is not respected, he or she will not be allowed to sell or serve.

Try to enter relationships with the attitude: "Esteem others better than myself." They then will promote you. This cannot be manipulative. It must be sincere and from the heart.

In this chapter, I ask you to establish a LIFE PURPOSE, clarify your MISSION and VISION, and further define some goals. It is best if you have a burning purpose that is compatible with your company mission and vision statement.

A life *purpose* define as your reason for living, your calling or your driving force. Once established, this will propel you onward and upward.

Your *mission* define as your or your company's aim or carefully crafted objective. A mission statement is a reflection of your values and organized priorities.

Your *vision* is your perception or mental picture of strongly desired future realities. It is more than a hope. You can permanently improve your world with positive clear written visions, preferably focused on realities.

SUCCESS STORIES

A man goes to the gym every morning and lifts weights. This helps his self-image and self-esteem. His *mission* is to build a great physical body. Another man, a friend from World Gym, recently set the American *record* in the bench press . . . on purpose.

Art Bartlett, a Los Angeles Realtor, got tired of competing against those who could spend more dollars in advertising than he could, so he *organized* other brokers around the city for a *common purpose*. They all had similar needs. He called his idea Century 21. He served others who he once competed with. They established a united mission. Bartlett expanded and established a vision for franchising real estate brokers in every city in America, then the world. This great leader sold his vision.

Domino's Pizza built a *dominant market share* by the K.I.S.S. methodology and a clear purpose, mission and vision.

K=Keep
I=It
S=Simple
S=Salesperson!. . .or Simplify!

They focus on **top quality, fast delivery and value.** They Become #1 in Selling! Their stores were built by market, then on a nationwide basis.

Clayton & Phyllis Jones, building contractors, designed Fiesta Beauty Salons in the middle '70s with no prior experience in this industry, and little capital. Their discount *budget strategy* and *consumer savings purpose* was modeled after Ray Holland's successful operations. Holland was Clayton's mentor and friend. They grew to over 250 salons. They Became #1 in Selling! They made *Inc. Magazine's* list of America's fastest growing corporations.

What do these people and companies who have Become #1 in Selling have in common? Many things, undoubtedly.

Domino's Pizza and Fiesta Beauty Salons used my services as a speaker, trainer and consultant. Each great company invariably has a great leader with a long-term vision.

Although I did not write my mission statement in 1977, when I first entered professional speaking, it was obviously: to teach or inspire others to Become #1 in Selling! Today, it is more elaborate or multi-faceted. I share this only to say your mission can change.

What is your mission statement and purpose for life? Do you have a long term vision to work towards? Be retrospective if needed! Establish your purpose, mission and vision.

GUARANTEE

A young friend, Nick, was born on April 22, 1968. As I write this, I begin a training program one-on-one with Nick. I serve him as his personal success coach.

Nick has as much raw sales potential as anyone I have met in a long time. Will he fulfill his potential? He needs *purpose* and accountability then I can guarantee success

Many of you will remember that the heavyweight champion Mike Tyson was thought to be invincible. Then, a guy by the name of Douglas from Columbus, Ohio, came along and knocked his lights out. Douglas had a short-term *mission.*

Several months later, Douglas, who neglected discipline in preparing for his first heavy weight championship defense, was knocked out in the third round by another fellow named Holyfield, a man with a long-term *vision.* In 1992 Tyson was really knocked out! He went to jail on rape charges. He had a major ethical and moral failure. It could be because his mission did not include ethical or moral values.

Become 🌺💃 *in Selling!*

Selling can be like that. . .you can be on top today, but knocked out tomorrow! Is that what you want? Let's keep disciplining ourselves to avoid that knock-out punch. Do not be susceptible to losing sight of your purpose or vision. Build a positive life purpose which focuses your life to benefit other people.

VISION IS MORE IMPORTANT
THAN A GOAL OR GOALS!

It is more important to have a long-term VISION for your future!

To continue the boxing analogies: Cassius Clay had vision. When he found religion, he got purpose. He became Mohammed Ali. He envisioned himself World Champion before religion and reached this reality. He sustained his career when he defined his life purpose.

He chanted, "I am the greatest!" before the first championship fight against Sonny Liston. No one believed him until he proved it by knocking out Liston. Liston was the heavy favorite. Old news? Listen for your *new* application.

Clay was such an underdog that most everyone was happy for the kid from Louisville, Kentucky. We overlooked his brashness, preferring to believe his affirming "I am the greatest!" was just his way of psyching himself up.

The **"I am"** principle is based on a name for God. When He spoke to Moses, He said, "*I am* has sent you." (Exodus 3:14)

What greater purpose than to model your behavior and receive your driving force from God? What greater mission than to aim to serve God? What greater vision than to see yourself as who God wants?

GO FOR GREAT!

Associate with those who want you to go for the greatest you can be.

Be prepared because some people may want you to be mediocre or fail. They are and have. They may throw verbal psychological banana peels in your path!

A great potential mentor or patron does not feel threatened by your goal to Become #1.

We can become too dependent on our mentors. They also are only human. Only God is perfect in His love. God is constant. He is always there. He is always ready to help us when we reach out to Him. Man cannot be like that, even though we are "created in His image." I believe God made us all GREAT.

Purpose can come from serving God first, and serving those in your life now, better, day by day.

Parents report how their children disappoint them. They often set unrealistic expectations. They do not allow their kids, sometimes, to discover their own purpose for life, to set their own goals. And if they fail, parents can box kids of any age into mediocrity due to their negative expectations.

Teaching positive goals in life is a great thing to do. I had become very goal oriented as evidenced by my Becoming #1 in Selling twice by age 28. When I began to market services that would help others sell better (and become better), I was really surprised just how very *challenging* my *mission.* Will your mission really stretch you?

There is no gain without a little strain! Forget that pain stuff!

As infants you are taught to avoid pain. "Don't touch the stove!" the mother shouts. "Stay out of my briefcase!" the father exclaims, "or you will get the spanking of your life!"

The grade school teacher directs, "Jimmy, you stop teasing Katie or you will lose your recess!" That's pain! "Not me, I want more pleasure!" you think throughout those early formative years.

Today as adults we are more motivated by the **pursuit of pleasure,** as opposed to the **strain (or pain) for gain.** Associate reaching your VISION with pleasure.

Salespeople who go on without purpose and significant goals will find life becomes a drudgery.

Fortunately, the *top 4% of all salespeople* are not like this. They have purpose. And they inspire others. We will always have winners and losers in the game of life.

Who would have thought the 1990 Cincinnati Reds would be the first team ever to lead their conference and league, from start to finish, then sweep the powerful Oakland Athletics in four games straight in the World Series?

And the Braves and the Twins in 1991!! Both from last to first in one year in their respective leagues.

Records are meant to be broken!

Anything is possible when a team or person learns to play together under the right leadership with purpose.

Pete Rose was ousted. . .baseball's most prolific hitter. . .and the Reds win the whole "ball of wax" the very next season! Just because one is a great hitter does not mean one is a great coach.

NO GAIN WITHOUT STRAIN

Just because you are a great salesperson does not mean you will make a great sales manager. Or that you can start and sustain and lead your own company someday. These are different skills, and sometimes the change psychologically can require more strain than one is willing to endure.

In my case, the fact that I became a Christian and began in earnest to read the Bible and to pray, along with regular church attendance, changed me so I could serve other salespeople (and managers and executives), and not always have to beat them.

Your belief systems control you. Examining beliefs will benefit you even if you disagree with the beliefs of others.

AFFIRMATIONS

Gold Medal Winners see victory, and keep their goal in mind, during the grueling hours and days of preparation and practice leading up to the big event.

If you know you had *the most important appointment of your life tomorrow*, how would you prepare today? Why not *prepare* as if that were to be the case with every tomorrow, for the balance of your career? The RESULTS WILL astound YOU.

Those who live life like this Become #1 in Selling!

They affirm TODAY who they want to be . . . who they must be . . . *tomorrow.*

Keeping the prior statement in mind, the lists of affirmations that follow in this chapter can greatly help. Customize your own.

LIST #1:

I can do it
I like myself
I am a winner
I am the best
I can close the sale
I will succeed
I am brilliant on the basics
I prospect diligently and effectively
I present with enthusiasm
I follow up thoroughly and timely
I have no fear of failure
I never fear rejection
I have all answers to all objections
I am funny when need be
I am an authority on selling and human
    potential
I have no guile
I will become #1 in selling
I imitate the winners only!

Since it takes 21-30 days to develop new and better habits, CONVINCE AND MOTIVATE YOURSELF TO AFFIRM your goals several times a day. Combine this with true prayer, and you will see positive improvement.

Yes, **you must be, before you can do, and you must do, before you can have.**

Recently, a Jewish woman named Tova, a graduate of one of my "Blueprints for Success" seminars told me: "Thom in Hebrew means pureness of heart." When someone gives you a compliment, remember it. Dwell in it. Affirm it so as to become more of it.

LIST #2:

I work for others' success
I am a servant first
I am thoughtful and courteous
I care about others
I use my time wisely
I build trust
I identify needs properly
I am prescriptive like a doctor

Then, you say, possibly, "I can't be!! I am none of these things!" Well, FAKE it for 21-30 days and these goals you affirm can and will become yours. **Fake it 'till you make it!**

Circle those affirmations you need to set as goals. GO BACK and review these two lists, NOW. And this third list . . .

LIST #3:

I do it now
I will never procrastinate
I am a great husband (wife)
I am a terrific father (mother)
I am physically fit
I will be healthier
I am healthy

I love god and he loves me
I have all the money i need
I am financially independent
I am very smart
I can solve any problem
I am very likable
I have a great career
I love my work
I always know what to say
I believe in god! he believes in me
I am friendly and like everyone
I know my business
I enjoy my recreation time

This is not mere mind over matter. Notice on the third list, I have affirmations for eight areas of life. Those eight areas are:

1. Spiritual
2. Family
3. Financial
4. Career
5. Social
6. Physical/Health
7. Mental/Intellectual
8. Recreation/leisure time

Our time to pursue goals in these areas of life is limited . . . very limited. Start today! Recently, this was driven home to me again when I phoned on a Friday for a man who had a Mercedes 380E that I had test driven only two weeks earlier. "My father died in his sleep last night," I was told. We know we have this present moment: today only.

Go back to list #3 and put a 1, 2, 3, 4, 5, 6, 7, or 8 next to each affirmation in the margin. These eight correspond with the list above. DO IT NOW!!

Become  **in Selling!**

Now, determine which of List #3 you will appropriate for your own life. Circle those you choose.

DO IT NOW!

HUMOR: I tell the story sometimes of the women who was asked to write the positive affirmation: I will never procrastinate again. Her response: "I will, in a minute!" Don't allow Procrastination to be the biggest nation in the world for you.

Take a few minutes to write some of your own affirmations, customized to meet your own needs, today.

1. _____

2. _____

3. _____

4. _____

5. _____

6. _____

7. _____

You get the idea. This is *more important* than learning sales techniques, and is the starting point for better goal setting, and acquiring a written mission statement, and more purpose.

Note many of the affirmations are attitudes or characteristics.

I am a person of integrity
I am a great listener
I connect with people
I know others trust me
I am honest

In Hebrew, the word "Thom" is also translated to "INTEGRITY." "Thom" means integrity, wholeness, completeness. What does or will your name mean?

HUMOR: One man, Charlie, with a low self-esteem said: My name means "good old boy." When asked what would be his epitaph, he said "Here lies Charlie, fat and happy as always!"

The first paid professional speech I gave, after many free talks, was before the Indiana/Kentucky Hardware Association many years ago. Although I lived in Columbus, Ohio, I eagerly traveled to Louisville, Kentucky, to speak at the Gault House, a well-known hotel and convention center.

This opportunity, and others, came to me because I dedicated myself to helping my mentor, Carl Stevens, reach his goals. I could have served him better had he had a written mission and purpose and shared it with me. I told him my purpose and my vision to become a professional speaker, like him.

I "booked" Carl so completely that when he was not available, I could say, "I am the next best thing!" Have an alternative product available when the best is not available or out of the price range of the customer.

Thank God for a mentor who did not feel threatened by my success and would allow me to become a top quality person who could create more income too.

What a good philosophy for life. Help others increase their value and worth. This was taught to me by another mentor, Drummond Gaines. Mr. Gaines had been the #1 National Sales Manager for N.C.R. in the '50s, then later Vice President for Litton Industries and S.C.M. Corporation. What a sales and marketing genius he was!!   It's too bad he died at age 65. Most of his knowledge and wisdom went with him, although he did author some very valuable materials and how-to books. Great sales leaders can teach and inspire you if you are open to their help.

GREAT QUESTIONS

These two questions will help you: **What am I willing to give up to get what I want? Is it worth it?**

We need *balance* with written goals in all eight areas of life. One may regret, as an example, missing critical times with children as they grow, so carefully plan your priorities.

WHEEL OF LIFE

Visualize life like a wagon wheel with eight spokes. If any spoke is shorter than the others, you could receive a bumpy ride. The wheel (your life!) could break down at that point! Some call it "burnout." Mark where you are now on the wheel that follows compared to (10) where you would like to be. Do it now!

Once you have X's on each spoke connect the X's. If you do not have a perfect circle, now, will this matter?

NAME_____   **This is on a scale of 1-10 (Ten being the highest)**

DATE:_____

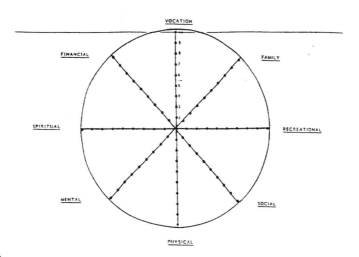

178

Have you had any *breakdowns* on the road of life? Without realizing it, it could be because of neglect of one or more of the eight areas of life. Some go *bankrupt* financially. Others *ruin* the spoke labeled family through neglect. Others *burnout* emotionally because they do not feed their mind the good thoughts. Some *crash* due to spiritual neglect. Or, maybe they do not realize this is an important spoke on the wheel of life.

Some *neglect* their health and physical well-being through *incorrect* eating habits, *lack* of exercise, or other *harmful* habits such as too much alcohol or smoking.

You may need to **recreate** yourself through more recreation or other positive activities. If you cannot afford a nice vacation, take consistent walks in the woods, neighborhood, or park. Go to a nearby lake and meditate upon the water, just as some meditate on the Word of God, and others through music, painting or simply relaxing. Ask yourself *"does this renew and build?"*

Athletics on TV helps many great sales people as they can relate to the competition against self and others.

BALANCE

I believe we need to budget time for all eight areas. Below is the right *priority* order at this point in my life. You can rate them 1-8 as you see it today on the lines provided, please. All eight are important and are due time allocation weekly. Because one is rated higher than another, does not mean it receives more time.

Rate these eight now:

_____ 1. Spiritual	_____ 5. Financial
_____ 2. Family	_____ 6. Career
_____ 3. Physical/Health	_____ 7. Social/Leisure Time
_____ 4. Mental/Intellectual	_____ 8. Recreation

Become in Selling!

Briefly complete this five-year personal projection. Think long term for a few minutes. . .

The date five years from today is:_____

Five years from today I will be:_____ (age)

My occupation is: _____

My main responsibilities are:

_____

_____

The activities I really enjoy doing (in five years) are:
(Remember: Do the same things, get the same results)

   1.
   2.
   3.
   4.
   5.
   6.
   7.
   8.

Five years from today, I rank the following areas of life in this priority (1-8 or several could tie)

Family	_____	Career	_____
Spiritual	_____	Physical	_____
Social	_____	Knowledge	_____
Financial	_____	Recreation	_____

My personal strengths are: _____

Your Mission and Vision Statement

My personal weaknesses yet to overcome are:
(only an absence of strengths) _____

_____

The main projects I have completed are:_____

_____

My major selling/marketing accomplishments are:_____

_____

FIVE-YEAR PROJECTED FINANCIAL STATEMENT

ASSETS	DOLLARS	LIABILITIES	DOLLARS
Savings Account	_____	Notes owed	_____
Real Estate	_____	Mortgage	_____
Home	_____	Auto	_____
Cash Value in	_____	Other	_____
Insurance	_____	Total	_____
Securities	_____		
Business	_____		
Autos	_____		
Other (itemize on back)	_____		
Total Assets	$_____	Net Worth	_____

Five years from today. . .ANNUAL INCOME _____

***B**ecome in Selling!*

Many of my readers must commit to associate new beliefs and new pleasurable outcomes with having financial abundance. If you believe good health, a great family life, spiritual and emotional well-being are rightfully yours, you must also believe you have the right to become prosperous.

You can attract prosperity. Some must offset lack or negative thoughts about the benefits of having a lot of money and financial independence. Daily condition yourself with positive affirmations and prayers that generate positive emotion within you. Example from a prosperous mentor: *God's prosperity is attracted to me!*

FIVE YEAR PROJECTION CONTINUED

Salary/Business/Commissions_____ Stocks/Bonds _____

Real Estate_____ Other Income_____

Income needed to meet your monthly expense_____

Are you a partner in any firm, planning to become a partner or affiliated with any other business in anyway? _____

My spiritual situation is:_____

Affirm: I have the habit of giving! There always is more than enough. I give _____%. I deserve abundance. I have a great vehicle. I live with passion! I stop sabotaging myself financially and in every other area. I remove all limitations. I will link all my successes and pleasure with God's will. I have changed my mental associations to accept total prosperity in every area of my life as my destiny. I believe God wants to prosper me. I will trust God. My health and physical fitness is (remember: 5 years from now):

_____

The social and recreational activities I enjoy include:

_____

Mental growth has included:_____

_____

The years from 1977-1982 saw more personal growth than possibly any other period for me. As I finish writing this, I plan for tremendous growth from 1995-2000. One could also have a 10 year personal projection. . .20 years. . .30 years, etc.

In 1979, I was chairman of the Long Range Planning Committee for my church. We surveyed the church members and community to determine and anticipate needs. On Lane Avenue in Upper Arlington, the Columbus, Ohio suburb where the church was located, we found that the elementary school population would be decreasing in the decade of the '80s, so we made plans accordingly.

We were near the Ohio State University which would be growing, so we made plans to expand programs and ministry to those students, but not elementary aged children.

Businesses could do the same. For many of my consulting clients, I assist with customer satisfaction surveys to evaluate how to increase and expand sales, service, product lines, and, therefore, profits.

Companies can benefit from an objective third party to help facilitate both personal and company development goal setting. This enhances teamwork and can help you "Become #1 in Selling!" Look for *value added service to offer!*

Let me remind you of the Peter Principle. The book by this title (Laurence J. Peters and Raymond Hall, William Morrow Co., 1964) presented the theory that most people get promoted or reach for one level of competency above their ability to perform. Because this may happen to you, you must prepare yourself for that next higher position of responsibility so you will not fail if it is thrust upon you.

183

Become  **in Selling!**

Or you may choose to change careers or companies in the next few months or years. Plan, just in case!

FIVE YEAR CAREER PROJECTIONS

HUMOR: A Catholic priest drove through his parish one day. He saw a farmer, a church member, in his driveway, so he stopped. "My!" he exclaimed to the man, "what a beautiful farm you have! The immaculate white picket fence, the massive red and green farm machinery. And, look at the corn. . .it is as high as a giraffe's eye! God has really blessed you with a beautiful farm!"

"Yes," the farmer remarked, "but you should have seen this place when God had it all to Himself!!"

It will take a lot of hard work for your five year career projections and greatest hopes to be realized. Henry Ford said, **"Thinking is the hardest work you will ever have to do!** That is why more people do not engage in it more often"

Many people may be tempted to leave these blanks empty because it takes massive brain power to do this. Right? *Wrong!* However, many people do hesitate to commit.

He who hesitates is _____.

Use pencil rather than pen, if you must, however;
DO IT NOW. . .

Answer the following questions as they would apply to you five years from now.

AFFIRMATION: *I CAN . . . BECOME #1 IN SELLING!*

The year is: _____ My age is: _____

My job/occupation/position is: _____

My career responsibilities are: _____

_____

Your Mission and Vision Statement

My approximate income is: _____

My five-year Projected Income Breakdown is:

Current
  Year   Next Year   2nd Year   3rd Year   4th Year   5th Year

19____   19_____   19_____   19_____   19_____   20_____

Income for these years I plan to earn below. . .

_____   _____   _____   _____   _____   _____

My career strengths have been: _____

_____

The sales skills and attitudes I have developed are: _____

_____

Awards I have received are: _____

_____

The things that motivate me the most are: _____

_____

My most rewarding experience is: _____

_____

The most important things I have done for my family are:

_____

Become  in Selling!

Are You Doing It Right?

Johnathan married Annette. They went to his parents' home for the first Thanksgiving dinner as a married couple. Annette noticed that her new mother-in-law cut the end of the ham off before she put it in the oven to cook, so she asked why.

Mom said, "I did it that way because my mama always did it that way." Conveniently, grandmother was there that day so Annette asked her, "Grandma, mom says she cuts the end of the ham off because you do so. Why did you do it?" Grandma said, "I did it that way because my mother did it that way."

Fortunately great grandmother was still alive so she called her at the rest home many miles away. "Great Grandma," she shouted, so as to be heard, "Happy Thanksgiving! I was wondering why you cut the end of the ham off before you put it in the oven to cook. Grandma, your daughter says she did it because you did it, and mom because grandma did it. Why did you do it that way?"

"Honey," great grandma squeaked, "I did it that way because my roaster was too small."

Annette solved the three-generation mystery. She could have begun doing it that way too, without question, and been the third generation to do something that wasn't necessary, or the right way to do it!

The obvious question is . . .**What have you done or are you doing just because someone before you did it that way?** And is it the right way to do it? If you are not getting the results you really would desire, then, too, be willing to change.

PERSONAL GOAL SETTING

☠**WARNING:** Many people do not reach their goals because they miss important steps in the process.

Do you have any idea concerning what you have to do today to reach your long range goals and objectives? In order to reach these objectives one must set specific goals today.

Let then our motto be, "If you fail to plan, you plan to fail," or at least not reach your full potential.

When we discussed your self-image, self-esteem, and affirmations earlier, written were some necessary steps in developing an action plan. Here are the specific six steps that work:

1. Itemization
2. Categorization
3. Prioritization

4. Crystallization
5. Visualization
6. Finalization

YOUR DREAM LIST

HUMOR: My mother, Betty Lisk, is a retired 4th grade school teacher. An elementary teacher caught two young boys copying; let's call them Bob and Mike. She may have scolded them, "Shame, shame on you boys for copying!"

She took the boys' papers to her desk, and proceeded to give both an "F" for copying. She looked at Bob's paper. The first question had an answer, "I don't know!"

She looked at Mike's test paper. The answer to the first question said, "I don't know neither!"

The point? We had better be more careful who we copy after! We all do so, more often unconsciously then consciously.

When developing your dream list, think of your long range purpose or mission for your life. Sacrifices today may be needed to bring your dreams to fruition tomorrow.

These exercises are designed to get you thinking on paper. Do not worry whether your dreams (wants and desires) are at this point realistic or unrealistic. The following action words will stimulate your thinking. This is part of the itemization process. Fill in the blanks with numerous responses. . .

Become 🏃 in Selling!

1. Who I want to become: _____

_____

_____

2. What I'd like to earn: _____

_____

3. Things I'd like to see/to do: _____

_____

_____

_____

_____

4. Things I'd like to have: _____

_____

_____

_____

_____

5. Miscellaneous Important Dreams: _____

_____

_____

DREAMS DO COME TRUE!

Imaging consists of picturing in our minds the desired goal, and then holding this picture until it sinks, so to speak, into your subconscious mind. It then releases great untapped energies. Dr. Peale said, "It works best when it is combined with strong religious faith, backed by prayer and the seemingly illogical technique of giving thanks for benefits before they are received."

To Become #1 in Selling image visualize it first. Do so to reach any goal. Combine this with prayer for best results. I know it works. . .I have proved it!

CATEGORIZATION OF DREAMS INTO GOALS

Your assessments and itemized lists now must be categorized. In order to expedite the process in this book, or in one of my seminars, we will do our categorizing in two key areas of your life. The two areas are:

1. Career Goals: Financial and Mental.
2. Personal Goals: Spiritual, Family, Social, Physical/Health, Mental, Recreational (all are emotional).

Go back and look at your assessments or dream lists and list everything here, and add anything else that comes to your mind.

Career Goals
WHAT

Personal Goals
WHY

1.

1.

2.

2.

3.

3.

4.

4.

5. ·	5.
6.	6.
7.	7.
8.	8.
9.	9.
10.	10.

OTHER:

Mental growth benefits both your career and your personal life. Actually all are interrelated. *The why goals drive you toward the what goals.*

If your mission statement is to put "Service above Self" as the Rotarians affirm with their motto, then examine your goals in the light of your life's purpose or mission statement.

If your goal is to Become #1 in Selling, "do you have synergism between goals?" *Synergism is when the sum of the parts equals more than the whole.* This happens in goal achievement when you reach your five-year goals in two or three years. That can be possible with proper planning, focused work, and God's help. *For every one minute invested in planning properly you save 4-5 minutes!!*

PRIORITIZE DREAMS INTO GOALS

Now, review your list and categorized and prioritize these goals based upon the degree of **your desire** toward reaching them. If #7 must be #1, indicate as such. Do this based on your current or projected levels of knowledge of income and motivation. You could have 100 items listed, not just 10. Affirm these goals for 30 days.

.These will be goals you feel you could accomplish within the next five years.

The book *"Magic of Thinking Big"* says it: THINK BIG!!

Are you like me in that at some points your life's purpose or mission is more important than at other times? Why is that? Would it be helpful to have that same level of motivation, energy, and concentration which you have had at peak times . . . all the time?

Keep your goals before you. This insures more motivation! Work on your goals daily, of course.

Some motivators prescribe placing all goals on 3 x 5 cards to carry with you so you can use them as flash cards like when we were learning the multiplication tables as kids. This *spaced repetition* not only **reminds and memorizes the goal,** but also drills it into the subconscious (which controls 95% of our actions).

Focus on what you want and need to become. When you become who you need to be, then the other things can take care of themselves.

More than anything I want to be a man of integrity and to develop fully the talents God gave me. How about you?

Another book speaks to that. *"Do What You Love, The Money Will Follow"* by Marsha Sinetar. Do you love selling and doing it with integrity?

My motivation, concentration, and quality levels increase when I attend the National Speakers Association Annual Convention, at various locations throughout the USA. How do you *increase your focus and commitment to quality?* And will you?

At an early convention, I was taught and inspired to seek out more positive free publicity. Business best comes from referrals and positive public relations you can purposefully generate.

Our company has sent out PR releases to newspapers and seek out radio interviews and TV appearances, trying to **gain more visibility** as you would for any product. Would this help you or your business, too? You must sell yourself and, in most cases, you can gain visibility free.

Become 🏃 in Selling!

.I asked for and received a Blue Chip Profile in the Sunday newspaper, The Columbus Dispatch. They said I was the youngest, at age 29, in the long noteworthy history of the publication to receive such an honor. Only one person each week was featured. This is shared to inspire you to do likewise.

Be careful how you *position yourself.* It can make or break you! *Product definition, positioning, and marketing strategies* are all parts of Becoming #1 in Selling and need to be kept in mind when working towards your mission and vision.

Keep focusing on your life's purpose and your company mission. Clarify your vision for the future!

As you grow many people will remember you for who you once were. Because they do not grow or change, they assume that is the case for you. *We cannot allow others to limit our future.* Help others see you as the person you can and want to become. "With God all things are possible!" Ohio motto.

You simply must become better each day. . .stay focused on our goals. . .work very hard and trust God for the positive results.

Before I provide you with additional tools to crystallize your long term goals into action plans, I must say a word about **the past**.

Sometimes you must resolve issues of the past properly before you can go on, insuring the same negative issues do not occur again in the future. Maybe you need to forgive yourself or someone else. Make something right with a creditor. Reestablish relationships or lines of communications with old friends or business acquaintances. Maintain or shape up family relationships. Review goals from the past that are unaccomplished. Repent from prior errors and mistakes.

MAKE A FRESH START!

Have a new beginning! Do not let the past limit your future! Everyday can be the first day of SPRING!

I have known salespeople, as an example, who were once last in sales, who Become #1 in Selling!

Frank Bettger's book, written many years ago, "How I Raised Myself from Failure to Success in Selling," is one documented case study.

Ben Franklin wrote that the method of affirming the characteristics he desired in his life was very important to his success. I have a friend (Ralph Archibold) who does a wonderful Ben Franklin characterization who can motivate any group!

Everyone wants the truth. But when others confront us with the truth when we are wrong, do we change accordingly? Those who become #1 in selling are willing to accept new truths. . .even those which hurt and bring about needed change.

Many professions have a *code of professional ethics.* Remember **ethics, values and beliefs-driven behavior.**

When the decade of the '80s began, I found myself in the plush corporate headquarters of Nationwide Insurance.

One of their Executive Vice Presidents was about to retire and was establishing a new mission for his retirement years. He called me in to consult with him about how to market himself as a professional speaker. I was 30 years old. What did I have to offer?

SUPER KEY TO SUCCESS

My own mission was not as clear as I would have liked; however, in *serving* this mature and successful man my own mission became clearer. See the point?

> It is in the mirror of serving others that our own mission and goals become more focused. Yes, "He who serves best does prosper most" and can Become #1 in Selling!

In three sentences or less, write your life purpose and your business mission. If your company has a clear mission statement, take a moment to meditate upon that, and think about and write

your goals in relationship to that mission statement. For your benefit, I provide this space. Please DO IT NOW.

MY LIFE'S PURPOSE:

MY MISSION STATEMENT:

Some people talk about their world view. Others say that their purpose is to glorify and serve God. If so, a Christian can say: "I am, I can, I will. . .because Christ lives in me and He empowers me."

You must consider the spiritual dimension since we all are spiritual creatures. A book of this nature would be incomplete without quoting the greatest teacher (and more!). Jesus is the best role model for a salesperson.

COMPANY MISSION

The largest hospital in central Ohio is Riverside Hospital. Their mission statement is: To deliver excellent health care in a cost effective manner guided by compassion and Methodist tradition.

What is your *company's mission?*:_____

_____

Top executives and CEOs everywhere are aghast at how few of their employees are committed to the organization's mission.

Dan Evans, CEO of Bob Evans Farms Restaurants, sees to it that his team members have a strong commitment to the company mission. Invariably, those in every company who do this seem to rise to the top.

I have had the privilege of helping companies define their mission through a group facilitation. Some employees and salespeople have not read the mission statement and admit they see little purpose for it. This is because a facilitation and discussion of the mission have not yet occurred. An autocratic delegation of a mission and vision statement will not empower people.

When one has a life purpose, their company's mission and vision become more important, too.

Want to get noticed in your company? Let everyone know you are 100% committed to doing your part to carry out the mission. See your goals and daily activity plans as a means to the end and become enthusiastic. Your enthusiasm will be contagious and help you sell much more.

If you are in selling, your light will attract new customers and more business, and you will. . . . .

BECOME YOUR BEST!. . .PERSEVERE!

Become **in Selling!**

We had a condensed mission statement printed on the back of some business cards. The card read:

THE THOM LISK GROUP

MISSION -- To provide outstanding service for our clients by offering the latest researched personal, human resources, sales training, business development services, in quality formats resulting in bottom line behavioral and profit increases on an affordable basis.

We have another page long elaboration. It is framed on our office walls for all to see and as a reminder to us. It was written at a time of retreat (some prefer to call it an *ADVANCE*) on a mountain top. Can your mission be improved? Consider a getaway to Focus! A friend says, *"FOCUS OR DIE!"*

Missions change and evolve as the market changes. Your *Purpose*, however, is not as variable. And, once you are fulfilling your mission, you will *get a new vision.*

Establish a time each year to evaluate and update your mission statement. Remember, goals grow out of your mission. Then strategies for reaching your goals are established.

It is never too late to find and commit to *more purpose for your life*!

"The most important human endeavor is the striving for morality in our actions. Our inner balance and even our very existence depends on it. Only morality in our actions can give dignity and beauty to our life."

. . . Albert Einstein

REVIEW QUESTIONS   CHAPTER SEVEN

1. Do you have a success example (company or personal) that inspires you?_____
   What is the application for you?_____

2. Are great sales managers different from great sales people?_____
   How? _____

3. What are your most needed affirmations?
   _____
   _____

4. Give an example of how helping your boss or employees to get what they want has benefited you. _____
   _____
   _____

5. Did you complete the wheel of life exercise? _____
   Can you see if you can adjust so you have a smoother ride through life?_____ If so, how will you do it?
   _____

6. If you have not completed the blanks in the chapter, when will you do so?_____

7. Please give an example of how a vision has materialized in your life: _____
   _____

We suggest you write and rewrite your life purpose until you really internalize and are living it. Please do it now. You can strengthen your resolve. . . your WILL POWER. This will cause you to be more successful in reaching your company mission.

CHAPTER 8

Goals That Convict
And Motivate!

BE ... DO ... HAVE!

Og Mandino's book, *"The GREATEST SALESMAN in the World,"* convicts and motivates. Everyone can identify with the central character in this best selling book. If you have not read it, I recommend it highly.

Before we know it, we will enter the 21st century . . . year 2000! The years and decades can march by so quickly that when we reflect back on any one year or decade, we focus only on a few highlights.

"I Did It My Way" was Frank Sinatra's well-known song. Frank did do it his way and he had great success in many areas of his life.

A *father* who loves his son told him recently in my presence, "Do it your way!"

That's why he retained me to help the business develop a reorganization plan that would integrate the next generation into leadership. His son was frustrated because he had a lot of what he thought were great new ideas. He was eager to try them out.

"Help my son by listening to him. Earn his respect; then, maybe, you can focus him better than I," the father said. The mother seemed more concerned about the need for goals for her 18 year-old daughter, "She has no ambition and we have given her everything!"

The sibling rivalry did not make it easy to work with this family-owned business.

Goals need to be **individualized** just like purpose. How many parents inadvertently hurt their children by projecting their goals upon the child?

Become in 🕺 *Selling!*

.I recently read about an entire church denomination that split when a young pastor married outside the church. He married a fine woman from another denomination.

Political, business, family, social and even church pressures can shape or influence our personal goals.

I counseled a 54 year-old successful salesperson who had been divorced less than a year. He understands the process of goal setting I present in this book quite well. He admits to the need for an ongoing sounding board to help him make wise decisions.
Have you ever set New Year's resolutions? Did you get by the 21st or 30th day so you could have a new habit?

Our minds and memories have a way of pulling us back to the past rather than projecting us into the future. Thus, we must stay focused on our future written objectives and do the best we can with each moment today. Motto: My Best for Now!

NEW YEAR'S RESOLUTIONS

I invested New Year's Eve one year with a client. This man in his mid-40s owned a business forms distributorship. His wife had filed for divorce for what he had thought were flimsy reasons. In prior months, we had met to research new marketing plans for the business and to establish new goals. Plus, I trained, organized, and motivated all his sales and management staff.

When he attended my two-day "Blueprints for Building Your Business" seminar in October, he set some new goals. One was (on the personal side) to find a new significant other.

Now I do not condone divorce, but it does happen, increasingly. I believe that the family that prays together does stay together. Here is what he wrote me sometime after the seminar. "*We have had a 100% increase in sales . . . I highly recommend your seminars and services.*"

Both Jim and Betty (his new girlfriend) spoke of new beginnings and new personal goals that New Year's Eve at Betty's home. A 100% increase in personal satisfaction.

Goals that Convict and Motivate!

.One other New Year's Eve, I had a quite dinner with Scott (my mentor at the Eureka Company) and his wife, Ginny MacLead. He was 70 and retired. We reflected on how we had worked together 20 years earlier, and I thought about what I had learned and accomplished in those 20 years, especially the past ten. (Sadly, Scott died of cancer on Thanksgiving Day 1991.)

December 31 or January 1 can be yours each day in attitude if you are constantly looking to *make resolutions* or *firm intentions* that will make you the best person you can be. Try it! For the past 3 years, we participated in a communion church service at midnight on New Year's Eve where we focused on getting rid of the past mistakes and starting anew.

It was shortly after one of these new year's **introspections** that it dawned on me what was happening in my life! Sometimes, it is clearer to see in **retrospect.**

I found I was to continue to:

☞ Serve individuals and companies who are, have been, or want to BECOME #1. Services can vary.

☞ Convince, train and motivate others to their full potential.

Can YOU look back and see a pattern?

A gentleman at a hotel recently introduced me as an expert in "human performance and motivation." One does not become an expert overnight or within a year or two, but in 5 years of dedication we can dramatically change our lives.

How about you? *Where will you be . . . what will you become in five years?*

The year 2000! 2005! 2010! 2015!

In Chapter 6, we discussed seven steps in a professional sales presentation. Step #5 is CONVICTION . . . #6 is MOTIVATION.

.What can help you defeat your fears about setting the goals that can propel you to Become #1 in Selling? **EVIDENCE CONVICTS!** And . . .

Many salespeople need to **overcome call reluctance.** Doctors make their rounds to see patients in a hospital. You, too?

THE FEAR OF REJECTION MUST BE OVERCOME!

Farming is one method of prospecting for Realtors and other direct salespeople. The Avon lady has certain streets and neighborhoods that represent her "farm."

"Thom," Ken Sampson, Executive Vice President for the Columbus Board of Realtors, said, "you have a great gift. I want to help you succeed! Our members need your message. Thom, you portray the attitudes needed of those who become #1 in selling real estate even though you are not a Realtor." The winners develop and maintain **PATRONS!** "Thom, I will be your PATRON," is what we want to know, and hear. Would you agree?

Can you convince yourself that each customer or prospect is a valuable seed on your farm? With the right nurturing these seeds bear tremendous fruit, and can become your benefactor . . . your patron.

We do "reap what we sow!" Sow goals that convince and motivate you to peak performance each day.

To defeat your fears, use . . .

D . . . Demonstrations
E . . . Exhibits
F . . . Facts
A . . . Analogies
T . . . Testimonies
S . . . Statistics
F . . . Formal Comparison
E . . . Expert Opinion

A . . . Analysis

R . . . Reports

. . . in the sales process!

When I taught salesmanship, along with Carl Stevens, at Franklin University, I would use many of the ten items I have just listed to convince the students that selling is a viable and valuable profession.

Ten years after my last class, I was speaking for the American Society of Training Directors (ASTD) in Columbus, Ohio about mentoring, when, afterwards, a woman approached me. She identified herself as a student from Franklin University. "Thom, I really appreciate the examples, analogies and reports you gave today. You demonstrate what a mentor must be !"

I hope people will say to you: "_____, you demonstrate what a professional salesperson is to be!"

We discussed in the prior chapter the first three steps in personal goal setting. They are:

             ✎ Itemization

             ✎ Categorization

             ✎ Prioritization

Now, step #4 . . . .

Crystallization of Goals

This is the process, whereby, you actually turn your dreams into specific goals which become complete with action plans. The exercises you have already completed were very important and necessary. Without this understanding and process you could realize 50% of the benefit of this formula for successful goal setting.

Action plans must be developed for the attainment of your goals.

You will have long-range and short-range goals, as well as tangible and intangible goals.

Most of your *internal changes* result from the intangible goals you set or will set. These achievements revolve around your attitudes, values, beliefs, and self-image. It is recommended at this point that you review those intangible goals or affirmations you set or checked or circled in earlier chapters when we discussed the self-image, self-esteem and affirmations.

Pastors sometimes work diligently to help people memorize and affirm certain key and powerful Bible verses to affect *character improvement* quickly. It works!

All your intangible goals can be pursued simultaneously with the development of short- and long-range goals to help you realize more of your tangible goals.

A tangible goal is that goal which can be perceived through ones senses. It is concrete or material. Sales goals are like that. One man flew from Montana to Columbus, Ohio, for one of my two-day "Blueprints for Building Your Business" seminars. Later he wrote, "Thom, I have had a *100% increase in sales* as a result of implementing what you taught me." That's very tangible!

When my son Todd was 11 years old, and my daughter Erin only 6, naturally, I had to take them into consideration, more so, than I do in the late 90's and beyond 2000 when establishing goals. **What affects your goals and motivation?**

Today, as a business management consultant, trainer and professional speaker, my goals are much different than the limited scope of services I had to offer in 1980. As we must grow and change as times change, so can and **must** our goals change.

In 1980, when I received $800 for a speech or mini seminar, I thought I had arrived. However, as Tom Winninger says, "*You don't arrive . . . you never arrive . . . you must keep polishing your act.*"

Goals that Convict and Motivate!

Business people exhibit their products at trade shows. This is often a great way to introduce a new product or meet new prospective customers. Often these are planned 1-2 years in advance. You are the #1 product you must sell. **You go on exhibit everyday**.

Would you want to buy from you? Are you the kind of person people look forward to seeing? Or speaking to by phone?

ASK YOURSELF MORE TOUGH QUESTIONS

Imagine a year from today, you will be auctioned off to the highest bidder. How would you improve you in the next year, so as to gain the highest price?

In the following exercises and for the majority of our exercises, we will label goals that are one to five years or beyond "Long Range."

"Short Range" goals are those which are more immediate. They are confidence builders and landmarks along the way.

Businesses have monthly and quarterly *profit and loss statements* to evaluate their businesses' progress. The first quarter of 1982 was the best quarter financially for me in 5 years. My first cassette tape program was selling well after my seminars, as was my first book (co-authored), "Those Marvelous Mentors."

1981 had been a good year . . . I had **momentum**. *Have you got momentum? Once you get it you do not want to lose it!* Please do not lose your focus on the best priorities.

Wilson Floors, the oldest and largest commercial flooring company in Columbus, Ohio was one of my on going clients. At their annual kick off meeting, they passed out T-shirts to everyone that said . . . **WE HAVE MOMENTUM!** Some of the "old timers" thought my motivational message was a little "cornball," but the winners responded like the champions they are.

They had a great year that year. Evidence of my contribution surfaced again 6 years later when they began a new division. I was the man they turned to mentor the divisional manager, and develop plans for market penetration. Given more opportunity I could do more. Is that our responsibility to *create more opportunities to sell more?* Of course! And you must remind people of your value and prior contributions, at times!

Bonded Oil, a 300+ location service station operation, based in Ohio, retained me to speak to their managers at an annual meeting. At the luncheon, just before my initial speech, I sat next to Paul Deere, the 80 year old founder.

Mr. Deere told me the story of how he began with two, then three gas stations during the heart of the depression. When he and I met, he was past 80, but still full of vigor, determination and energy. He told me how he finally sold out to Marathon Oil, the industry giant. He seemed very unpretentious for a multi-multi millionaire.

I asked him, "To what do you attribute your success?" He said, "Thom, I do not believe in the word: **can't**! As a matter of fact, our employees were *not allowed* to use that word! You must have a **can do** attitude!"

Could Paul Deere have envisioned all the goals that he would realize since the day he opened his first gas station!?

Opportunities abound today more than ever for the person who is willing to WORK. However, your success in many cases, may be determined by your . . .

DIVERSIFY

Irv Weisheimer, co-owner of one of the most successful vacuum dealerships in the USA, told me recently he will continue to diversify his product line so as to serve the demanding customer who can and will buy from his 60 year old retail/wholesale establishment.

Thinking long-term makes some of the needed sacrifices today more bearable.

ANTICIPATE OBSTACLES

Goals that Convict and Motivate!

A key element to effective goal setting is to anticipate any roadblocks you might encounter along your path to success. Can you plan to avoid them? One of the best techniques for overcoming objections in a sales presentation is to *bring up the objection yourself* . . . to anticipate it . . . and answer the objection early in your presentation. The same thing is true in goal setting. Anticipate your problems so *you can devise solutions.*

Let's concentrate on short-range and long-range goals in both personal and career development. The sections for both will consist of several phases. They are:

LONG RANGE . . . . . . 5 YEAR GOALS
LONG RANGE . . . . . . 1 - 5 YEAR GOALS
SHORT RANGE . . . . . QUARTERLY GOALS
SHORT RANGE . . . . WEEKLY GOALS

In the next chapter, we will discuss daily planning.

When I facilitated, over a 4 month-period, management training sessions for the 26 salon managers of Fiesta Beauty Salons, who could have projected that they would have over 200 salons by the end of the decade!? They really took these goals setting procedures seriously! They *decreased their advertising expenditures to redirect funds towards the human resource development and train the trainer program* I customized for them. The **results?** In one year . . .

25% increase in gross sales overall
20% increase in average ticket sales per store
15% increase in customer count per store
30% increase in product sales per store

It wouldn't have to be that good in the next few months for you to complete these exercises, too, would it!?

WIIFM . . . determining "what's in it for me?" before beginning generates the motivation needed to keep pursuing goals in spite of unforeseen setbacks or delays.

LONG RANGE PERSONAL GOALS

FIVE YEAR

Make a list of your personal goals that will take more than five years to complete (review lists from prior chapter).

1.
2.
3.
4.
5.
6.
7.

Who will you be accountable to for reaching these goals?

(Insert Names)_____

_____

BE . . . GLAD YOU DID

For years I had a speech that was quite popular with management and sales groups. It was called "PAINT THE PICTURE OF SUCCESS." One of the stories highlighted: **Gee I'm glad I did** and **Darn I wish I had.**

These two people . . . Gee and Darn . . . started together in the... **LOVE AND AFFECTION STAGE** . . . of life. Either could have Become #1 in Selling! They had similar family and educational backgrounds. Both got married right out of high school, but Gee decided to keep growing, Darn was not motivated. (What happens if a Gee marries another Darn?)

When they entered the second stage of life, the **RAGS TO RICHES STAGE** . . . they found themselves both working for the local widget manufacturing company. One day over lunch, Gee turned to his old buddy, Darn, and said, "Gee, Darn, I have this terrific idea on how to bottle widgets. Go into business with me selling widgets . . we'll get rich! . . . all our dreams will come true!"

Darn said, "Darn, Gee, I like working here . . . punch in . . . punch out . . . no hassle . . . good benefits . . . secure job . . . no risk, besides, that will never work."

Gee exclaimed, "I think it will! I can become #1 in selling bottled widgets with or without your help, DARN. I've got to GO FOR IT!" So Gee quit his secure job. All his relatives and friends thought he was foolish and even said so. (Know the feeling?)

Nevertheless, this did not discourage him. He kept on going! He knew "if it is to be, it is up to me!" So he was willing to work 12 hours a day, 6 days a week. For the first few years, he earned less than he would have at the Widget Manufacturing Company, but at the 4th and 5th year, he gained more acceptance and established momentum, which he never lost!

Ten years from the date he quit the Widget Manufacturing Company, he was worth a tidy sum. The whistle blew at the Widget Manufacturing Company one day to let the workers off work. Out came DARN with his lunch pail under his arm. He looked up from checking the sidewalk cracks to see a shiny new Cadillac drive by. In it was his old friend . . . Gee, I'm Glad I Did. The old friends exchanged waves, and all Darn could mumble to himself was . . . "Darn I Wish I Had!"

Many more years passed before the old friends would see each other at their 50th high school class reunion. They encountered each other at a park bench in the town square.

Gee said, "Gee, it has been a great life! Lots of hard work, sure, and I almost went broke twice, but today I am financially independent. I have 20 beautiful grandchildren from our five. And soon my wife and I will celebrate our 50th wedding anniversary! We have a couple of homes, a beautiful boat, we are involved in church leadership and in the community and I have even written a couple of books for young aspiring entrepreneurs. My health is fantastic . . . I still jog 4 or 5 times a week. And my trade association recently recognized me as a "member of the year." Two of the kids run the business today and even the grandkids are involved. We have a trust set up so that everyone will be taken care of should I die. My wife and I travel whenever we want to!"

This is the . . . **LOOKING BACK STAGE**

. . . it will be here before we know it!

All Darn could do and say after listening to Gee was . . .

"DARN I WISH I HAD!"

Don't you be a DARN I WISH I HAD . . .

Make a list of your **personal goals** that will take five years to complete:

    1.
    2.
    3.
    4.
    5.
    6.
    7.

If need be, visualize yourself in a rocking chair at age 80, 90, or 100. Reflect back upon your life. How do you feel? Are there things you left undone? Well, it is not too late. You can do it if you think you can! Stay committed and focused.

Goals that Convict and Motivate!

.If you are a student about to graduate from college, according to a recent poll conducted by Computer World Magazine, you may choose to set as one of your career goals to join . . .

      International Business Machine Corp. (IBM)
      American Telephone & Telegraph Co. (AT&T)
      Hewlett-Packard
      Digital Equip. Corp.
      Apple Computer, Inc.
      Other choices? So many choices!

Why did graduates choose these companies? PERSONAL needs and personal goals!

"Traits the students look for among potential employers include opportunities for further education and training, a global corporate outlook and meaningful responsibilities," the magazine reported. "For students looking for a rewarding job with clout, a solid background in business and technology is quickly becoming a ticket to a fast ride up the corporate ladder."

Must your personal goals include *increased computer literacy?*

In the early '80's, it was predicted that hi-tech and service-oriented jobs would lead the way with increased job opportunities. That will be true, too, in the late '90's, and to the year 2000 and beyond. Each market segment and company will have someone Become #1 in Selling! Will you be on that winning team, or the person who becomes #1?

What decisions need to be made today to position you, or educate you to capitalize on opportunities that will present themselves five years from today? Are you willing to discipline yourself on a quarterly, monthly, weekly, and daily basis towards your long-term goals?

A lady complained about her parents moving her between her junior and senior years of high school. On three separate occasions she commented to me that she had been a big fish in a small pond. "I probably would have been homecoming queen my senior year; however, no one knew me at my new school."

Become in Selling!

Let's not look back and constantly think about what might have been.

Let's shape our futures to be much better than the past!

Make a list of **personal goals** that will take One Year to Complete.

1.
2.
3.
4.
5.
6.
7.

So often, our personal goals become subordinate to our career goals. I have purposely placed personal goals ahead of career goals because, again, *it's not what we want but why we want it that will motivate us to action.*

Why   have a new Auto?
Why   have a new wardrobe?
Why   have a new home?
Why   have new furniture?
Why   have a large investment account?
Why   have a happy family?
Why   run 25-30 miles this week?
Why   write another book?
Why   love my neighbor as myself?
Why   Become #1 in Selling?
Why   build a successful business?
Why   become #1 with my spouse and kids?
Why   be assured of eternal life?
Why? Why? Why?

I have my reasons, do you? The old hymn says: "Trust and obey for there is no other way, . . . "So much time asking why questions, rather than focusing on having a thankful attitude can be harmful to your success. Sure, ask your prospects why. You are paid to be and do, then you can have.

Personal goals can be very personal! So much so that we dare not share them with another human being. However, if you have a significant other (married?) in your life, it is very important to communicate your goals with each other. Agreed goals reduce conflict.

On October 15 one year, I received a letter from Don Dotty, Vice President of Sales, Ross Laboratory, a mammoth company and Division of Abbott Labs. He wrote:

Dear Thom:

It is always a pleasure to observe an artist ply his craft. For me this is true whether it be Sinatra singing, Staubach. passing (footballs) or (Thom) Lisk speaking. Thanks again (for speaking for the Columbus Sales Executives Club), and I look forward to seeing you again sometime. Regards, Don Dotty.

Your goals could include **letters of personal recommendation.** How could this benefit you?

DEFINE SUCCESS

How will you know if you are a success. What is your definition of success. I like this one . . .

Success is the progressive realization of a worthwhile and predetermined personal goal.

Do you have a better definition? Write it down:

And please remember some people are more *interested in* **significance** than success. Significance can also be defined in several ways. It is in the eyes of the pursuer. However, one who has a significant eye, not just a successful life, makes a lasting impact on people, our society and maybe the world. Please keep this in mind establish written goals.

WRITE IT DOWN

HUMOR: A young man was drafted. He went to see the doctor to pass the physical examination before he could be sent off to war. There are circumstances that can circumvent reaching your goals, beyond one's control.

He said, "Doc, send me off to war; I want to kill somebody; I want to get some of that blood and guts; I want to shoot or stab someone. Send me now, Doc."

The Doctor looked at him and said, "Boy, you are nuts!!!" The young man pulled out his pen and said, "Write it down Doc . . . write it down!"

He was promptly dismissed!

Writing does crystallize thought. Thinking on paper is a sign of genius. A short pencil beat a short memory every time! And someone once said, you really do not know it unless you can write it down!

Become #1 in Selling! . . . Write it down if it is a goal!! Then give me and others a progress report! Only those who love you and want what is best for you will support you in this effort. Certainly another sales person in the same company or industry will not support you if this is his or her goal too!

Goals that Convict and Motivate!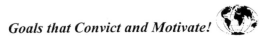

WRITTEN GOALS

What can written goals do for you? They **make the difference!**
Here is why . . .

1. Written Goals Add to your Self-Respect

    There is an intense satisfaction and self-confirmation in
    reaching a goal you have committed yourself to
    ACCOMPLISHING.

2. Written Goals are great Confidence Builders

    When you know where you want to go and how you plan to
    get there, you are more confident of YOUR ABILITY.

3. Written goals add a sense of Values

    Goals encourage you to reflect on your values and take a
    look at yourself in relation to YOUR EXPECTATIONS!

4. Written Goals reduce conflict

    There is real security in knowing what you want to
    accomplish and how you PLAN TO ACCOMPLISH IT!

5. Written Goals Create a sense of Purpose and Anticipation of
    Life

    It's easy to stay enthusiastic about something that's really
    IMPORTANT TO YOU.

6. Written Goals help you Concentrate

214

. Once you really decide you are going to reach a goal, you can see, hear, and think of more possibilities for reaching it then you ever DREAMED EXISTED.

Focus on what you are becoming, doing and need. **Motivation** to pursue goals is the primary ingredient for those who Become #1 in Selling!

One of my personal goals one year included serving my church as chairperson of the Long Range Planning Committee. Establishing a long-range plan for a 250-member church in the center of a prosperous Columbus suburb took a lot of time and research.

The process was similar to researching the needs of 250 customers all of whom you'd like to be more committed to your company. How do you create commitment in your customers?

COMMITMENT

It starts with you! If you are more committed and more focused on your goals . . . you will be more likely to expect others to do so too.

As a matter of fact, you will cause people to see how purchasing your products or service will help them reach goals they may not have though were important to them.

The best salespeople are the most goal oriented just as the most successful in every profession, vocation, business or any area of life

.

Goals that Convict and Motivate!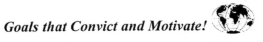

SHORT RANGE PERSONAL GOALS

QUARTERLY

Now that you have made a list of your one year personal goals, break them down into quarterly goals.

First Quarter Goals   Quarter

Today's Date: _____   From: _____   To: _____

Date to be completed   Goals   Check when completed

1.

2.

3.

4.

5.

6.

7.

OTHER:

WEEKLY GOALS

Each week develop an itinerary of goals in advance of the week. Review the list of your quarterly goals (personal). Now break them into weekly goals. Fill out one work sheet and then additional sheets as you progress through the quarter of year.

PERSONAL WEEKLY GOALS

Today's Date: _____ Week Starting: _____
(Duplicate for next 13 weeks)

Date to be completed	Goals	Check when completed
1.		
2.		
3.		
4.		
5.		
6.		
7.		
8.		
9.		
10.		

Goals that Convict and Motivate!

Other weekly goals, or goals next week:

ADDITIONAL QUARTERLY GOALS

Break the remainder of your personal goals into quarters of the year.

One simple example might be that you have set a personal goal to save or invest $6,000 in the next year towards the purchase of your dream home in five years. So you would simply list $1,500 ($6,000 divided by four equals $1,500) in each quarter. Since there are 13 weeks in each quarter (52 divided by 4), one weekly personal goal would have been $115.38 saved per week towards the new home.

Family goals could be broken down into quality time investments. Investing 30 minutes a day with your son or daughter adds up to 3 1/2 hours per week or 46 1/2 hours per quarter! Can you see the benefit to keeping track and checking it off your list when complete? You can do this for all eight areas of life, using time as the measuring instrument if you like.

SECOND QUARTER PERSONAL GOALS

Date: _____   To: _____

Date to be Completed	Goals	Check when Completed

1.

2.

3. .

4.

5.

6.

7.

THIRD QUARTER PERSONAL GOALS

Date: From: _____   To: _____

Date to be Completed	Goals	Check when Completed

1.

2.

3.

4.

5.

6.

7.

Goals that Convict and Motivate!

FOURTH QUARTER PERSONAL GOALS

Date: From: _____   To: _____

Date to be Completed	Goals	Check when Completed

1.

2.

3.

4.

5.

6.

7.

Possibly, you will need more space than I have allowed. Consider developing your own *goals' notebook.*

LONG RANGE CAREER GOALS--FIVE YEAR

Life begins at _____. You fill in the blank. The so-called baby boomers, those born between 1946 to 1964 are turning 40 right and left. It is believed that their influence will grow dramatically as we approach the year 2000 and beyond.

Many people, research indicates, hold a job no more than 5 years. So there is a good chance you will be doing something different from what you do now 5 years from today . . . or you will be working for another company. Promoted?

Can you foresee that and plan for it today?

Become in 🏃 Selling!

In the early '80's, I became very well acquainted with an ex-NFL football player. He became a great friend. Like many athletes, his pro-football career did not exceed five years by much. So what?

He had name recognition so he was awarded an automobile agency selling a luxury brand of autos. This agency Became #1 in Selling! Five years later, he had financial troubles, sold out, and went into gas and oil exploration and investments, and real estate investments. Five years after this, he was in the ministry full-time!! Now he pastors a wonderful growing church!

Many people are experiencing mid-life career changes. I do believe **"If you aren't having fun doing it, you are doing it wrong, or it is not for you!"** So, now is as good a time as any to plan a change. Maybe your change is to work better.

If your career goals are not being met where you are . . . you may not Become #1 in Selling (and, therefore, unlikely to reach your other personal goals) . . . then, consider a change, if possible.

That's what I did in July of 1982. I had worked successfully for myself for 5-1/2 years, the first 1-1/2 years of that period as an independent contractor for Carl Stevens, while housed at Management Horizons, an international consulting firm, now a division of Price Waterhouse.

In May 1982, I met Roland DeMott, Vice President, National Sales Director for Highlights for Children. He introduced himself at a seminar I facilitated for the Columbus Sales & Marketing Executives Club. (I was Chairman of their Sales Training Committee.) I recruited Dr. Roger Blackwell and Dr. Buck Matthews, Chairman of Marketing at Ohio State University to assist, along with some other "experts."

The second seminar I recruited other sales trainers to assist, including Mike Frank, Bob Hillier, and Bill Mayo. These were powerful seminars for salespeople and sales managers. We learned from each other. You can learn from everyone if you are ready. Are you open to learn from all?

WHEN THE STUDENT IS READY
THE TEACHER WILL APPEAR!

Since I had completed a list of five-year personal goals which included: more time with the family; more long term stability; less travel; have Todd in a private school . . . I was open to Highlights for Children recruitment offer to have me replace Roland DeMott. He wanted to retire. Initially, they hired me as a consultant for $1,000 a week for a few hours for me to evaluate, objectively, their needs. It seemed like a great opportunity.

I did the following . . . and I ask you to, also, please make a list of your *career goals* that will take **five years to complete.**

1.
2.
3.
4.
5.
6.
7.
8.
9.
10.

We cannot totally anticipate all that may impact our lives and careers. So it is best to be flexible, ready to change, if needed, and, continuously set goals.

Next, make a list of your *career goals* that will take **one year to complete.**

1.
2.
3.
4.
5.
6.

7.

8.

9.

10.

You may recall, that at age 20, I had prophesied to Red Connell, "I want to have your job someday (Vice President of Sales, National Sales Director)." Now, 12 years later, I found myself at the top of a 300+ direct sales organization. I now had the "dream job" I had focused upon 12 years earlier.

Be careful what you dream about; it might come true.

If you really want to Become #1 in Selling and maintain balance while you Become #1 in some other areas of life simultaneously *remove the distractions*, as quickly as possible! Once I got back into the church, I stopped, as an example, going to the bars. The images one sees there is not conductive to Becoming #1 in Selling in most sales situations, or #1 in your family life with spouse or kids.

Some must stop watching so much distracting negative TV. **HABITS!** Have you written on these goal lists which personal and career habits must be changed or removed? What *new attitudes* would help? Do you have, as an example, *a place for everything and everything in its place?*

The #1 problem or *challenge* for all aspiring sales people is "poor work habits." Earlier, we said habits or attitudes of thought must improve before habits of action will improve.

POSITIVE HABITS TO DEVELOP INCLUDE

1.

2.

3.

4. .

5.

6.

7.

LONG RANGE CAREER GOALS
QUARTERLY

Now, make a list of your career goals breaking them into quarters of the year. Example: Let's say your sales goal is $2,500,000 for the year. (I'm going to think BIGGER . . . How about you?) Your quarterly goal for each quarter would be $625,000. From this point, you could easily break your goals into monthly goals. Or $208,333 per month!

First Quarter Career;   Today's Date: _____

Date to be Completed	Goals	Check when Completed

1.

2.

3.

4.

5.

6.

7. .

8.

9.

10.

When I joined Highlights for Children (America's #1 children's publication for ages 2-12 with over 2 million subscribers), I had many goals for July, August and September, the third quarter of the calendar year. You can start your quarter at anytime.

My career goals were set in conjunction with the CEO, Gary Myers III, grandson of the founders, and the then President Jerry Solinger. Both were great planners and strategic thinkers. Who can help you now? Strategic team planning is important.

Team goals need the team's input!

Family financial goals are set with the family team members' input and/or needs in mind. For any team of people to take ownership of their goals, it is best to involve team members in the process of establishing goals.

WEEKLY CAREER GOALS

Review your list of Quarterly Goals each week and break them into weekly goals.

Today's Date: _____   Week Beginning: _____

Date To Be Completed	Goals	Check When Completed

1.

2. .

3.

4.

5.

6.

7.

8.

9.

10.

Many sales organizations require their salespeople (for their benefit) to complete an **itinerary** in advance of each week. Some might have 10 sales calls planned each day. This, along with other plans, are a part of a strategic individual sales plan, and it should also be written.

Be sure to slow down and ask for the order! Activity is to bring the *desired results*, not become busy work. Do not confuse activity with actual accomplishment!

The habits developed in preparing, using, and analyzing required reports will benefit anyone. Better planning will provide more time to do what you really want to do.

We need to make better decisions on how we invest the 168 hours each upcoming week. *Invest hours* toward the target accounts, markets, prospects, and people *better*, so you can Become #1 in Selling. Plan It.

Become in 🐝 *Selling!*

.Each week at Highlights for Children, when I was the National Director of Sales, we had a computer printout on all sales results throughout the USA in various categories including:

1. Direct Mail Sales
2. Telemarketing Sales
3. Representative Sales

Then we dissected these sales by:
1. Response to mailings
2. Telemarketing Sales
   A. Which person, shift, territory, enrollment length, lead, CUSTOMERS.
   B. Renewal, new sale, etc.
3. Representative Sale
   A. Which person, manager, lead, length, commission split, CUSTOMERS.
   B. Renewal, new sale, how lead or referral came.
4. Profits per person per sale, etc.

HUMOR: I once knew a person who suffered from paralysis of analysis! He had all the answers but no one to listen to him.

With the right software for our computers we can forecast, plan, track, and manage better.

As a consultant, I help with customization of these systems and much more. I want to help your company and you Become #1 in Selling in your market niche(s). I sometimes recommend TELEMAGIC or TICKLE, a sales, client, and customer follow-up system by LC software, Inc. Contact The Thom Lisk Group for more details, if needed.

The first quarter of my project for Highlights for Children went quite well. I gave two-day seminars in six locations across the USA for the 60 field sales managers. I trained these trainers to sell, recruit and train their people. Sales began increasing throughout the USA!

Discipline to forecast and plan further into the future now can help everyone avoid costly mistakes later. Here is a work sheet that will help.

SECOND, THIRD OR FOURTH QUARTER GOALS

Date: From: _____ To: _____

Date to be Completed	Goals	Check when Completed
1.		
2.		
3.		
4.		
5.		
6.		
7.		
8.		
9.		
10.		

One could invest an entire chapter or book on the significance of the next step in goal setting.

VISUALIZATION

I am reminded that the "lust of the eyes," the "lust of the flesh," and "the pride of life" can get anyone way off track. When I discuss visualization, I am not prescribing a methodology that would have you focus on the wrong priorities.

I do believe we become a part of our surroundings, therefore, it is important to place yourself in an *opportunity-rich environment*. Associate with those who are, or have a part of what you desire. HOWEVER, never sacrifice what is right. Never make idols of things or people or companies.

You have now set your career and personal goals, both short and long term. Now paint a picture in your mind, then, put it on paper. This is the *positive picture* of what tangible event or events must take place for you to have achieved your goals. What do you see? What would you like to be experiencing? As a result of your efforts, how will it benefit you, your family, your company and others?

Literally VISUALIZE (prayerfully image) and draw pictures or paste them depicting goals achieved from each area of life one month from now. Use this space, and more, if needed. DO IT ASAP. DO NOT PROCRASTINATE! THIS IS VERY IMPORTANT! Let me caution us again that we must focus on *Being* before we *focus* on *doing or having* . In other words, to Become #1 in Selling, first **focus** on who you can become . . . attitudes . . . self-image . . . self-esteem . . . integrity . . . character. . then because you have become better, now, you can and will attract the people and things you desire. You *BECOME PREPARED, EQUIPPED AND EMPOWERED* to do more things correctly each day. The motivation to do so is a result of personal goals, needs, hopes, desires and aspirations.

Goals that Convict and Motivate!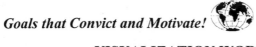

VISUALIZATION WORKSHEET

"The best and most beautiful things in the world cannot be seen, nor touched. . . but are felt in the heart." Helen Keller

"Seek first the kingdom of God and His righteousness, and all these things (you hope for) will be added unto you." Matthew 6:33

230

FINALIZATION

This step is to inventory the goals you have accomplished. It is suggested you complete this *worksheet each quarter*, listing goals fulfilled. This will help you to evaluate your progress, redirect your efforts, if necessary, and give you a sense of accomplishment. There is great intrinsic value in this which will, in turn, build your self-confidence and self-image. Give yourself a reward for each successful completion . . . something to look forward to , if need be, to maintain your motivation.

Goals established, worked towards, and reviewed, in the ways described, will bring conviction, motivation and belief. As a *result*, you will do more of what it takes each day to Become #1 in Selling. It worked for me . . . and has for many others. It can work for you if you work at it.

Your *written goals will convict you* to . . . **become** . . . **do** . . . and, **have!**

Date: _____

Review of Goals Accomplished   From: _____ To: _____

Major Goals Written Here	Percentage of Goal Reached
1.	1.
2.	2.
3.	3.
4.	4.
5.	5.
6.	6.
7.	7.

Goals that Convict and Motivate!

What I Need To Do In The Next _____ Days To Complete These Projects Or Fully Reach These Goals:

1.

2.

3.

If you desire to BECOME #1 IN SELLING as YOU place SERVICE ABOVE SELF to your customers, please consider:

"Commit your way to the Lord, trust also in Him, and He WILL bring it to pass." Psalm 37:5

"And life is what we make it, always has been, always will be."
Grandma Moses

"The greatest discovery of my generation is that human beings can alter their lives by altering their attitudes of mind." William James

"Go ye into all the world . . ." Jesus

"See all the prospects in this city, then in the county; then in the state; then in the nation; then in the world. These who will not buy after your best presentation effort, forget, and say . . . who's next?! Improve all about your sales effort A-Z, each day, week, month and year, and you will become the greatest!"

. . . An Unknown International Sales Manager

REVIEW QUESTIONS   **CHAPTER EIGHT**

1. Have you defeated all your fears? _____ What does DEFEAT FEAR stand for?

   _____

   _____

2. Can a mentor help you reach your goals? _____

   Which Ones? _____

   In what way? _____

   _____

3. Did you complete all the goal setting exercises in the chapter?

   _____. If not, please do so now.

4. Now discuss your goals with others who want or need you to succeed.

5. Can you describe how you have *become* a better person because you first visualized the end result? _____

   _____

   Describe what you have become and acquired as a result of your vision or mental picture imaged. _____

   _____

6. Do you have any suggestions for improving this book? _____
   Please send your ideas to **THE THOM LISK GROUP** or the publisher. Thank you. Our goal is constant improvement.

CHAPTER 9

Big You...little i

MOTIVATION AND OBJECTIONS

Now we will move to more meat and the **main course**. The final chapter will provide a closing. . .closing the sale. . . and much more! If YOU are like me YOU like to eat dessert any time of the day, and sometimes, before and during a meal, as well as at the end!

Closing sales are that way, aren't they? Every master salesperson knows he or she must be *closing all the time*. . . and you recognize others who are attempting to "close" or sell to you.

"Do not expand your direct sales organization, it is cost prohibitive. Focus on building the telemarketing department which has had some significant levels of success." These words prophetically given to top management at Highlights for Children were my analysis in 1983 that were not totally heeded until the 90's.

When selling in person or by phone people seldom want your opinion. They want to know. . .

WIIFM

What's In It For Me?

THE ANSWER...WIIFY!

i have worked to remember NOT WIIFM, BUT WHAT IS IN IT FOR YOU, thinking of many who have "Become #1 in Selling." i use the word "i" to help sell myself, or share personal experiences or stories to make the points. i realize i am really nothing without God.

my **six most important WORDS** are:

YOU are king. . .YOU my customer!

The **five most important WORDS** are:

YOU did a terrific job!

The **four most important WORDS** are:

How YOU benefit is. . .   or. . .
Which means to YOU. . .

The **three most important WORDS** are:

Will YOU please. . .

The **two most important WORDS** are. . .

"Thank YOU ! !"

The **one LEAST most important WORD** is. . .

i . . . or. . .my

The **one MOST IMPORTANT WORD** is. . .

YOU. . . then. . .WE

The above is important for us to remember, do YOU agree?

When YOU are focused on what's in it for me, YOU CAN lose your focus on communicating properly to the customer or prospect . . . W I I F Y . . .

What's In It For YOU!

Let's face it, others seldom do not care: What's in it for me.
They think about themselves and their needs, challenges or
opportunities most of the time. Some managers tell their
salespeople to ask their customers to buy more to help the
salesperson win a trip or prize. i disagree with this tactic.

When with the Eureka Company, i won trips to Hawaii and
Puerto Rico for a week each. When with Kurfees Coating, Inc., i
won a trip to Florida (or was it Grand Bahamas Island?). In the '80s
i had many all-expense-paid trips by clients to desirable places. My
customers at the time, even though i was friends with many, could
have cared less. They would have preferred to have the trips
themselves! YOU are the first to know about some of these trips.

These kinds of incentives, nonetheless, do provide increased
motivation, don't they?

MOTIVATION

If i had to summarize selling, and How to Become #1 in Selling,
in 4 words. . . i would say . . .

Prospect

Present

Follow-up

. . . Better!

To do all four better, YOU always need motivation. The goals
YOU set in the prior chapter, if reviewed often, and taken seriously,
will give YOU MORE motivation.

Rather than allow others to provide the motivation YOU need to
become #1 in selling, at some point, YOU must fly on your own.

The mother eagle literally pushes the baby eagle out of the nest, and he/she must fly. A mentor can do just so much for any of us! Losing a job can be the best thing for YOU!

WHAT DO YOU ATTRACT?

In the wild, like attract like, although at places like the San Diego Wild Animal Park, YOU can see giraffes, as an example, mingling with North American antelope on an open plain. Ordinarily this is not the case.

Great salespeople like to be around other great ones. . .or potentially great ones. You've heard the advice: "If YOU want to soar with eagles do not flock with the turkeys!" Sharpen YOUR ax upon better people.

You may not Become #1 in Selling, if YOU spend too much of your leisure or entertainment time with those who are "Darn i wish i had" types.

Some salespeople win so often that their egos get so big they have a hard time getting their enlarged head through the door. They turn people off before they can turn them on to their products. *HUMOR:* A friend of mine once told me, "Thom, egotism is a disease that makes everyone sick except the person who has it!"

Egotists, those with so much false pride about who they are have little OBJECTIVITY. Great people are humble!

To Become #1 in Selling, YOU need objectivity.

Prentice Hall once surveyed many of the managers in America's top corporations. They asked them "What one word would epitomize the great manager?"

Would YOU have guessed the synopsis of the survey? "The hallmark of a great manager is that he or she is OBJECTIVE."

Earlier YOU agreed that the most difficult person to manage is the "guy in the glass." You must manage your prospecting and client management activities better than others to Become #1 in Selling! Have a strategy that positions YOU uniquely better.

Big You . . . little i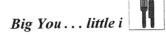

In hundreds of paid professional speeches or seminars, i have closed my speeches with this poem . . .

THE GUY IN THE GLASS

WHEN YOU GET WHAT YOU WANT IN YOUR STRUGGLE FOR SELF,
AND THE WORLD MAKES YOU KING OR QUEEN FOR A DAY,
THEN GO TO THAT MIRROR AND LOOK AT YOURSELF,
AND SEE WHAT THAT GUY HAS TO SAY.

FOR IT ISN'T YOUR FATHER, OR MOTHER, OR WIFE,
WHOSE JUDGMENT YOU MUST PASS.
THE FELLOW WHOSE VERDICT COUNTS MOST IN YOUR LIFE,
IS THE GUY STARING BACK IN THE GLASS. (AND ALMIGHTY GOD!)

HE'S THE GUY (OR GAL) TO PLEASE, NEVER MIND ALL THE REST
FOR HE'S WITH YOU CLEAR TO THE END,
AND YOU'VE PASSED YOUR MOST DANGEROUS, DIFFICULT TEST
IF THE GUY IN THE GLASS IS YOUR FRIEND.

YOU MAY BE LIKE JACK HORNER AND CHISEL A PLUM,
AND THINK YOU'RE A WONDERFUL GUY,
BUT THE MAN IN THE GLASS SAYS YOU'RE ONLY A BUM
IF YOU CAN'T LOOK HIM STRAIGHT IN THE EYE.

YOU CAN FOOL THE WHOLE WORLD DOWN THE PATHWAY OF YEARS
AND GET THOSE PATS ON THE BACK AS YOU PASS.
BUT YOUR FINAL REWARD WILL BE HEARTACHES AND TEARS
IF YOU'VE CHEATED (GOD AND) THE GUY IN THE GLASS.

... (Author unkown)

Do YOU really like yourself? You can. . . you must! As Ethel Merman said. . . "God does not make JUNK!"

Objectivity involves. . .

1. Suspending your ego from the throne of your life
2. Setting aside all prelearned, and conditioned values, attitudes, and opinions

3. Assimilating (bringing together) all the facts, data and other inputs; then. . .

4. Make a great decision, then you can help others do the same!

And some of YOU complain about the cost of this book, or investing $100-$200 in cassette tapes to learn how to sell better! i have no sympathy for YOU. The best investment for returns in this life is investment to improve yourself in all the right ways.

BAD ADVICE OR GOOD ADVICE

Your clients and prospects want to know if they can trust the recommendations YOU give them.

i trusted the man who sold me consulting and career marketing services. However, he may have been more interested, at the time, in reaching his quotas, and overhead expenses, than my true fulfillment. But, in the long run, it worked out ok. YOU must not constantly revisit old decisions. You must trust God who will help you to trust those he allows in your life.

Burn me once, shame on YOU. Burn me twice, shame on me! i went off to Chicago for in-depth tailored marketing strategies. i asked for and allowed other professionals to identify all my options, objectively, and help market me, (the product), to companies.

They knew the secret behind arousing desire and motivating the emotional man.

What are YOU more emotional about than your own career? It is an extension of your own personality. That's why we love selling, don't we? You can, if in the right sales situation, express your personality through your sales activities and relationships. Again. . ."If you aren't having fun doing it. . .you are either doing it wrong or it is not for you!"

In Chapter 6, YOU received four steps to CONVINCE OTHERS. Now here are the steps to motivate others. . .

Motivational Planning Sheet for: _____

Big You . . . little i

_____ (your prospect).

Affirm: i CAN CAUSE MY PROSPECT TO WANT WHAT i
AM SELLING.

YOU WILL WANT MY PRESCRIPTION AND BUY
FROM me . . .TODAY!

i DO HAVE YOUR BEST INTEREST AT HEART!

1) *Problem Review*: _____

_____

_____

(Verbally review his/her stated problem)

Your Answer: **"THIS IS IT!"** (Referring to what YOU are selling)

2) *Project to a later time*: _____

_____

(use words like "It is the year 2000, Bill, as a result of this decision
today. . .")

3) *Paint a word picture now*: _____

_____

You see (87%) _____

You hear (7%) _____

You taste _____

You smell _____

You feel _____

Since 87% of the mental impact comes from what YOU see, and 7% from what you hear, (on the average), you paint a picture like. . . With this decision today YOU are able to see your dreams come true. Can YOU see YOURself with the promotion YOU desire...with more income which YOU can invest on a nice vacation for the family, and that new home? Can YOU hear your grandchildren playing outside YOUR winter home or on the beach?

4) *In motivating, remember. . .*

The **big appeal** to his/her dominant buying urge:

_____

_____ (the answer to his or her problem)

It's not what they want, but why they want it that really motivates others to buy. In 90% of the cases, according to another Prentice Hall Survey of outstanding salespeople, people buy for emotional or psychological reasons . . . not for rational reasons!

10% RATIONAL OR LOGICAL
90% EMOTIONAL OR PSYCHOLOGICAL

Some sales trainers talk about the Hot Button. Others say "Sell the Sizzle not the Steak!" The **dominant buying urge or motive** is a more accurate description, isn't it? Now, here are the seven wonderful closing words to use after YOU have painted the picture properly. . .

5) *That's What You Really Want, isn't It?*

Some purchased this book because they really want to Become #1 in Selling! Others because they want to stay #1 in Selling! This may be what YOU wanted. Why YOU wanted it, really motivated YOU to purchase my book, didn't it!? OR, to read and use it!

If YOU purchase more of my materials, or attend my seminars, or YOUR company uses me on an ongoing basis as a consultant, it will be because YOU have gotten results from using these ideas. Or YOU know i share the truth and YOU know i have more truths for YOU or your associates. This stuff works. . . if YOU do!!

What Motivates? Think of an example. . .

1. Desire for gain (pleasure) _____

2. Fear of Loss (pain) _____

When motivating others? We remember. . .

PEOPLE DO NOT CARE HOW MUCH I KNOW UNTIL THEY KNOW HOW MUCH i CARE. . .ABOUT YOU!

BIG YOU. . .little i!!

Remember, also, when motivating (or closing), in order to communicate that YOU sincerely care. . .

LOOK_____   LEAN_____

LOWER_____   SMILE_____

NOD_____

Look the person in the eye. You do not trust people who will not look YOU in the eye!

Lower your voice. This invites confidence. . .they are more inclined to concentrate and listen.

Nod your head up and down. Signify your expectation for agreement with this non verbal gesture.

Lean forward towards the person. This adds warmth and understanding.

Smile because it invites confidence. . .they will smile, too!

You convince, motivate, and close with effective non verbals. Please list what non verbals YOU can use more effectively:

CONDITIONS

Sometimes conditions dictate whether YOU can close a sale. To Become #1 in Selling YOU do not have to close them all.

YOU do need to know when to walk away, and understand YOU did all YOU could do.

Many times in the examination step YOU are given a condition that may appear, on the surface, impossible to overcome.

CONDITIONS, just like the weather, can change quickly, and drastically!

Here's an example:

YOU attempt to sell a $5,000 product to a person who needs it badly, and, is beginning to understand that. He only has $5,000 and has committed it to another priority.

YOU qualified the prospect properly with all the right questions, so YOU know he knows that YOU know his condition. But the prospect says, "I'm sorry, i can't afford it now!"

YOU could say something stupid like "When do YOU think YOU will be able to afford it?"

Rather, YOU position YOURself like the consultant, the *consultative salesperson* (the doctor) and YOU empathize by saying:

THE 3 F'S

"i can understand why YOU *feel* that way. We had a man who had a similar situation. He did not take our recommendation and his career never did get back on track. He had the money but preferred to hang onto it. However, he spent it while unemployed. He *felt* he could wait. He *found*, when it was too late. . . after his savings were all gone. . . that he could not objectively market himself. YOU do not want that, do YOU?"

FEEL. . .FELT. . .FOUND!

This technique for overcoming. . .

OBJECTIONS!

. . .can help YOU Become #1 in Selling! Now rather than paint a negative picture, like the one i just verbalized, let's say it more positively. . .

> The best remedy for any objection is to anticipate it, and overcome it before it can ever surface!!

"i can understand how YOU *feel*. We have a client who had a similar condition. He *felt* he could not afford our services, too. Here is how he *found* he could finance the purchase: (fill in the blank) _____. Now he has a new position and earns 25% more per year. He recovered his $5,000 investment in less than 6 months. That's what YOU really want, isn't it?"

Being the right person insures YOU hear alarming objections less. However, in life, YOU can make a perfect sales presentation, answering each potential objection in advance, and still encounter. .

HOPELESS OBJECTIONS

In life few situations or people are truly hopeless. There is almost always something that can be done. Of course, when my grandmother reached 105, there was little that could be done to keep her alive. People sometimes give up on others too soon many times. And they give up on sales or customers too soon.

Exactly 20 years after leaving the Eureka Company i spoke with the current President of the company by phone. Gil Dorsey said "Red should not have offered YOU the job at age 23 as a Regional Manager." Anyone at that age would have been hard pressed to resist corruption with what was asked of them to succeed in that company then. Sometimes others can box us into a nearly hopeless position. However, there is always a positive way out, and lessons to learn.

How would YOU define a hopeless objection? Is there really such a thing as a hopeless objection in YOUR sales activities? Certainly!

If YOU are like most great salespeople i know, YOU do not give up easily! YOU find objections challenging, right? Right!

However, when YOU do finally determine an objection is hopeless, decide to redeem YOUR time. . .get away as soon as possible! Learn how to say. . ."Next!" WHO IS NEXT?

CAN BE ANSWERED

Most objections heard by the salesperson who wants to Become #1 in Selling can be answered. Objections in this second category are either:

1. Unstated, or
2. Stated

The unstated objections are the most difficult for the inexperienced or new salesperson. Until YOU know what the objections to your proposal or presentation might be, YOU will have difficulty surfacing them in a standard sales presentation.

Big You... little i

The consultative salesperson naturally. . .

1. Asks questions
2. Listens
3. Gets the real reason
4. Brings it up first

Therefore, the consultative salesperson can identify clearly the objection, and prescribe a solution. This is a major reason why the PROBLEM SOLVER (Chapter 4) can eventually sell (serve) all type buyers.

HUMOR: Someone said a consultant is someone who will "borrow your watch, tell YOU what time it is, and charge YOU $100." In 1984 i traveled to Detroit, Michigan and La Salle, Illinois, each, several times on consultative assignments by auto, often earning over $100 an hour. So what?

HUMOR: Someone said, "A consultant is someone who is at least 100 miles away from home."

Jesus said, "A Prophet is honored everywhere except in his own country, and among his own people!" *Application?* The #1 salesperson would share his plans so others could duplicate them, however, few people ask or listen, especially those in one's own family or company!

When i spoke at the annual meeting of Gates McDonald, a subsidiary of Nationwide Insurance, at their annual National Sales Conference, i could not envision that it would lead to their wanting to retain me to develop their Michigan market.

Cricket Magazine, a division of Carus Corporation, paid me over $11,000 in 1984 for 10 days of my time to consult with them. Marianne and Blouke Carus and i had some delightful lunch meetings together, while considering how to improve their marketing, direct mail, and sales effort.

Interestingly enough, this last assignment came as a result of the mailings generated, some months earlier, during my $5,000

objective career assessment and marketing consultants. A 220% R.O.I.!

R.O.I. = Return On Investment

i hope YOU will invest more so YOU can receive more too! Can YOU see the benefit?

Ben Franklin said, "Empty the coins from your pocket into your mind, and your mind will empty coins into your pocket."

YOUR customers can understand your benefits as YOU ask better questions, ok?

Sometimes when i am invited to speak at a large meeting, i prepare a questionnaire or assessment to send to all anticipated attendees. In this way, i can better anticipate their needs and customize a message more fully.

DO OTHERS KNOW YOU LISTEN. . .

. . .carefully? Many have had classes in public speaking and join groups like Toastmasters. However, how many of YOU have had a class in "LISTENING"? Listening properly is hard work!

Articles written by Carl Stevens and me were published in the Ohio Business Review Magazine. Our monthly article fell under the category of "Sales and Marketing in Business." One article's title was "Is Listening A Lost Art?":

"We only hear 25-30% of what is said to us. Listen for the total message being transmitted to us. There are two aspects of communication. Effective communications is like a good pair of scissors. There are two vital components that must work in concert if optimum results are to be achieved. One half of the pair of scissors by itself is not very functional. It takes both halves to develop the synergy that is needed for maximum results. Listen, then speak more appropriately.

FUZZY WORDS

Big You . . . little i

One possible difficulty to achieving maximum exchange of ideas is that maybe we are using "fuzzy words." No wonder prospects have objections, and do not buy! Fuzzy words create different pictures in different minds.

WORDS are symbols that trigger pictures in YOUR mind. WORDS can have different connotations to different people.

If YOU say to a listener, "Think of the home of your dreams--what type of architecture would YOU see? Would it be colonial, modern, Tudor, Cape Cod, Spanish, or just what picture would come to your mind?"

When i asked audiences, "What person comes to YOUR mind when i say, handsome man, beautiful woman?" . . .the responses are seldom the same. Some name a spouse, boyfriend or girlfriend. Many name TV or movie stars. Why?

Language is a system of symbols that stand for ideas and objects whose meanings we attempt to agree to and understand. A specific word may illicit different responses. Some people are not good with words and their meanings.

No wonder many objections to your sales offers are *UNSTATED!* How do YOU. . .

GET THE REAL REASON?

Yes! Ask the right questions! Become an active listener.

ACTIVE LISTENING

Active listening is a label that has been placed on a time-honored technique. It is feeding back the information YOU have been given and the feelings expressed by the other person. Active listening assures the other party that YOU understand what they are attempting to communicate. This understanding is a necessary part of any exchange if YOU hope to motivate the other person. It is especially important in emotional exchanges.

"Listening does not mean simply maintaining a polite silence while YOU are rehearsing in your mind the speech YOU are going to make the next time YOU can grab a conversational opening. Nor does listening mean waiting alertly for the flaws in the other fellow's arguments so that later YOU can mow him down."

. . . Dr. Samuel I. Hayakawa

This . . . listening . . . is the essence or at the heart of *practicing putting others' needs and wants #1.* Others must be #1 more so with most of YOU so YOU can Become #1 in Selling!

BIG YOU . . . little i . . . active listening is the application of the BIG YOU . . . little i "philosophy."

TELL ME. . .

When YOU sincerely want to hear a more detailed explanation from the other person, YOU CAN add **"tell me about it!"** Then listen.

An objective listener will make an overt effort not to put a label or labels on what the speaker is saying. For example, "He sounds like a liberal to me," or "He's just another conservative spouting off," or "She's just putting out the same old stuff. I've heard that before."

Listen, this person may be different. That's one reason why i do not use all the standard sales techniques of overcoming the objection.

The three-step method, *Feel. . . Felt. . . Found, works in most cases*, if used properly.

WHY?

"Why do YOU feel that way?" is a good question to get to the *real reason* the person is objecting. They will only give YOU the real reason if they perceive they can trust YOU.

Most salespeople really forget (or do not know how) to dialogue properly. The goal of dialogue can be for **clarification**, not victory. Great sales people love a. . .

CHALLENGE

Challenge YOURself to come away from dialogue with new information. Information about what others are thinking and doing and more importantly. . .why. If YOU can better understand other people and where they are coming from and why, then, just maybe, this will help us better understand ourselves. It will help you sell more!

How can i adequately explain to YOU what i learned about others and myself when i formed an association named the Christian Business Management Association? CBMA was incorporated just after my friend Ohio District Court Judge (he ran for the Supreme Court) John McCormick and i prayed over the Articles of Incorporation and By Laws before the filing.

Ken Sampson, Executive Vice President for the Columbus Board of Realtors, and Zelma Bishop, Executive Vice President for the Ohio Funeral Directors Association, helped me and some other trustees . . . do it right. They challenged me to become an executive director (part-time) during the startup phases.

If YOU do not do it right the first time, when will YOU have time (or get a second chance) to do it again!?

People want to help YOU reach YOUR goals. Some people, your patrons, that is. Great people will challenge YOU, and great prospects challenge YOU with their objections. Be thankful that they care enough to help YOU! Because that is what they do by making YOU WORK for the sale. YOUR BEST customers were often be the hardest WON!

YOU can overcome the unstated objection, If YOU have, and can take the time needed.

STATED OBJECTIONS

Have YOU ever heard the expression "You can eat crow!" What are they saying? Recently i slept with the bedroom window open. Rather than awake to a rooster crowing, i heard a crow crowing. It's not a pleasant sound. No wonder some farmer invented scarecrows to scare the crows away from the corn field (and house)!

How many objections have ravaged YOUR sales career? REFUSE TO LET OBJECTIONS STOP YOU IN THE FUTURE. UNDERSTAND THEM! Win or lose, give them all YOU have! You can find yourself with many uncertainties. The experts had helped me reassess my options, affirm my strengths again, and market myself via letters and resumes, but they never prepared me for the rejection i was to experience. . .the stated objections. . . when looking for a national sales management and training job.

A salesperson is only partially prepared unless he/she has all the answers to the potential objections.

Abe Lincoln was rejected time after time during various elections, including a defeat in 1858, just before his election to the presidency in 1860. He learned how to handle disappointments so that he did not panic during the difficult days of the Civil War. He was prepared through adversity, each a great learning experience.

To Become #1 in Selling, view lost sales as learning experiences . . . view stated objections joyfully. Now it is put on the table where YOU can deal with it.

In one week i had meetings as follows: Omaha, Nebraska, on Monday; Los Angeles on Tuesday; Wednesday in New Jersey and in White Plains, New York; and Thursday in Chattanooga, Tennessee; and Friday i gave a speech in Gatlinburg, Tennessee, before a brief stop in Cincinnati, Ohio, before flying home to Columbus, Ohio. So what?

Each company i visited had stated objections to buying my services long term. Because i was, i thought, offering the best solution, i was not completely prepared for the rejection i received.

Rather than bore YOU with the details, let me simply assert: i can understand almost any rejection or stated objection YOU might encounter. i have walked in YOUR moccasins if YOU are selling...

regardless of what YOU sell or who YOU serve and sell. My best advice?

YOU must remember to. . .

- ☛ Reject rejection!!
- ☛ Learn from rejection!!

Do NOT take rejection personally!!☹☺

Some employers put their salespeople in the unfortunate position of having to cower away from stated objections because they do not train salespeople properly. Of course, many salespeople do not have enough *drive to search out the answers to each objection*; then prescribe the solution properly at the appropriate time.

YOU want to Become #1 in Selling! YOU must be prepared to overcome objections and maintain a positive expectant attitude!

YOU must learn to reject rejection! One of the greatest compliments i ever heard as a young salesperson was "Thom *does not hear the word 'NO'!*"

HUMOR: Now, some salespeople are great at generating at least two orders. . ."Get out. . .and Stay out!" Not you, I hope!

Stated objections come in these categories:

1. Genuine	3. Half-Baked
2. Trivial	4. Put Off--indication of indecision

When YOU receive these types of objections, are YOU R.E.A.D.Y.? Here is how to answer. . . (options)

R.everse the objection

E.xplain further

A.dmit it. . .YOU or them

D.eny. . .they will try to cover up

Y.Ask "Why?"

?.Restate it as a question

Examples:

REVERSE the Objection: "We cannot afford it!"

YOU say. . .

"OK, the investment in our seminar is a lot of money. However, YOU cannot afford not to attend! YOU need more Sales. . .and more income. . .a 25% increase in YOUR income is what YOU said YOU wanted. . .YOU now earn $30,000 a year. . .25% equals $7,500. $500 for this product is only 1/15th of the increase YOU will experience, in the next year alone. In the next 20 years, $500 is a small investment to learn how to Become #1 in Selling, I feel

GENUINE objections need more of an explanation. . .

"i don't see the value in your 'BLUEPRINTS FOR BUILDING YOUR BUSINESS' seminar system," she says.

YOU say. . .
"Apparently i have not explained adequately or thoroughly. Here is an in-depth outline of the seminar sales system. . . .
YOU will appreciate knowing how each feature will specifically benefit YOU. Knowing more about what is taught, how it is custom-tailored and installed, and how it has benefited others will help YOU with your decision!"
ADMIT IT. . .YOU or them:

"i don't care if i ever Become #1 in Selling!. . .or build my business!"

YOU say. . .
"i appreciate YOUR openness (admitting it). . .not everyone can be or wants to be #1. Undoubtedly YOU would like to earn more

money, so YOU can provide for YOUR personal and family needs, correct? Well, this is it!"

OR, YOU SAY...

"i admit that every company we work with. . .or every individual does not Become #1 in Selling. However, just learning what those who are #1 are and do, must help YOU to improve, wouldn't YOU agree?"

DENY

"i don't need any help," the individual asserts. Or, the Corporate President tells us, "We have all the answers now. We are #1 now, so we don't need your help." Or, "Our business is different."

Actually, they will not admit these things, but this is what they say when they deny our proposals that have been proven to help or solve problems or meet needs, similar to theirs. So. . .

"i can understand YOUR indecision. The LSW Company president had a difficult time understanding how we would get him a return on investment, too, initially. However, after some internal and external surveys for his company were completed, he had to admit he had many problems a business consultant could resolve. Here's what we did for them. . ."

ASK: WHY?

i am a "baby boomer," born between 1946 and 1964. The early baby boomers are in their 40s in 1995. The boomers like to ask "WHY?" according to demographic researchers.

In the decade of the '90s, it is estimated the age group between 45-60 years of age will grow by 18 million by the U.S. Census Bureau. By contrast, Americans between age 25-43 will show no increase in numbers.

Who are YOU selling to and what are their characteristics? Knowing this can help YOU, on any day, sell better, and more.

i have written this book so it would apply and appeal to any reader in any year. Is what you're doing designed that way? If not, why not!?

ASK THEM "WHY?". . .

Sometimes it is tough to ask the "why?" questions. COURAGE! It can be even tougher to answer openly. We naturally resist becoming vulnerable to others. After all, if YOU know too much about me, YOU might take advantage of me, right? WRONG!

i prefer to *trust people* and give them the *benefit of the doubt.* "Why?" is not doubting; asking "why?" is helping. We are helping the person to understand.

"WHY DO YOU FEEL THAT WAY?"

This is an interesting and effective question if YOU are prepared to empathize rather than sympathize. Those who Become #1 in Selling seldom sympathize. They empathize.

"Love Must Be Tough," the book by Jim Dobson, Ph.D. not only offers new hope for families in crisis but also is a good motto to live by. He speaks of an appropriate time to sympathize on page 188. There are few times in selling to sympathize. If YOUR father dies, ok, but not over "i can't afford it!"

RESTATE AS A QUESTION:

One of my favorite methods for dealing with:

TRIVIAL,
HALF-BAKED, OR
PUT OFF. . .

objections or indecision, is to *respectfully restate* their concerns in the form of a question while softening it.

YOU can say. . .

"Thom, i do not want to Become #1 in Selling!" (HALF-BAKED)

i say. . .

"Nick, why would anyone resist improvement?" (Sometimes they do not think through what they are saying.)

YOU say. . .

"Thom, don't YOU think YOU MUST cover_____ (topic) more in YOUR book or seminar for people to really Become #1 in Selling!?" (TRIVIAL)

i say. . .

"Donna, YOU wouldn't want my book to be 1000 pages would YOU? Or our seminar, seven days long?"

YOU say. . .

"Thom, i know as much as YOU do about how to Become #1 in Selling!" (PUT OFF)
i say. . .

"If that's true, why didn't YOU write the book!" or, more politely, "That could be, Tony; however, i think YOU would have to agree that a reminder or refresher would be valuable, wouldn't it? And all of us can get new ideas from one another, can't we?"

TIMES TO ANSWER

In this chapter, primarily taught are:

1. How to motivate

2. How to overcome objections

The timing with both are important, aren't they? Those who Become #1 in Selling have great timing. i pray and plan for better timing in my communications all the time. How about YOU?

The TIMES to answer are:

1. Before the objection surfaces

2. When the objection is raised

3. Later . . . promise to give an answer later

4. Never . . . it need not be answered

With practice YOU can improve YOUR timing. "Perfect practice makes perfect!" the famous football coach Vince Lombardi said. This is good advice if YOU are to Become #1 in Selling!
HUMOR: Remember, the difference between a BIG SHOT (YOU) and a little shot is the BIG SHOT keeps shooting. . .and shoots more often, and more accurately.

i pray YOU will *persevere!* Please write me with YOUR questions, comments, and how YOU have and are using this material as YOU strive to Become #1 in Selling.

And, before i conclude this chapter, allow me to share a comment on the many excellent personality profile assessment tools available. Understanding YOURself and the different type profiles better can help YOU acquire happier relationships, and sell to more people more often.

Earlier we covered the five sales styles and the five buyer styles. Assessments can be given to determine YOUR dominate style. We can evaluate management styles for team-building purposes, too!

Big You ... little i

Would it be helpful if YOUR team worked together better? Help build your team!

The science of human behavior has come a long way in the 20th century, particularly in the past twenty years. Dr. William Morrison is credited with the original modes presenting *four personality categories*. Others have elaborated further and have tests available. Basically, they are:

1. Sensing type
2. Intuitive type
3. Driver type
4. Creative type

People who are high S types (sensing), high I, high D or high C, manifest similar strengths and weaknesses.

Myers-Briggs Type Indicator assessments offered by Consulting Psychologists Press, Inc., can help YOU understand (and accept) PEOPLE better. Or checkout Performax's profile.

Entire books and seminars are offered on this subject alone. Will YOU please check it out further? **YOU are King or Queen!** Thank YOU for reading and applying this chapter and this book! YOU did a terrific job! i appreciate YOU! i am in business to serve YOU!

DO'S AND DON'TS SUMMARY

Throughout this book i have mentioned DO's. The DON'TS are usually obvious. Remember these:

1) NEVER ARGUE! An objection is often someone's way of saying: i NEED MORE INFORMATION!

2) NEVER ATTACK! Separate the person from the objection or complaint. NEVER try to prove prospects wrong.

3) ALWAYS LEAD!   People will often answer their own objections, if given enough time to talk.

STAY WITH IT! Help others to win. It is. . .BIG YOU. . .little i.

REMEMBER . . . IF YOU DO WHAT YOU HAVE ALWAYS DONE YOU WILL GET WHAT YOU HAVE ALWAYS GOTTEN!

i hope i have been a catalyst and a positive change agent in your life as i have been for so many others. YOU, also, can and will help others deal successfully with *change* in direct proportion to your success dealing with the inevitable changes YOU will encounter.

May God bless and assist YOU as YOU make the necessary changes in your life. YOU can do it! Remember . . .

"God opposes the proud but bestows favor on the humble." Peter 5:5c

REVIEW QUESTIONS

1. Do YOU agree with THE GUY IN THE GLASS?

2. How can YOU gain more objectivity about your sales career?

3. What emotions or feelings motivate or control people the most?
    In your case can YOU build more positive feelings?
    Can you appeal to the positive feelings of others?

4. Name and explain in your own words the 3 F's for overcoming objections.

5. Do YOU believe that most objections can be answered?
    Can the sale be made to these people?

6. Listening? How much do we hear of what of what is said to us?
    What can YOU do to improve your listening ability?

7. What is active listening?
    Please write out a phrase that would demonstrate that YOU are actively listening.

8. How do we need to view rejection?

9. What has been the most difficult objection for YOU to handle?
    What can YOU do to improve your response?

10. Customize and write answers to every objection YOU hear. Can you memorize them?

CHAPTER 10

Synergism (and Strategy) in Selling

PROSPECTING & MARKETING

Over the years we all could have benefited by being more articulate. Clarity and clear communication spoken in distinct syllables or words brings better results.

Transition years bring new beginnings. My bookshelves and cassette tape library expanded at an accelerated rate as I searched for more answers during transitions in my career. Have you had times like that? Your greatest growth can come through change.

If you drive 10,000 miles per year, you probably average 40 MPH, or less. That translates into 250 hours in your auto, minimum, when you can be listening to educational and/or informational cassette tapes! Reward yourself by educating yourself further during these travel times and transition times.

There is more to life than Becoming #1 in Selling!

Have you learned this truth . . .

"Commit thy way unto the Lord; trust also in Him; and he shall bring it to pass." (Psalms 37:5)

Bring what to pass? Your goals . . . your dreams for the future! Commit your customer and prospecting activity to a wise God, too! Then: plan better, prepare better, hope greatly, discipline yourself sufficiently, work smarter, and balance your efforts.

On an unusually snowy April, a group of sales people gathered together for an *award banquet at a prestigious country club*. Each

 *Become* *in Selling!*

had been awarded points for performing activities which would lead to more sales. Now was the time for well deserved recognition.

Before the contest had begun, they had often viewed the completion of itinerary forms and out bound telephone calls as drudgery. But, now that these and other activities were measured and rewarded, they took on new significance. Can you see each person, one by one, strutting to the front of the room to receive a new suit as their prize?

Why not give yourself more rewards for the successful completion of the tasks you dislike. Something to look forward to! If your employer does this, great; however, when I learned the truth of how to find satisfaction in the little things needed everyday to succeed in selling, I started having more fun!

Keeping records, statistics, reports, etc. can give you great joy if done to the best of your ability. And, they can help you **analyze how to generate more sales!**

A book on selling could not be written without discussing . . .

PROSPECTING

A man divorced and was amazed at how many women he had to choose from. Wherever he went he ran into single attractive women who smiled at him, and treated him respectfully. For years he had dealt with rejection in his sales career, and to top that, his wife divorced him!

Now the "Prospects" phone him! He sold himself to many and rebuilt his damaged self image and self esteem. He compared notes with these women and found they needed acceptance, too. He says he became "single again."

Gradually, his judgmental attitudes subsided and he came to accept and forgive himself . . . then he could forgive his ex-wife. Doing so, he was better able to accept others, their limitations, and all else. (This has happened to many women too.)

"When I got to the other side of the fence I found that the grass really was not greener after all. I now could see things through my ex-wife's vantage point. I discovered how to empathize better with the opposite sex, listen better and meet real needs."
"I am thankful for a second chance!"

Unfortunately, in prospecting for new business or a new spouse, you seldom get a second chance with the same person. Therefore, it is very important to do it right the first time!

Synergism in prospecting for most salespeople would necessitate a number of simultaneous methods. And, often a different approach with each is needed. In many sales situations prospecting is like courting. Once you consummate the marriage, make certain you service the account lovingly!

CURRENT CLIENT BASE

There is a diamond mine in most of our back yards, as the famous story "Acres of Diamonds" points out. Before you prospect for new business, you can contact every past or present customer, if possible, to determine if more opportunities exist.

And ask for referrals.

We all know that the best form of advertising is positive WORD of mouth advertising. We all hope to generate more of this positive PR but seldom do we have an organized plan. Those who Become #1 in Selling ask for, and receive, referrals (and much more) from satisfied clients.

Since people often forget the positive contributions you make to their lives or businesses, you need to remind them.

Professional problem solvers help others discover the solutions to their problems by 1) asking the right questions, 2) by being in the right place at the right time and 3) through active listening. As a result, clients often think they discovered the solutions on their own.

That's great! Others are more likely to implement new ideas if they think the idea was their own!

We must look for other ways to maintain loyalty and patronage. The best way is to keep serving . . . keep being the *catalyst to solve their problems. . . meet their needs.*

Winston Churchill's famous one sentence speech was . . .

"NEVER . . . NEVER . . . NEVER . . . NEVER

G I V E   U P!"

Many so called "self made millionaires" went broke, or nearly did so, one or more times before they made it.

Napoleon Hill reports in his famous book "THINK AND GROW RICH" that "more than five hundred of the most successful men this country has ever known told the author their greatest success came just one step beyond the point at which defeat had over taken them." (page 23-24) **PERSEVERE**.

Many of the best marriages survive tremendous storms. Some shipwreck, or nearly shipwreck, before the partners become dedicated to the principles that build healthy relationships. And they now focus on positive role models. Without some marriage partners realizing it, they expect failure because, after all, "my mom and dad's marriage failed."

Build your customer base as if you'll have to live with them for a lifetime! Or beyond!

Parents neglect their children, at times, in pursuit of their career or business goals, only to later ask..."Why me?," when their kids end up as druggies, in jail, pregnant, or worse!

I have a doctor friend who specializes in preventive medicine. He does not treat symptoms all day like many doctors. He prescribes preventive measures so that his patients do what will bring about great health and a long life. Can you offer preventive solutions in your sales effort? Certainly!

A recent Leadership Seminar I gave for The Ohio Veterinarian Medical Association helped me realize that Vets practice preventive medicine, too. Plan ahead to prevent problems.

Friends of mine work in nearly every sales career field imaginable. One once said to me...

"Thom, my business is different... only you could never Become #1 in Selling in my business.

To that can I quote one great salesperson? "Bullroarrr!"

Many salespeople (sales managers, executives, and others) have, rather than 10 years experience, one year experience 10 times!! TIMES HAVE CHANGED!

You may be in the ideal situation with a fine company and suddenly another opportunity presents itself. What makes you think, really, that you can succeed more so in another company or in another industry or in another city, if you are having mixed results where you are now? Believe me, make it work where you are now, if possible.

People forget who you are, quickly, no matter who you are, unless you keep in touch!! Retailers do this through advertising to target markets. How do you keep in touch? Never give up selling yourself...your ideas...your solutions! Is there a better cost effective way?

In addition to giving speeches, I decided to re-enter sales for a period in 1985.

I chose a sales opportunity as a Sales Consultant for an Allied Van Line Agent. At the time this company had 10 salespeople from three offices. Some were veterans with 20 years experience. I knew business and sales management and how to sell, but, nothing about the specifics of these services! I'd give speeches on the side; and offer other speakers occasionally.

The company had a four month sales contest from June through September 1985, only four months after I began. Guess who out sold everyone? Guess who won the big bonus? Thom Lisk!

Become *in **Selling!***

. Have you ever heard the saying "He could sell snowballs to Eskimos?" Don't sell people something they do not want or need! Be like Pete Rose when he was, ON THE PLAYING FIELD! A Charlie Hustle! Out hustle everyone else! How about you? Think...plan...prepare better.

Selling is the most secure career profession of all! However, to build a...

$$ SALES CAREER $$

...you must maintain and service your clients. The PRO looks, constantly, for new ways to be of service, or new products to offer the same people...or new ideas; at least, for referrals.

It's best to not have to offer it through a new company, however. People want to see stability. They want to know you and your company will be here next year!

If need be, charge more...earn more...retain more...so when you have a set-back you will have more staying power. Conserve your resources. Companies do this, so can individuals.

PROTECT YOUR CLIENT BASE

Think of the long term implications of how you treat each client, customer or prospect, today! And do not take the gift of your relationship with the company you represent for granted. This could determine if you are there tomorrow!

Each person's needs and wants are very important. Listen carefully! Help them see how you are a means to reach their ends!

Fred runs a division for a profitable company. He is up by 5 am. He started out in sales. He is at the business before everyone else, just like his father before him. His customers love his knowledgeable courteous answers to their inquiry. When you are with Fred, you KNOW he is listening. Is that true of you?

CLIENT SATISFACTION

In recent years my company has helped numerous companies improve client or customer satisfaction. General Motors grades their dealers on the satisfaction % of their customers.

They award or disallow benefits to their dealers based on the **CSI**...Customer Satisfaction (or Service!) Index.

A recent client had us survey a sampling of their customers by phone after a letter of introduction. The **objective** feedback we provided them helped us to develop needed client penetration strategies in a highly complex and technical market niche. An outsider facilitating this process properly insures openness from each client (or prospective client). They have become #1 in their niche as a result. *SURVEY YOUR CUSTOMERS!*

A number of buyers and executives from Lazarus, central Ohio's largest department store for 100 years, moved to Cincinnati. Their merger with Federated Department Stores, and other consolidation moves, forced a reorganization plan. I visited many of the executive's homes after negotiating the moving contract with the "Powers To Be." Once this project completed, I went on to other challenges. (I often ride with salespeople of client companies before presenting tailored seminars.) This Allied agent became #1 in the most important way with their customers.

More recently, I have assisted with executives in formulating actual reorganization plans. What a selling job this becomes! People resist change; however, it often is necessary and for the best. Welcome change! Expect change! Be prepared for change!

TEAM EFFORT

One project found me assisting with out-placement of over ten executives when a major manufacturer had to downsize. Teaching executives how to sell themselves into the next right position can be very rewarding. Many must learn how to become #1 in selling so they can get a new job!

Employees that are satisfied insure that clients are satisfied. We like to help create a *family atmosphere* or environment in companies where every team member or associate becomes more aware of each person's job responsibilities (and pressures), and therefore, better able to carry their fair share.

There is nothing more frustrating for a great salesperson than to not have the support staff or harmony needed to deliver on his or her promises to the customer, or to capitalize on the market opportunities. Sell a team effort! Build your team!

For us to Become #1 in Selling what must we do to develop and maintain our support staff? List your ideas here, then take action...

1.

2.

3.

4.

5.

6.

7.

GENERAL COMPANY CLIMATE SURVEY

Management theorists, speakers, professors, researchers, et al, have increasingly been saying...LISTEN TO THE EMPLOYEES.

The proverbial suggestion box is still a great idea. Salespeople often have the best ideas for top management because they listen to the customers all day.

How well does management listen to their salespeople, or to their employees in your company?

To help facilitate this process, I adapted what I call a General Company Climate Survey, from another one of my great mentors, David Thompson. I give this to targeted groups of employees (preferably all employees by department). No name on the survey is asked so the employee has no fear of retribution. The tabulation of fifty key responses helps prioritize internal and external problems (opportunities?) What can be done to improve your climate?

In selling we know "the squeaky wheel gets the grease." Salespeople manage by crisis just as much as managers do.

We must manage by objectives! Get organized!

SALES PERSONNEL CLIMATE SURVEY

Once I put my consulting business back into a higher gear in 1986, I found I was in a new race. In the late 90's we are in a hyper competitive era.

Major pit stops during the decade of the '80s helped me to sharpen my tools. Learn more. Reorganize. Serve better. Many people have learned, that quarterly, mini vacations help guard against burnout. Some take off 2 months off per year and still outsell those who do not, because they are fresh. Think about it. I am simply asking you to know yourself, and adjust your schedule, if possible, and, if needed.

Abe Lincoln said, "The woodcutter who stops to sharpen his ax will cut more wood!"

Three significant new mentors in the 80's broadened my business and selling acumen. And in the 90's my HEROES pull me upwards! My career path in the 1980s was circuitous, but always with purpose! And Passion! You must have PASSION!

Dozens of sales people who are #1 in their companies or market niche have helped me research my conclusions in this book. I have confirmed, with their help, how to... Become #1 in Selling!

We surveyed several dozen sales organizations from several markets in several cities in the 80's and 90's before formulating my presentation in this book. And, before presenting solutions to sales management, it is a great idea to survey all sales people. Pinpoint

attitudes that can weaken the team, then develop strategies to improve the sales climate.

CHOICES...CHOICES

Those who Become #1 in Selling make the right choices because they know their market. They know who to see and what to say. They have "timing"! They do because they are good learners and listeners. They are risk takers. Calculated risks!

I have spoken to some of the Fortune 500 companies. Their problems are the same as the emerging small to medium sized business, multiplied. The Fortune 500 were all small companies at one time, too! If you have small sales now, persevere! You could be great! You know by now...YOU ARE TERRIFIC! AFFIRM IT IN THE FIRST PERSON . . . I AM . . .

START TODAY!

Start where you are today! Make the best of your current situation. Then, and only then, will you earn A) more clients, B) a bigger territory, C) a better compensation plan, or D) more sales. Or, what ever else YOU SEEK! Results speak for themselves, don't they?

Synergism happens when the sum of the parts equals more than the whole. "How is that possible, Thom?" you ask. The Scientific mind may not understand that $2 + 2$ can equal 5. BUT YOU CAN!

I had an architectural company as a client company where one of their people shared with me the real meaning of synergism. After a group meeting where we discussed a great deal, including

MANAGEMENT STYLES

a project architect (one of ten present) told me the meaning . . .

SYN = Greek for Similar

ERG = Work
ISM = Philosophy

When we work at goals in all eight (8) areas of life, we create a synergistic effect that can propel the wheel of our life forward faster.

The goals that we anticipated would take five (5) years to complete are completed in four (4) years, or less! Why? The balanced approach to life brings better time utilization and decision making, synergistically attracting success! Your timing is improved.

Like a heat seeking missile you find the target faster.

Like a magnet, we attract exciting new possibilities! Become #1 in Selling! create a synergism that others only dream about or can not imagine exists.

In more recent years, I've also discovered the synergism that is needed to . . .

<u>Become #1 in Leadership!</u>

It is something different for a sales or marketing manager than it is for an entire company. I hope to detail that in a book for interested and needy persons and companies. (Write or phone **The Thom Lisk Group** for details today!)

MARKETING SYNERGY

Once a Strategic Marketing Plan for a company or individual is developed, we focus on implementation to each target account. Often times each company being sold to requires a different and unique strategy. Earlier in this book, I discussed five different type buyers and how to sell or approach each.

As most of my readers know, there are many more than five company types! Each one has its own unique climate and policies and procedures. However, each is a reflection of the management style of one person, ultimately.

Become 🐛 *in **Selling!***

. Who was it that originally said, "Any organization is only the lengthening shadow of one person?"

Your company reflects its philosophy in its mission statement. Start there if you are researching a particular company which you hope to sell. Ask to read their mission statement. A public company usually will have it in their annual report. Companies for whom I have helped develop a mission statement, often allow me to help prioritize (objectively) company development goals. These are important for salespeople to know if they are to market successfully, and . . . Become #1 in Selling! The salespersons' goals and strategies come from the company mission and company goals.

Once the marketing strategies are established, then you must prioritize organizationally and administratively to implement the strategy. Get all involved as a team in the plan.

THE BUCK STOPS HERE!

This was President Harry Truman's famous saying, as it could be for most company Chief Executive Officers (C.E.O.'s). I once visited his home town in Missouri. He began just like many of us, with few advantages.

Joe Cole is a great sales person in Columbus, Ohio with a background in radio sales and sales management . . . he became #1 and was offered a job to run a new company . . . COLUMBUS C.E.O. MAGAZINE. Do your best, maybe you will become a C.E.O. one day. Then in addition to serving your customers, you will need to serve all your employees, as you build your team.

The C.E.O. and/or President is interested in an R.O.I. . . Return on Investment. This is true for a public or private company, a for profit or nonprofit entity. If incorporated, the Board of Directors holds the C.E.O. accountable for results.

In every organization the "Buck" must stop somewhere. Those who are constantly passing the buck . . . making excuses . . . will have it passed to them sooner or later! Learn to cope better . . . solve your problems today! Responsible people win!

The family is in jeopardy in America because husbands and fathers have abdicated their responsibility. The man was designed by God to be the head of the household, as every entity runs best with only one ultimate decision maker. Of course, the wife is the neck and she turns the head! Who influences those you must sell? Are you remembering to sell them, too?

Many organizations, just like families, are partnerships, and therefore, the partners must be in agreement, or there will be conflict. Conflict can be OK, Dr. Marilyn Manning asserts, as it often brings about growth.

Often, a spouse must hold up the head of a discouraged partner who sells for a living. Help others bounce back. Be optimistic.

Great leaders delegate most decision making to others but retain veto power. Others influence important decisions. More and more executives look at their employees, as wells as their customers, as partners. The wise leader empowers people to make decisions on the front line so that customers are served quickly and to the customers satisfaction.

The C.E.O. has many concerns and pressures but none more vital than the marketing strategy, and its implementation. Finances follow marketing and sales, not the other way around.

Humor: A man was asked, "Who makes the BIG decisions in your family?" He emphatically declared, "I do!" Then he was asked "How many BIG decisions have there been in the 25 years of your marriage?" He admitted "none." Apparently, he had delegated all decision making power. This man is equally responsible for the decisions of his spouse.

In our company, we developed a list of financial policies and procedures. Every C.E.O. needs these benchmarks to steer the ship when in treacherous waters.

Have you ever ridden on an old fashioned Mississippi River paddle boat?

You could liken the finances in a business to the steam that drives the paddle to move the boat forward. As important as that is, let's compare the steering and navigation to marketing a business.

Become ✦ *in Selling!*

To Become #1 in Selling in its market niche a business must have a navigator who can read the twists and turns in the winding business river. Someone who will take the time to research the future and plan accordingly. The course must be charted in advance due to the possibility of foul weather (competition, economic slumps, etc.). No matter how experienced or skillful the navigator, one can never totally anticipate every storm that can develop.

So, the marketing strategist pre-thinks all the avenues of how to succeed before setting sail. He or she may answer questions like these . . .

1. What can we do or offer in the market better than any other?
2. Based on our projected revenues and current cash position, how many dollars are available to market professionally?
3. How many people will we need to assist us in our marketing efforts and what will be their responsibilities?
4. Once we gain some momentum, how will we sustain ourselves?
5. Can our product (or service) be positioned (and packaged) to maintain (or improve!) required profit margins
6. What colors communicate best who we are to become?
7. What further improvement in the product or service can be made? Or, what new product or service lines could we offer?

Synergism in marketing would consider the following ten components. Just as a dime is not a dime without ten pennies, marketing is not marketing without these ten present. They are:

1. Advertising
2. Sales Promotion
3. Public Relations
4. Marketing Research
5. Product Development
6. Pricing

7. Service
8. Channels of Distribution
9. Physical Distribution
10. **Personal Selling**

Most, or all, of these apply to your business, whatever you sell. The majority of this book is about developing your personal selling effort. Personal selling is the most important component of marketing.

MARKETING QUESTIONS

Ask yourself these questions about the ten areas from which your strategic marketing plan gets implemented.

➤ How can we advertise our product better? And to whom?

➤ Do I really act as if word-of-mouth advertising is the best form of advertising?

➤ Does my sales promotional literature really say what I want it to? If not, what will I do, and when?

➤ Components of my capabilities brochure could include: mission statement, testimonials from satisfied clients, a summary of what we are offering, pictures, etc.

➤ Do I use each thoroughly in my presentation?

➤ Are my public relations as great as they could be?

➤ What can I do today to enhance the image of myself and my company? This month? This year?

➤ How do our customers really view me and/or us?

➤ Would a customer satisfaction survey identify new opportunities? Create new business?

➤ What key questions can be asked of each potential or prospect client?

➤ Can we pinpoint market conditions more clearly so as to respond more professionally and accurately?

Become ☘️ *in Selling!*

- Are there products we can improve? Can we create products or develop products (or acquire) to serve better, and increase sales, and profits?
- Is my product and/or service packaged properly? If not, what and when will we improve?
- What do clients like most . . . and least . . . about my product/or service? What can I do about this?
- If I could change or improve one thing about my product today, what would it be? If I have no control over the products I offer, what can I do to make them or my company more attractive to others?
- What void do I see in the market? What cost would be required to bring new product(s) to market? What is the short and long term potential benefit to both the customer, and to my company, and me?
- Are my products and services priced properly? Competitively for comparable products? If not, what can I do to offset these differences?
- How can we better justify the price(s) we are asking?
- How can I/we retain a larger portion of the profits earned?
- Can we effectively discount our price while not jeopardizing the integrity of our pricing structure?
- How can I/we serve better than my competitors?
- How can I/we serve in a unique way?
- What service can we offer that no one else offers?
- Do my customers believe that we offer superior service? If so, how can we communicate this better to prospective customers, verbally and non-verbally?
- What can we do to distribute more of our products?
- Where can we distribute our products (or services) that we do not now pursue? What would be the investment to do so?
- Can we distribute our product/service better, faster, or uniquely to make us stand out?
- Whom can we contact to distribute our products/services?

➤ How would we set up a new method of marketing distribution. Or can we?

➤ Can our product/service be physically distributed with less inconvenience to our customers?

➤ Do we understand all the channels of distribution available?

➤ We always can improve our personal selling efforts. What areas need the most focus for improvement now?

➤ How can we upgrade each salesperson on our team?

➤ If I were as motivated as I can be, would I sell more?

➤ What sales skills do I need to improve? Or, do those I supervise need to improve?

➤ What would happen if we made more sales calls on more decision makers each day?

➤ How can I/we prospect more effectively?

➤ What time and/or territory management ideas could I apply to my sales situation now?

➤ In what area of my sales presentation or personal customer service am I weakest? What will I do about it?

☛ Can He Decide?   ☞ Can She Decide?

There are a lot of questions! I hope you can decide!

A study once found that 67% of all sales approaches are made on the wrong person. What would transpire if you saw more of the right people each day? And asked them more of the right questions?

A 100% sales increase is not unthinkable for many of my readers. You can Become #1 in Selling if you focus on the right people. Stop wasting time! Invest time wisely!

There have been many weeks when I invoiced over 40 hours of my time. Ask any C.P.A. or attorney how difficult that is, let alone a sales, marketing or business management consultant, like yours truly. The lessons I have learned make me a more valuable consultant, speaker and seminar leader. YOU are to become more valuable each year.

Become in ***Selling!***

Rather than bill on an hourly basis, many put a value on their themselves just like you would with any product. $3,500 for a one hour speech because of the hundreds of hours of preparation. Or, you can work for the profitability of each project.

Affirm: My time is worth $_____ per hour.

Or better yet: I would like my time to be worth $_____ per hour. Think **B I G!**

Remember, to be paid like a professional later, you must perform like one today! It begins with your own self image and self esteem! Do you need to review that material, more so, from earlier chapters?

SYNERGISM IN PROSPECTING

Show me a Master Salesperson and I will show you a Master Prospector. Show me a Master Prospector and I will show you a Master Salesperson! Often today, in certain sales profession, **networking** is the preferred word.

How many of us have lost customers? Through no fault of our own!! It happens to the best of us!

Therefore, we must constantly be looking for new business. Prospecting! Networking! Schmoozing!

One year, I traveled throughout the great southeastern section of the USA for a few months helping a company assist their dealer network to market and sell better. From Nashville to Richmond, Virginia . . . from Alabama to the Carolinas . . . I heard, "Teach me how to prospect better!"

Now, entire books could be (and have been) written on prospecting alone (as with many of the other subjects I touch on in this book). Books on the subject I recommend include: *The Blitz*

Call by Bill and Sue Truax; *Successful Cold Call Selling* by Lee Boyan, and many others.

To Become #1 in Selling in most sales situations, one needs to consider ten basic methods. Work all simultaneously and you will develop synergism. You will gain so much business you will only need to use #9 and #10.

The ten overall **methods or prospecting** are:

1. The Cold Call or Warm Call
2. Directories
3. Observation (when driving, networking, etc.)
4. Social Method, Networking
5. Nests
6. Clubs, Associations, Organizations (Networking)
7. Centers of Influence
8. Past or Existing Customers
9. The Referral
10. Patrons

Liken this to the ten rings on an old fashioned hammer and gong at the circus. Each time you hit the ledge with the mallet, you reach a different level of effectiveness in prospecting. Ten rings and the bell!! And win the prize! The sale!

In our seminars and consults we can and have customized prospecting plans for individual salespeople, and entire companies.

A professional salesperson does not run blindly into his or her prospecting efforts. They develop prospect (and marketing) strategies complete with a . . .

PRE-APPROACH SYSTEM

You also must determine the potential of each prospect or customer and invest your time accordingly. Study your products

and services in order to see how they may best fit your potential prospect's needs.

Pre-approach letters can be sent to announce your future contact. One part of the strategy can be to map out the territory or city into sections. Plan your time so as to not overlap your efforts. I

If you are prospecting by telephone, use the exchanges to direct your telephone contacts. In doing this, you can schedule your appointments in the same area of town.

When in Atlanta, one creative salesperson showed me his computer printout of all scheduled customer and prospect calls. He put it all (his activity and plans) in the computer, which in turn, helped to schedule him. He intended never to neglect any opportunity, or customer! There are many great computer software programs available today on a generic on industry specific basis that can assist you in *Client Management*. I've served companies who customize these for their specific needs.

COLD CALL

Some sales "experts" believe if you ever make a cold call on prospects you are not using your head. I have seen where this is the only available approach in some sales situations. A warm call is when you have some pre-approach information.

To Become #1 in Selling! you need more patrons than all others, and referrals from these patrons. Build loyalty. Be loyal!

DIRECTORIES

One consulting client, a Mayflower Moving and Storage Agent, thought so much of my service that they provided me a copy of their directory of all agents for me to market customized sales seminars to all. Your patrons will do this for you. Acquire directories that can benefit you.

OBSERVATION

Another consulting and training client referred me to their state and national association where I served as a speaker and seminar leader at an Annual Convention. I observed that they were members and asked for their help, "a referral." You may travel about and observe prospective businesses or homes to sell.

SOCIAL METHOD

One client was met while playing golf, recently. Another, I met for the first time at a Lions' Cob Meeting, and another at a Rotary Club Meeting where I was the luncheon speaker. Networking has become a familiar phrase and is something more and more sales people are doing in all kinds of situations to enhance their prospecting efforts. Are you networking!? Can you share similar stories? Where will you go? What will you do?

NESTS

When I spoke for a state association, I uncovered an entire nest of prospects, and generated many new clients. If you have credibility with one person in a group, you may be able to hatch many other customers.

CLUBS, ASSOCIATIONS
ORGANIZATIONS
(more networking opportunities)

The Chamber of Commerce has been a good source of meeting new people for me, and many other sales people, that result in more business. How about becoming a member of a trade association where you can meet prospects? There are special interest groups for anyone with all most any interest in some of the major cities in the

USA. It is great to join or participate in these groups to learn, and meet new people.

CENTER OF INFLUENCE

Our friends in state and national politics are tremendous centers of influence and give creditable introductions to certain people. Network with the most influential people possible who can assist you in reaching your goal. Can you think of people who are well thought of who can influence those you want to impress or approach?

PAST AND EXISTING CUSTOMERS

Let's not forget to give our old customers proper follow up so they do not become new clients for our competitor! Do you need a newsletter, computer or assistant to help you keep in touch? Your base of clients will grow. Strengthen your base. It then becomes more imperative that you manage better, invest your time better, and maintain and develop . . .

REFERRALS

A person aspiring to BECOME #1 IN SELLING! realizes the referral lead is the easiest to close. My research and experience indicates that you will invest half the time selling the referral lead, if pre-qualified, as you will selling company generated non-qualified leads, in most cases. You can usually close referrals twice as fast.

PATRONS

A patron is a supporter, a benefactor and a well wisher. He or she is someone who has your best interests at heart. The "secret" to developing and maintaining a great many patrons, and thereby

282

insuring you Become #1 in Selling! . . . is 180 degrees opposite from what most people believe to be true! It is to get that person to do you a favor!

You may ask, "Thom, how is this so?" It is true because the greatest need or desire in human nature, as people search for meaning, is to serve others . . . to be in a position to help another person.

MASTER KEY

By asking others to help you reach your goals to Become #1 in Selling!, and the other areas of life, you actually do them a favor! This results in them feeling needed, good, important and appreciated.

And this is exactly how we all want to feel!!

Are you humble enough to ask?

In the fall of '87, I asked several patrons to evaluate a new business plan for "The Thom Lisk Group," the new name of our company. Their objective feedback helped me make some critically important decisions that shaped 1988 and 1989. This then positioned me properly, to Become #1 in the '90's . . . and into the 21st century.

Others will help you if you let them! Ask them!

PATRON PROSPECTING SYSTEM

To Become #1 in Selling! you may need a system to force you to do what you already know to do, but don't do (enough of)!

A 3 x 5 card system that forces you to remember and follow up works for many people. Have you heard it called a tickler system? Rate each prospect or customer A,B,C, or D based on potential. And, again, this can be accomplished nicely on computer, or even a digital electronic portable pocket secretary these days.

Collect as much data as possible but don't get bogged down in too many details and shuffling cards! J.C. Penney said "The secret to success is to get others working for you." If you were to start thinking of everyone you come into contact with as a possible prospect for something you may one day be marketing or selling, you would probably treat them differently today by being more appreciative and attentive.

Prospecting is the most important part of the so called sales cycle. To reach all your career goals you must develop and maintain an organizational system for both customer files and for developing new business. Harvey McKay recommends the Rolodex, as do many others, or new computer software to accomplish the same objectives.

REFERRAL SYSTEM

Make certain you stay focused on referrals from satisfied clients or customers, if at all possible. Put all other prospects in a separate pile or file if needed, or at least code referral prospect cards somehow so you remember.

Sometimes you can ask a referral to set an appointment for you, or provide a letter of introduction. Or, simply drop your customers name . . . "Mr. Jones, Mr. Smith is a client of mine. He likes my product so well he suggested I contact you . . ."

A *prospecting attitude* is critical. Especially when:

NETWORKING

With everyone you meet you have one of four opportunities:

1. Make a Friend
2. Develop a Potential Associate
3. Develop a Client or Customer
4. Meet Someone Nice to Know

Many salespeople are licensing skilled networkers! I recommend Ann Boes book *"Is Your Net-Working?"*

NEGOTIATE WIN/WIN RELATIONSHIPS!

QUALIFICATION

I touched on the fact earlier that qualifying prospects . . . getting to the decision maker with the right offer . . . is the most difficult part of prospecting.

We must ask "Probing" questions. Our challenge is to learn the "Truth" without irritating the person. We become:

> A. Diagnostic
> B. Analytical, then
> C. Prescriptive

President Franklin D. Roosevelt made a *habit* of having his aides supply him with a complete dossier (or profile) on each person he was to meet before meeting them, for obvious reasons.

Salespeople must become great politicians and win everyone's vote possible, while not sacrificing their integrity. Let's remember, however, the most skilled vote getter can never please all of the people all of the time, or get all the votes. To Become #1 in Selling! you need to know what you stand for, and stand strong in spite of opposition, setbacks, and disappointments.

Keep working your system! Prove to others that you care!

THOM'S CARING SYSTEM

> Discover
> Respond
> Assimilate
> Nurture

Become 🐛 in Selling!

Get excited about DISCOVERING new prospects . . . new people whom you can sell and serve. You could mark one group of prospects or files of names . . . DISCOVER.

The second tier of contacts label . . . RESPONDING.

Either they are to respond to you, or you to them further. RESPOND in such a way as to get and stay noticed.

Thirdly, ASSIMILATE people into your client base just as you would new information. You cannot read and digest a book like this in one sitting; why would anyone expect to have a PATRON assimilated after only one or two meetings? Have a desk top file or computer labeled ASSIMILATE.

You must become a NURTURER if you want to Become #1 in Selling! in most situations. Have a goal to motivate those you enjoy or need to work with on an ongoing basis into the NURTURE stage. Especially, those with *big* potential. How many clients and prospects are you nurturing now? Typically, big prospects need contact more often.

Synergism in personal selling includes terrific:

- 🖋 Attitudes, Self-Esteem, Self-Image
- 🖋 Personal Goal Setting
- 🖋 Professional Sales Presentations
- 🖋 Prospecting and Developing Patrons
- 🖋 Clients and Employee Satisfaction
- 🖋 Marketing

. . . and what you will receive in Chapters 11 & 15.

Do me a favor? Help me Become #1 as a speaker, author and consultant! How?

Believe that you can Become #1 in Selling! DO IT! Then tell others this book helped you, *please.* THANKS A LOT! This was written for you! I believe in you!

Work to maintain the right attitudes in the sales cycle you perform, and especially in your prospecting efforts.

"Attitude is more important than facts, than money, than circumstances, than failures, than success, and than what other people think of you. Attitude is more important than skill, appearance, or giftedness . . . I am convinced that life is 10% what happens to me and 90% how I react to it."

- Dr. Charles Swindoll -

REVIEW QUESTIONS

Simply answer all the Marketing Questions listed in the Chapter.

"Selling is getting rid of what you have, simply. Marketing is deciding what it is you will have to get rid of."

Dr. Roger Blackwell, Author & Professor
of Marketing, Ohio State University
Author or Co-author of over 20 books

CHAPTER 11

SALES MATURITY

BUILD FOR THE FUTURE!

Eleven is #1 twice. In baseball, how many home runs are hit after the 2nd strike? How many basketball or football games have you seen that were decided on the last play? Championships are often decided by one point!

One year on January 1, the Buckeyes of Ohio State football missed being in the Rose bowl due to a last second field goal by their arch rival, Michigan, in their showdown game. Iowa lost that day, too, yet went anyway due to O.S.U.'s loss. **Losers can become winners**.

Across the nation, the same Saturday in November, UCLA lost to their "enemy," University of Southern California. Neither got the *best prize*, the Rose bowl.

Every year a similar story develops. Alabama beat #1 Miami and was crowned #1 in each college football poll another year on January 1. And one year Washington was undefeated ending their season to #1 Miami. How many miles apart are these two teams?

Miles are nothing in today's fast paced hi-tech society. Fax machines, car phones, video conferences, E-Mail and hi-tech gadgetry are to make life easier, but does it really? Some sales people travel as many as 50,000 miles (or more) in a year to be there when their customers need them, or when a prospect is ready to buy. Whether you travel by phone, plane, computer, mail or car to your customers (or they come to you), you must be prepared to respond properly and serve effectively.

"He who serves best will profit most"

Become 🐝 *in Selling!*

Competition demands that we stay alert and abreast of changes. For each company, it will be increasingly important for each team member to OPTIMIZE his or her potential. True, whether in athletics or business.

You will need to get *tougher, more informed and wiser* to compete as the future will soon be upon you.

My mother sent me a Thanksgiving Day card when I was living in Southern California. Think about this:

A Thanksgiving Prayer

Across the miles.
I'm glad we have God
to keep us together
when we're so far apart.

Have a
Wonderful Thanksgiving

Love you,
Mom

You have seen that AT&T ads that say . . . "you are only as far as a phone call away." Thankfulness is a big part of sales maturity.

We were amazed when the astronauts communicated with us from the moon. We, the taxpayers, paid for that trip! You've been sold on how to allow our tax dollar to be used.

"One small step for man,

One large step for man-kind."

. . . Neil Armstrong

Although each of us only takes one small step at a time, I am a believer that one life can make a BIG BIG BIG difference. We see evidence of the impact of one person's life in every walk of life.

Why couldn't you . . . or I . . . have a lasting impact . . . maybe an eternal impact . . . across the miles . . . for years to come? *YES, YOU CAN!*, the title of my friend Art Linkletter's book.

How many times have you entered the eleventh hour, so to speak, and not had a certainty about tomorrow? A certainty about an agreement or how about how-to format a proposal? Or what to say by phone or in person!?

Join the club! The real world! Or is it?

Do you manage by crisis? There is. . .

A BETTER WAY!

The basics in selling, I suppose, will never change. However, each of us can become better prepared.

I'm convinced that all great salespeople or those that aspire to greatness . . . to Become #1 in Selling, will always continue to *search for a better way*. For most, that involves attempting to clone themselves at some point. Or, at least, hire an assistant or more.

No matter how hard we work, or how smart, we only have so many hours each week . . . **168.**

If we have been smart enough, we have retained some of those hard earned dollars, and we, then, can put money or people, or both, to work for us.

We all have known those who have Become #1 in Selling who had someone in the "Ivory Corporate Tower" cut their territory or opportunity, in some way. Reorganized or downsized out of a job!

In many companies, *entrepreneurial relationships* exist in order to retain creative driven individuals. In the early 70's, I had this situation as a Branch Manager for the Eureka Company, and, finally, in the 90's, it will become nearly the norm.

.Wilson Floors penetrated the commercial marketplace due to the % of profit incentive program offered to their account executives, as do many others, in their markets, in part due to creative compensation programs.

New business startups and failures are increasing at alarming frequencies. The entrepreneurial and capitalistic spirit is alive and well in America! Can you offer services to this growing market segment? If so, to whom and how? Entrepreneurs drive our economy. It is wise to understand these people, maybe you will want to sell to them.

Business experiences *four phases.* They are:

1. *Startup*

2. *Growth*

3. *Maturity*

4. *Restructuring or Decline*

In a person's maturity phase, just like with a business, this is when he or she is best suited to Become #1 in Selling. Recently, a forty-year old man attended my 1/2 day sales seminar. I learned he out sold everyone of the 20 other salespeople the next month, his first month in the industry and with this company. Maturity.

Success too early in one's life can be bad for a person if it comes too easy. Success can delude you into thinking you are better than you really are. Maybe you are simply in the right place at the right time and success comes, just as it would have to anyone in that situation doing what you did.

Maybe you have a hot product or service that is somewhat exclusive and highly in demand. This is the time to save your money and not live too far beyond your means because it may not last long-term. You may need to restructure.

The region rose from 9th to 2nd in six months under my leadership as a Regional Manager with Eureka. I made a lot of money and my children still benefit 20 years later.

One of the common mistakes I see in companies I serve is that #1 salespeople are offered the sales managers job. The company loses a great salesperson and gains a poor manager. The attributes needed to become a great sales manager are different. Some companies are not mature enough to understand and appreciate this fact.

Certainly, some #1 salespeople do become great managers and leaders, however, what I am prescribing is *more wisdom in utilizing human resources* in all companies. The thinking is that the superstar will teach all others how-to.

As we mature, we need to ask new questions about how to invest those . . .

168 HOURS!

We do or we decline!

Family priorities caused me to temporarily shelve my aggressive business plans at one time in my life. Rather than work 60-90 hours a week and travel overnight, I decided at times to invest 15-30 minutes every morning with my wife, and one hour a night with my children as they grew. In recent years, I have invested 90 minutes a day in prayer, church and reading or educational growth.

You will find, as I did, that this kind of time commitment during the normal work week, and more on the weekends, is unusual for someone who is driven to Become #1 in Selling. Focus on selling and serving your spouse! Losing your spouse or children is much much worse than losing your best customer!

FAMILY HOURS

Where did the time go?! We have asked ourselves. More than anything I want my friends in selling to say things like: "Thom,

you helped me to have no regrets!" And "Thom, you helped me prioritize better." "You helped me live a balanced successful life in all ways." "You helped me avoid costly mistakes and avoid potential problems." "You motivated me to be and do my best." What do you want others to say about you?

If family was #1 on your priority list in the goal setting exercises, you now will want to make the time commitments to follow through. Here's an *example:*

Number of Hours:	Daily	Weekly
TIME with Spouse	1.0	7.0
TIME with Son	.5	3.5
TIME with Daughter	.5	3.5
TIME with other Family	.5	3.5
TOTAL Family TIME	2.5	17.5

Some commit much more. Most much less. One study from Focus on the Family confirms that the average DAD (who is or wants to be average) invests 38 seconds on uninterrupted quality time with each kid. Kids need positive male role models.

This problem is not getting better! The solution(s)? One is the increase of the family-owned and operated business where the kids become active.

How much time is wise for you to invest with your family? Please make a commitment now. Fill in the blanks:

My Family Time:	Daily	Weekly
Spouse	_____	_____
Child (Name)	_____	_____
(Name)	_____	_____

Sales Maturity

	Daily	Weekly
(Name)	⎯⎯	⎯⎯
Others	⎯⎯	⎯⎯
Total Hours	⎯⎯	⎯⎯

Necessary Time

This would include (examples):	**Daily**	**Weekly**
Sleep	⎯⎯	⎯⎯
Eating	⎯⎯	⎯⎯
Grooming	⎯⎯	⎯⎯
Toiletries	⎯⎯	⎯⎯
Laundry	⎯⎯	⎯⎯
Cleaning	⎯⎯	⎯⎯
Total Hours	⎯⎯	⎯⎯

Can you think of other "Necessary" time expensed weekly? Reading, exercise, etc.

GROWTH

If spiritual growth this was a high priority for you, as it is for many I know who have Become #1 in Selling, you may want to allocate time beyond Church or Mass on Sunday, or the Synagogue on Saturday. The young salesperson decided a 15 minute Bible Study and prayer time in the early morning and just before bedtime was best for him along with Sunday school and church attendance on Sundays that totaled 8.5 hours weekly. The *change in thinking* that resulted made him #1 in selling, he reported. "It helped me focus on others, serving people and not so much on myself."

Some tithe their time to their church or in spiritual growth. That might equal 11.9 hours per week. 168 hours per week minus 49 (7 days x 7) hours sleep, leaves 119 hours x 10% = 11.9.

You decide. All will agree that we have a free will. God loves you and allows you to make choices. As you make better choices and decisions, you will become better equipped to help others make decisions, too!

The young man I just mentioned had, in 30 days, everyone noticing a *positive and significant improvement* in his personality, stability, and attitude, including patience and caring.

8760 HOURS A YEAR

It is hard to believe that we only have 8760 hours yearly in our hour glass of life!

We invest 2000 hours, on the average, yearly, to earn an income, to *build financial security.*

That is 500 hours a quarter of productive time for most people. You can say you "work 50 hours a week" (or more?) and there are 13 weeks in a quarter, so you work 650 hours. However, we are talking about productive time.

No matter how well I manage my time as a business/education management or marketing/sales consultant/trainer (and professional speaker), I could only bill 500 hours per quarter maximum. The same is true for other honest professionals. Some consultants must acquire retainers before the project begins, just as a general contractor would before building a new building. He must have *operating capital.* The points? *Time is your most valuable operating capital!*

You must *value your time per hour more* as your expertise increases, and turn away from undesirable business and expenses of time.

These lessons are difficult for everyone to learn . . . harder to implement. Discipline and empowerment to wisely invest time is a noble goal.

ONLY 10%

One Prentice Hall Study points out that the average salesperson has "only 10% of his time really productive" because only 10% is invested eyeball to eyeball with a decision maker.

Of course, we aren't average - right? Or at least we do not plan to be! So we must manage our time better so we can be in front of and serving our clients or customers.

But do we really manage our time? I think not. It is here, and it is gone! We make decisions about how to invest the time. I use the word *INVEST* because we believe time is a most valuable resource. Focus prayer power to decide how to use this much better! Think! Plan! Change!

One of my studies of salespeople in top companies uncovered some statistics. They point out that better planning and time utilization are keys to success.

Weakness' Most Frequently Found in Sales Representatives

1. 💣 Poor planning and organization of **time** and effort: 40%

2. 💣 Lack of effort, drive, aggressiveness, stamina, motivation, etc.: 24%

3. 💣 Failure to make sufficient sales calls, develop prospects and acquire new accounts: 10%

4. 💣 Uncooperative attitude, failure to get along with colleagues and customers: 8%

5. 💣 Insufficient study of new products and applications and failure to sell them: 6%

6. ☞ Failure to conduct self properly (excessive entertaining, general irresponsibility, drinking):   5%

7. ☞ Lack of BASIC sales ability and potential for growth: 3%

8. ☞ Poor judgment in analyzing prospects and selecting accounts: 4%

☞ All the Weakness' =   100%

Throughout this book we focus on the strengths and solutions.

However, I'd be negligent if I did not occasionally share the weakness that our prescriptions are designed to remedy.

When serving as interim Director, Sales and Marketing for one client company, I worked very closely with 12 salespeople for 10 months. The 20% of the business held true...in other words... Charlie, Bob, Michael...3 out of 12 sold as much as the other 9 combined...actually nearly 80% of the total volume!

The only reasons some of the other salespeople's figures looked good were that they got some of the spill over...some of the accounts that Charlie did not have time to serve.

Charlie was a great salesperson but poor manager and trainer of other people. Yes, he has the potential, but why take your #1 salesperson and make him a manager? This has been tried over and over again, and was not the wise thing to do in Charlie's company's case. So they hired an outside consultative sales manager. One who does not have to win, one who can serve and help each one to succeed. A fine restaurant has a dining room manager to solve the servers' problems and keep all motivated.

Another company I served one year had several beauty salons. I was *referred* to them by Clayton Jones, President of a 200 plus salon chain, Fiesta Beauty Salons.

Are your clients referring you to others? Set a goal for them to do so! **Ask for referrals**.

Sometimes I have served several companies in different industries simultaneously as an interim this or that.

Clayton was smart. He would not try to "make a silk purse out of a sow's ear."   Sometimes companies have hired me as a consultant and trainer to upgrade their PEOPLE.

Usually the top 20% want to continue to grow and improve...if they can find the time. The middle 60% can improve with better training and motivation. However, they often will not seek it out on their own so management must offer it. And the bottom 20% should not be selling at least for their current company.

Bear Bryant, famous football coach said, "If you are going to make chicken salad, start with chicken!" In other words, if you are the coach, start with the best raw talent!

Everyone could be #1 in Selling, but most do not have the discipline, dedication and willingness to change. And, most do not have the coach to bring out the best in them.

Remember the story of Charles Atlas, the 95 pound weakling? He built a world champion body!

Bob Weiland was determined to walk across the USA, and did so, even though he had lost his legs in Vietnam. A friend of mine from Ohio, Steve Newman, walked around the world! THE WORLD WALKER! What is possible?

Kyle Rote, Jr. became the world's greatest athlete by competing with superstars from every professional sport, even though few people had ever heard of him. When I met him, and had my picture taken with him, it was hard for me to envision him as the "greatest" because of his size. It must have been his *iron will and heart that made him #1*. Kyle is one of hundreds of speaker available through our company and our Professional Speakers Bureau.

Stories abound about people who overcome great obstacles and handicaps due to their positive CAN DO attitudes. They *develop a winning plan and execute it.*

We all need to be certain we are in the right career field, company, industry, or vocation if we are to Become #1 in a selling career. As a small example, a senior at Ohio State University told me "I made big money selling home improvements for about a year, but could not continue to tell the lies, so I left." Did the company condone or encourage this?

Some salespeople who must close in one meeting, and therefore, fail, would be great in a relationship-building sales situation where more empathy is an asset.

FINANCES FOLLOW

When you do what you love to do, the money will follow! Do you allocate hours each day or week to focus on your financial goals?

It *requires more* than just paying the bills and budgeting better to end up with more.

KEY PRINCIPLES

Time management centers on effectiveness over efficiency. Efficiency refers to how well you do something, whereas effectiveness refers to whether you must do something at all.

You must:

- Be analytical and critical about your time usage

- Focus on how to do the highest priority things first and better.

Peter Druker said, *"It is better to do the right thing than to do things right."* In selling of most sorts this means *investing more time in front of qualified buyers.* But, because of time demands, selling and delivery systems are changing.

As an example, the Dean of Ohio State University business school told a group recently that "we are looking at ways to serve our customers better. The STUDENT!"

Determining innovative solutions to the time and financial restraints people face may dictate who survives and succeeds in your world in the future.

Ask yourself always: "Am I focusing on RESULTS or activities?" It takes self-discipline and a great self-image to not be swept up by day to day activities where the pay off may be low. Keep your big and long term goals in mind as you sort through decisions daily.

Some say "my day is determined by my customers." The Vilfredo Pareto principle, I learned years ago still applies. Some examples:

THE 20/80 RULE

➤ 20% of the customers account for 80% of the profits

➤ 80% of the results comes from 20% of the time

➤ 80% of the new customers come from 20% of the prospects (invest more time with 20%)

➤ 80% of usable info comes from 20% of the total

➤ 20% OF THE SALES PEOPLE MAKE 80% OF THE SALES!

THE MORAL? Expand your high payoff time! Learn to delegate if at all possible. Learn who your best prospects are and focus on them. *Small changes* can have *geometric effects* on sales RESULTS.

We have time management ideas after the goal setting ideas in this book because your goals cause you to want to invest your time wisely. You may have written "I want to increase my sales and income by 25% this month."

Non-specific goals that cannot be interpreted into time utilization can frustrate you. An example would be to say "work harder" or "do better." The basis of time organization and management is a PLAN.

Planning is a *conscious effort of bringing the future into the present!* Review your written goals in the context of the time management ideas shared in this chapter. Your goals can be transferred to weekly plans in your pocket or desk calendar.

Become deadline oriented, however, be flexible. Challenge yourself! What is your best record? Or the company record? What is your time line?

Can you afford *unnecessary travel* or getting a *late start*? To Become #1 in Selling you cannot waste time waiting or talking to the wrong person very often, can you? Think about how you can get eye to eye with more decision makers each day. Learn to say "No" to protect your time. My research and experience indicates that one uninterrupted hour is worth three of interrupted time.

In conclusion: *overcome procrastination.* How? Break down large tasks into bite size parts. Make a commitment to someone, thereby, giving you positive time pressure. Set up deadlines which force you to prepare, then plan to prepare.

Avoid getting bogged down or hampered by details. Keep swinging, even when decisions bring no results. Babe Ruth struck out more than anyone, and he also hit more home runs. So did the man who beat his record, Hank Aaron. *Be prepared to fail* occasionally. Expect better results next time! Maturity!

"Men do not fail; they give up trying."

... Elihu Root

CHAPTER 12

TERRITORY & TIME MANAGEMENT

You must become a master at time management in most sales situations. Is this important to you? Organize essentials:

- √ Productive selling time with qualified customers and prospects, and
- √ Invest the least time traveling. Be in the right place at the right time.

A territory consists of people in a specified geographic area, typically. There are countless opportunities to tell your story, however, you must use wisdom and discretion to know who to see, phone or mail to, when and how much time to invest.

Dissect your territory carefully and create time saving routes and boundaries. Driving to the farthest point and working your way back in is often a good strategy, if in outside sales.

Many companies and salespeople know the profit and prior sales volume from each customer and their potential when planning their sales calls. The list of questions you can ask yourself about your territory (and customers or prospects) is almost endless in preparing thoroughly. Examples include:

- Which products/services are selling best with which accounts in which territories or markets?

- Where are more of these (20%) top accounts?

- How many calls can I make each day?

Recently, at a Sheraton Suites Hotel, I spoke at length, pool side, with a pharmaceutical District Sales Manager. He spoke highly of his company and products, however, he admitted that he and his ten people only sell three products to their doctor customers. They, along with companies in every industry type, focus their people to insure better market penetration.

The KEY to investing time better, however, will always be to first **manage yourself better** affirm:

> I possess right now the power to transform the quality of my life by making better decisions about how I invest my time and with whom!!

TIME AND MOTION ANALYSIS

A company asked me to evaluate their nationwide tele-marketing operation. I researched some new markets, and helped them acquire some large accounts as I took their salespeople into states like Michigan, Missouri, Indiana, and Arkansas to offer field sales training support, sales coaching, business development, and a little cheerleading when needed. I also did group motivational sales education sessions for the company.

On one trip through Arkansas, we saw 23 companies throughout the state in 5 days; and acquired 10 new accounts! Pre-planning and phoning in advance did it. Some call this appointment setting, as well as advertising, "pre-selling."

Manufacturing and QC (quality control) people, as well as IE's (Industrial Engineers), evaluate their assembly lines to see how things can be automated or assembled faster and cheaper.

Salespeople need to evaluate where their time is invested, and make *better decisions* to see *more rewards*.

MARRIOTT

."We don't continue to win your business simply by resting on our laurels," Marriott advertises!

They have been a client of mine recently and I have learned that they work to embody excellence in customer service and selling. In their ad they picture all the many awards they have won and they state:

AWARDS DO NOT WIN BUSINESS -- SERVICE DOES!

In their case, it was reported in the newspaper that they become so diversified with various type properties to serve various type travelers that they had to refocus. Having stayed at Fairfield by Marriott (budget), Courtyard by Marriott (mid-priced), and the luxury Marriott during my travels, I can see clearly the *market segmentation* and differences. *Your customers can see the differences*!

My seminar *HOW TO HANDLE CHANGE* for Marriott was well received when it was offered by their #1 business council in the USA. *How can you handle change better?* I could have in this situation, I know in retrospect, completed more research and prepared a more custom tailored pass-out for participants, and been better prepared. Can we *change so as to prepare to serve better?*

You must be so excellent at what you do that you will be *memorable* and people *will want to tell others about you.* Word of mouth pre-selling! Maybe this requires accepting fewer clients so you or others on your team can invest more time to prepare. Then you may be able to justify a higher price for the improved services or products. Good advice!

TIME FLIES

Have you ever let valuable time fly? Remember your chief assets are:

➤ Your TIME

➤ Your Know-HOW (and "Do-How")

What value do you place on each?

Is your time worth $36 per hour, as an example? A survey conducted over a one 3-year period with over 300 salespeople reported that their average earnings in the presence of a qualified prospect was $36 per hour.

What is the person who is #1 in Selling worth per hour? $100? $200? $300?

You could easily figure what your time was worth last week or month, or this upcoming week or month.

Just keep track of how much time you invest in front of qualified people then divide your gross income by the total hours. You may be surprised!

Once you do, determine what your selling time is worth . . .

My **Selling Time** is

Worth $_____ Per Hour

I want my time to be worth $_____ per hour one year from today!

You have a choice. What will you do with your time in the future?

INVEST IT ☐   WASTE IT ☐ (check one)

Want to earn more money?

Affirm: ***I will make better sales calls on better prospects!***

If I made MORE CALLS on BETTER PROSPECTS what would happen to my sales?

WHAT'S MY TIME WORTH?
(Refer to chart on next page, please)

My goal is to earn $_____ this coming year. Based on what I would like to be earning, my time is worth $_____ per hour. It is worth $_____ per minute. I'll make MORE calls . . . on the RIGHT prospects!

PERSONAL TIME

Please remember, the tendency, when in transition times in our lives, or when wanting to form new habits, is to want to return to the familiar. We must *keep on growing. Stay focused on your higher purpose.* If in management, motivate everyone by remembering their personal time is important to them. Do focus them on your mission while showing them how to invest time better so they can earn more money so they can have more time to invest in their personal lives. This is great motivation.

Earlier in the book, I challenged you to establish personal goals for (1) Career

        (2) Financial

              (3) Family and

                     (4) Spiritual.

You also need to block out time for goals to be accomplished in these ways or areas:

(5) Social   (7) Mental/Intellectual

(6) Physical/Health   (8) Recreational/Leisure

Become 🏃 in Selling!

IS TIME REALLY MONEY?

If I made MORE CALLS on BETTER PROSPECTS what would happen to my sales?

WHAT'S MY TIME WORTH?

If I Earn	Every Hour Is Worth	Every Minute is Worth	In A Year - 1 Hour A Day is Worth
$ 2,000	$ 1.02	$ .0170	$ 250
2,500	1.28	.0213	312
3,000	1.54	.0256	375
3,500	1.79	.0300	437
4,000	2.05	.0341	500
5,000	2.56	.0426	625
6,000	3.07	.0513	750
7,000	3.59	.0598	875
7,500	3.84	.0640	937
8,000	4.10	.0683	1,000
8,500	4.35	.0726	1,063
10,000	5.12	.0852	1,250
12,000	6.15	.1025	1,500
14,000	7.17	.1195	1,750
16,000	8.20	.1366	2,000
20,000	10.25	.1708	2,500
25,000	12.81	.2135	3,125
30,000	15.37	.2561	3,750
35,000	17.93	.2988	4,375
40,000	20.49	.3415	5,000
50,000	25.61	.4269	6,250
75,000	38.42	.6403	9,375
100,000	51.23	.8523	12,500

Based on 224 eight-hour working days.

Territory & Time Management

Based on what I would like to be earning my time is worth $_____
per hour. I'll remind myself of this fact _____ times tomorrow.
I'll make MORE calls . . . on the RIGHT prospects.

64% of sales calls are made on the wrong person.
Documented Survey by a Leading Sales Magazine.

When you complete the ideal week form that follows, consider all areas of life. And, please consider that to be *paid like a professional* you need to prepare and plan like one! Plan to determine who really makes the decisions and see more of the people.

IDEAL WEEK

Please invest time NOW to complete the chart. Ask yourself these important *questions*:

Did you schedule Thursday 3:00-5:00 pm to set appointments for next week?

How about 7:00-7:30 am each day to plan that day? Or do you prefer to do it the night before?

Do you set an itinerary for next week every Saturday morning like many #1 salespeople or do you do it Friday afternoon?

How many days a week do you have productive breakfast meetings? And lunch appointments?

Is Wednesday night a good time to focus 100% on your family from 6:00-10:00 pm?

How about a date night with your spouse?

Do you jog, like I do many nights, from 7:00-7:30 pm, or longer? Is time for exercise scheduled?

Did you block in Sunday morning for church or do you not yet see all the value in church attendance?

308

IDEAL WEEK

	Monday	Tuesday	Wednesday	Thursday	Friday	Saturday	Sunday
6:00							
7:00							
8:00							
9:00							
10:00							
11:00							
12:00							
1:00							
2:00							
3:00							
4:00							
5:00							
6:00							
7:00							
8:00							
9:00							
10:00							

Is Sunday afternoon a good time for a nap? How about 30 minutes Sunday night to plan for the upcoming week so you can be at your best on Monday morning?

Did you schedule time to read, listen to cassettes or take a class that will help you reach your long-range goal?

Are there certain customers you need to see every week, or every other Tuesday? Or phone? Or mail to?

You get the idea Right?

Plug in your . . . IDEAL WEEK. That's all it is . . . a GOAL to strive to achieve.

Do you need to see (or phone) ten people or clients a week or a day or twenty? Or, just how many, ideally, to reach your sales and income goals?

And, would it be a good idea to have one of these IDEAL WEEKS completed for each week of a month? You could label one - 1st week - another 2nd week, etc.

Are you like many salespeople (and all others) who do certain things only every 4th Thursday or at months end?

We have worked with people in almost every classification of job, as we move towards the year 2000. Everyone, whether Accounting Manager, C.E.O., Operations Manager, Executive Vice President, Sales Manager, Customer Service Rep., Salesperson or first line Supervisor can benefit from having an ideal week established. Sort through the unnecessary and discard it!

SUCCESS COMES IN CANS

Joel Weldon has a can that is the size of a small vegetable can with this label imprinted . . .

Success Comes In Cans
Not In Can Nots!

And it is written "I CAN do all things through Christ who
strengthens me!" A great reminder when considering more
disciplined . . .

TIME INVESTMENTS

To travel mile after mile to reach a client when one is just
around the corner that could be served at a profit may not be wise or
needed. THINK!!

Miles add up to lost time. Turn this wasted time traveling into
educational time by listening to educational and motivational
cassette tapes or CD's.

You can receive a college education equivalency in less than 4
years, if you drive as much as many salespeople!

INGREDIENTS

In Joel's can the ingredients are:

Commitment	Persistence
Courage	Knowledge
Goals	Defined Values
Imagination	Focused Thinking
Creativity	A Sense of Humor
Honesty	Positive "I Can:" Attitude

Without planning it, I have touched on all these things in
Becoming #1 in Selling! So once you have enough successful
experience, maybe, you will do the right things automatically!

When I wrote another book, *Become #1 Christian!*, I focused a
great deal on defined values, especially as it pertains to daily
planning. Our *values shape how we make our decisions, and* how
we *invest our time.*

I drove to California one time as follows:

	Drove
1st day (dropped daughter off at school before leaving at 7:30 am)	1005 miles
2nd day	1110 miles
3rd day	250 miles

Exactly at 9:00 a.m., the 3rd day, Sunday, I pulled into the parking lot of the world famous Crystal Cathedral Church, pastored by Dr. Robert Schuller. I had not shaved in 3 days, but I made it . . . ON TIME! I listened to the church service on the radio. They still have a drive-in church, as when Dr. and Mrs. Schuller began the church in 1955. I recommend Dr. Schuller's books to you and his HOUR OF POWER TV program.

It's important to *start out correctly*! BEGIN RIGHT! FINISH STRONG! And when things go wrong as they sometimes will, TURN YOUR LEMONS INTO LEMONADE.

DAILY PLANNER

When you employ a DAILY PLANNER, you put a quirk in human nature to work for you.

With the use of a planner, you make a statement of self-affirmation that you are going to do something. By putting it to writing, you trigger a mental mechanism which will cause you to accomplish what you have set out to do. As long as you have the schedule with you or before you, you will persist until you have achieved your goals.

That is why the planner could also be called a PERFORMANCE PLANNER! Daytimers, Inc. of Allentown, PA offers excellent tools, as do many other companies.

The list of things to do is similar to the red light found on the dashboard of a car.

You can be terribly busy and behind schedule, but when the little red light flashes on indicating that you are about to run out of gas, you somehow manage to find time to refill.

What you are accomplishing when you use a Daily Planner is *making the most profitable use of your time.*

By using the Daily Planner you *gain the satisfaction of having accomplished what you set out to do.* Without the planner, you could be on a carousel to which there is no beginning and no end.

It is this *lack of structure* that causes many salespeople to leave the field of selling. They cannot tolerate the frustration of the merry-go-round.

A good illustration in point is the experience of one large business computer manufacturer that has both a sales and a service organization. The salespeople are much better paid than the servicemen. However, the company loses forty percent (40%) of its salespeople every year as compared to only two percent (2%) of its servicemen.

An in-depth study revealed the cause. The servicemen had the *daily satisfaction* of knowing that they had completed what they set out to do. On the other hand, salespeople never experienced this same sense of accomplishment. Upon reaching their sales quotas for each month, the slate was then wiped clean at the beginning of the next month, thus starting their drive for accomplishment and job security once again.

You will . . .

ACCOMPLISH MORE

. . . in your business or sales career if you will employ the daily use of an activity planner and, thereby, *follow the lead* of all who have achieved outstanding success.

If you are to be a real winner and *make all your dreams come true,* you must take control of your time. Without specific plans for each day, you are out of control. Events, circumstances, and other people will dictate to you and you will be at their mercy. That's

OK, I suppose, if it's the boss and he or she has your best interest at heart through organized sales and customer service.

You can go, literally hither and yon, often feeling that nothing ever seems to get done, or complete.

It is only through the use of a carefully thought out plan of action that you can gain control in order to become the *master of your own destiny* and *captain of your own ship.*

NO OTHER WAY!

With a specific plan of action you will eliminate frustration, indecision, tension, and needless fears; instead you will devote the same energy drained by these factors to more efficient and productive work and activities.

Peter Druker wrote "Time is our working capital. Managing it is everybody's number one (#1) PROBLEM."

It is impossible to manage, organize or control your time without a plan. The basis of TIME MANAGEMENT is PLANNING.

I may plan a ten day vacation with my family over the holidays. I may be excited about all we can do . . . and all we can share together. However, to maximize this family time, I must plan it!

The *miles traveled will be worth it* because of the known goal... the planned events when we arrive.

How you organize your time and make it work for you will have a *profound effect upon your life*!

It literally can mean the difference between . . .

SUCCESS OR FAILURE

Working a Daily Planner, budgeting and scheduling your time is *far more important* than budgeting your money. If you lose $100 you can regain it. But, if you lose an hour, there is no possibility of ever recovering one minute of it!

.You will be astonished to discover how much more effectively and effortlessly you will work if you *force yourself* to be *orderly and systematic.*

Perhaps you have heard the saying, "If you want a job done, give it to a busy person." That statement does not seem to make sense. If the person is already busy, how can he or she *find the time* to take on yet another job? They can because they plan their work clearly and work the plan!

You must be your *own tough boss* if you are to become #1 in Selling! You must *report to yourself,* and *constantly evaluate yourself.* If you are not endowed with the ability, then you need *a tool or a system* to help force you to do more of what you know is the right thing to do everyday. Develop your own categories, if you prefer, or purchase and use ours, or use maybe DAY-TIMER, FRANKLIN PLANNER or a computer programmed form.

DAILY PLANNER **CATEGORIES INCLUDE:**

- Family Activities
- Business/Career/Vocational Activities/Tasks
- Financial Plan/Things to Do
- People to See . . . Places to Go
- Leisure/Recreational/Social
- Letter to Write/Proposals/Follow-up Notes
- Phone Calls to Make
- Goals Accomplished Today
- Mental Growth . . . Reading, Listening, Etc.
- Physical Fitness
- Time Schedule (by the quarter hour) Today
- Spiritual Personal Growth Plan

An example of a two-part planning form I designed for one client, HIGHLIGHTS FOR CHILDREN (the largest children's publisher in the USA), and their salespeople, follows.

You can use ideas from this to design your own. I have relationships with many time management experts in the USA and Canada whom I can further recommend you to for tools to assist you. No tool or system is good unless we use the tool, whether a computer or paper tool.

What tools will you utilize to transform your tomorrows into success and significance?

In writing this book, I have reflected on, and condensed a good bit of what I have learned about how to Become #1 in Selling in over 25 years.

Briefly, may I suggest to go back to review each chapter and write key ideas for use NOW. Maybe write your best ideas in your planner and carry it with you always. Review them 21 days for best results.

Chapter 1

Chapter 2

Chapter 3

Chapter 4

Chapter 5

Chapter 6

Chapter 7

Chapter 9

Chapter 10

Chapter 11

Become 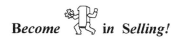 in Selling!

HIGHLIGHTS DAILY ACTIVITY PLANNER

DAY: _____ DATE: _____

Phone Calls To: Manager, Reps, Recruits, Home Office

Name _____ No. _____ Regarding _____

1. _____
2. _____
3. _____
4. _____
5. _____
6. _____
7. _____

ROUTING LEADS/Referrals/Farming: Zip Groups; Map # _____

1. _____ 12. _____
2. _____ 13. _____
3. _____ 14. _____
4. _____ 15. _____
5. _____ 16. _____
6. _____ 17. _____
7. _____ 18. _____
8. _____ 19. _____
9. _____ 20. _____
10. _____ 21. _____
11. _____ 22. _____

LETTERS AND NOTES TO WRITE, SUPPLIES TO ORDER: _____

1. _____
2. _____
3. _____
4. _____
5. _____

THINGS TO DO: BUSINESS

1. _____ 4. _____
2. _____ 5. _____
3. _____ 6. _____

THINGS TO DO: PERSONAL

1. _____ 4. _____
2. _____ 5. _____
3. _____ 6. _____

COMPLETE THIS BEFORE BEGINNING EACH DAY!!

PRIORITIZE: **A** - MUST DO-WILL INCREASE SALES; **B** - NEED TO DO;

C - NICE TO DO ☺   ©Thom Lisk

Territory & Time Management

TIME SCHEDULE - Appointments, meetings, things to do

6 AM	3:00
5:30	3:30
7:00	4:00
8:00	5:00
8:30	5:30
9:00	6:00
9:30	6:30
10:00	7:00
10:30	7:30
11:00	8:00
12:00 PM	9:00
12:30	9:30
1:00	10:00
1:30	10:30
2:00	11:00
2:30	11:30

YOUR PERSONAL SALES GOALS **Today's Prev. Sold Month**
KEEP SCORE DAILY   **Goal/Sales Total   To-date**
I.O. SALES
P.I. SALES
NON-LEAD SALES (FARMING,
REFERRALS, CLUE, ETC.)
SALES TO LEADS RATIO
DAILY RECORD OF BUSINESS EXPENSES
What, Where, When, Purpose   AMOUNT

©Thom Lisk
TIME IS MONEY. DON'T WASTE IT!
YOU CAN AND WILL REACH YOUR GOALS . . . . .
IF YOU THINK YOU CAN!
21 days of consistent use insures that you develop habits of success.
Fold in 3 parts and carry with you.

318

The number forty is the number of completion. Have you seen the slogan . . . "Life begins at 40!?" Or do you prefer to be negative and say it is "The overhill gang!?"

Can you divide your life into 12 or 15 sections and distill the essence of what you have learned during each period that has been of most value to you and, therefore, to other people?

YOU are a person OF VALUE. YOU are IMPORTANT. God has a special purpose for your life!

THE BEST IS YET TO BE!

Have you *reconciled your past*? That is have you put it behind you? Have you learned what you were suppose to, so you can go 100% into the future? Have you forgiven everyone that has hurt you in the past? Have they, if at all possible, forgiven you where need be?

Regardless of your present set of circumstances, can you be joyful in the present moment?

Remember BECOME is future tense. We never arrive. This life is a joyous journey! Others may look at your past and attempt to limit you . . . don't let it happen! They may say "He (or she) will never change!"

> **Pray and Affirm: I can make great decisions to shape a terrific future. God wants to give you wisdom to spend your time better.**

You can Become #1 in any area of life because you give service that is superior.

Across the miles you may find *THE ROAD LESS TRAVELED.* That is OK! And that is the title of the M. Scott Peck best selling book. In it he describes how to "embrace reality and achieve serenity and fullness in our lives."

Keep reading, growing and investing your time wisely. *Your goals* are important!

AND, remember to humble yourself. *Help your customers and your patrons.* Serve more of them better so they Become #1. Then you can Become #1 in Selling!

Please remember: PEOPLE DO NOT CARE HOW MUCH YOU KNOW UNTIL THEY KNOW HOW MUCH YOU CARE!

"He who wants to be first must be last," the best servant of all!

"Getting wisdom is the most important thing you can do! And with you wisdom, develop common sense and good judgment."

. . . Proverbs 4:7 (LB)

"I have always thought the actions of men the best interpreters of their thoughts."

. . . John Locke

CHAPTER 13

THE BEST SALESPEOPLE

THINKING & FAITH

The question has often been asked me, "Thom, how can I close more sales?" I am sometimes tempted to give a laundry list of tried and proven closing techniques with a challenge to memorize them, once customized. I know there is much more. Thinking skills that cause you to diagnose better are a key.

Most often selling is a *process*. An art! A masterpiece is not painted with one swift stroke, or one unique brilliant maneuver. Many people do not understand the sales process and the psychology of selling and buyers. How can they hope to understand HOW TO CLOSE MORE SALES!? Well, here are a few ideas and stories to start you *thinking*. Do you recognize any of these people or maybe, yourself?

Master sales people do not just read about it . . . they prefer to simply do it! It is almost an instinct with them. It is *intuitive*! The great closers have a hard time explaining what they do and how they do it, but they know why they do what they do, so I will start with answers to the WHY questions through some brief stories of closers I have met. Closers are negotiators and the best ones create win/win agreements. They've answered key questions.

> Why close sales? Why understand how to close better? Why become a master closer? Why examine your closing methods? Why negotiate a better "deal?" Do I have faith to close?

EXAMPLES OF SALESPEOPLE

Become 🏃 in Selling!

CHARLIE

In selling, my friend Charlie is a master. He is well liked. He knows his products *and* his customers, works hard, and closes more sales than any three other sales people in his well-known company, combined. How does he do it? First, he needs the close worse than others. His self image and ego demands he be #1. He feels better about himself when he closes, and he needs this feeling more than others, somewhat because of his insecurities. Of course, he would never admit to this. Charlie is thought to be a pro, because he solves people's problems. Sometimes he creates situations that his products will solve, and he is closing all the time!

This man does it through correctly crafted questions. He understands both *open-ended* and *close-ended questions*, and when to use each. He understands how to be an active listener, and use empathetic statements. Boy, is he smooth! His non-verbals are closing sales for him, too. His head is always nodding up and down, and his eyes sparkle with concern. You understand, don't you? His questions elicit positive responses for many reasons, starting with the fact he has *a positive expectancy*.

MIKE

Then there is my friend, Mike. He wants to be everyone's friend. He doesn't close as many sales as Charlie, because he is overly concerned about everyone liking him. You have met the type, haven't you? He knows all about my family before he tells me about his services. He closes through the bond he *attempts* to form with me . . . or you.

LINDA

Linda is another story! She makes me laugh, which is good, isn't it? I find I am at ease around her, and she gets her way with me. The reason she can close with me is she is always telling me about how and why others buy her products, and she even shows me letters of recommendation from her satisfied customers. Reputation buyers respond to her closing question like: "Paul, you can see how you will benefit too, can't you?"

DONNA

Donna, on the other hand, is too pushy for me and other buyers I know. You see, it seems she is trying to always impress me with how great her products' features and benefits are. But quite frankly, I could care less, because she never bothers to ask me an open-ended question like "Thom, what is important to you?" or "Thom, tell me about what you like least about my competitor's product which you now own?" She must not care is my conclusion.

DAVID

Then how about David? He must think I am stupid the way he tried to sell me a suit. He didn't bother to find out what I do for a living, so when he used all his slick closers, I backed off, and he never knew why. He thought he was qualifying me by asking me questions like "Sir, do you prefer this suit or that suit?," We can call you when we get a suit that will meet your taste, Sir. I will need you to complete this card today, OK?" But he really irritated me, because I sensed all he wanted was my money, so he could get a commission! Didn't he know I know all the sales techniques, too (just like many other)?

That is it, isn't it? The best closers are often the most caring! They understand "People do not care how much I know until they know how much I care . . . about them!" They are pros because they solve my problems. They ask for the order, when they see I understand they have a solution that I can afford. Pros understand they are *always closing during the entire sales process* and sales cycle! And they *then* can negotiate the best deal for themselves,

while making the buyer feel they also win. I have worked to do this throughout this book, haven't I?

DECISIONS

I must decide how to close this book and insure I include all that will help you BECOME #1 IN SELLING! However, I have come to *understand* that it is rare when one can please all the people all the time. Many sales people speak too much and talk right by the sale. I focus to never be guilty of that again! So, the balance of this chapter is my analysis of what you need to yet consider.

Every day people make decisions which impact our future. Decisions we have little or no control over. The government decides to send troops to a foreign land, as with the Persian Gulf conflict , or the Somalia relief effort. One man, the President of Iraq made the decision to invade Kuwait, and millions of lives were affected. Gasoline prices increased by 25% in a few short months due to activity half way around the world. "That's history!," you say. As always, we learn from history.

The decisions you make or those whom you help decide, can have long term implication, for good or bad.

A drunk driver could drive left of center and kill one of your loved ones in a head-on crash.

A father divorces a mother and marries a younger woman. A few years later when he dies, the children receive zero inheritance, if there is no prenuptial agreement. The new bride receives what some thought was rightfully the husband's children by the first wife. Decisions!

Life can seem unfair at times. Let's not dwell on the circumstances of what "time and chance" deals us today. Let's *take control* to shape our own future with *better decisions*. And many of us can *help others* do the same *through the acquisition of our products and services*. What can you do to make the best of today so your tomorrows will be brighter? **Focus!** Call it stewardship.

Have you read Dr. Robert Schuller's book *"Life is Not Fair, But God is Good?"*

A phone call one Sunday evening one mid February placed me in a position to make a decision that took me in a new direction, and changed my life forever. This can happen to you! Be prepared! A Certified Public Accountant called me in response to a letter I had decided to mail him in August of the prior year.

TYPES OF DECISIONS

Whether managing our lives, a company, other people, or a sales opportunity, decisions can fall into four categories. Since you are working to help others make decisions, it makes sense to understand that these are:

1. *Some decisions only the buyer can make.* If I am selling something, it helps me to know what only you must decide upon. Many people reserve the right to appeal to a "higher authority" when they are only putting you off.

2. *Some decisions are better made by others.* Maybe it is not important, not in your job description, or your spouse handles that decision in your household. Again, in selling, you want to find out who is the decision maker.

3. *Some decisions are too risky.* You feel you cannot afford to make the decision. The consequences might be too terrible if you decide. So in a case like this, what do you do? Procrastinate. I would never want to sell someone something that could hurt that person, nor would you.

4. *Some decisions can be and must be delayed.* Deciding today is not best because you do not have all the facts, or other's input, or this is simply your policy. Sales people need to understand this and be willing to get back at an "appointed time."

TIMING

Become 🏃 *in Selling!*

Timing is important in selling! When that Sunday evening phone call was received, I was looking (and quite frankly, praying) for the answer to a problem. Why did the phone call come then?! Why was this man asking me now to go to California and help him in his business development? I had to decide after several phone conversations and forwarding material back and forth.

Many things and *people influence* our decisions. How could he know that earlier in the day, my wife and I had sat holding hands and praying about moving to southern California? How could he know that I had just come in from a long and thoughtful prayerful walk? This was highly unusual timing in all respects. I am usually a jogger. Not this night!

When my daughter told me to return the call of a Mr. Bob Rusk from San Diego, I decided to do so. So often, leaving your name and number for others is a waste of time, isn't it? Buyers seldom call back unless they already know and respect you, or, have an urgent need. I won't bore you with all the details, however, I must say that I have become attentive to these seemingly providential appointments or coincidences.

Many top sales people and corporate leaders do feel a *sense of destiny*. Or, they might call it "a passion" or "expectation for the fulfillment of their plans and purposes." They decide when they see that others are concerned about the *self-actualization* of their dreams.

Do *this* for others! You can more readily BECOME #1 IN SELLING and reach your other goals.

FAITH

One of the most important ingredients . . . if not the under girding principles of all success, is FAITH. It is something I have yet to dissect. Faith was mentioned earlier as one of the positive attitude activators, along with HOPE and LOVE.

It would be easier for me to discuss marketing and sales approaches; or how to make sales presentations or proposals; or

326

how to use the telephone or negotiate step by step and word by word, to wrap up this book. Yet, I would be less than honest. . . if I did not tell you about the role of FAITH in my life, and in the lives of those I know who have BECOME #1 IN SELLING. Without FAITH you are doomed to mediocrity.

It takes faith to go into uncertain or unfamiliar situations. You must believe that *you can make the right decisions* to be and do or say the right things, as needed. No amount of preparation can totally prepare you. You could memorize every feature and benefit about your products. You can memorize all kinds of research about your prospect, along with a beautiful presentation, however, you must still move FORWARD IN FAITH.

Twelve days after the phone call, I decided to drive from Columbus, Ohio to San Diego. My "test marketing," I thought, was complete in Columbus, Ohio, a city similar in demographics to the USA overall. So, I was confident, I can succeed anywhere. Success breeds success!

One study of entrepreneurs confirms that most of them made their big money in a new location, often in a new city and with a new product or service. Why? Higher positive expectations! This also happens for a salesperson, manager or leader who believes that THE BEST IS YET TO BE!

Of course, if you are doing too many of the wrong things, regardless of changes in location or even expectations, you will not succeed. Reality says you must *do the right things right* . . . and . . . more of them week after week than your competitors.

Since the cost of outside sales calls in many industries is up 100% in the past 10 years, one must become an *authority* on deciding how to invest time. Position yourself as the authority!

Since salespeople are the key to distribution, salespeople may need to be confronted so they will admit their weakness, so they can do something about it! AND THAT GOES FOR *THE SALES MANAGER* TOO?

Become 🌸🏃 in Selling!

SALES MANAGEMENT

Although I have not said much about sales management, preferring to use the word mentor in many cases, let me remind us, that *for many sales people the difference between success and failure in sales is a great sales manager.*

HUMOR: There is a great double standard in many companies in that sales managers point their finger at the salespeople and say, "you gotta sell more!" They may fail to realize they have three fingers pointing back at themselves. They must serve salespeople three times better! Train/Motivate! Plan/Direct! Strategize/Give Tactics! I have a speech I will soon give in New Orleans for the International Annual Convention of Sales & Marketing Executives Internationals (SMEI). We call it: *SALES MANAGEMENT FOR THE YEAR 2000 . . . NOW!*

Sales Managers! You must win through helping your salespeople win! I want to win by helping you both win!

Here is a tragic example of this double standard: I gave an in-house 30 minute mini sales training session to a group of 8 people. They include 6 Sales Representatives, the Sales Manager, and the General Sales Manager.

The "deal" was that after my session I would ask people to sign up to come to an open sales seminar in the morning or evening. There was a sales management seminar in the afternoon. Three of the people signed up to attend with the company agreeing to pay 1/2 the small investment in the seminar. When I was about to leave the General Sales Manager said to the three (tongue in check?), "Guys, there will be a test after the Thom Lisk seminar to see how much you retain and apply." Of course, since he was "too busy" (translated "cheap") to go himself (or maybe he thought he had all the answers), he would not know what they were exposed to, so his so called "test" was impossible!

And, *of course*, he made excuses for his not taking two hours to go to our sales management seminar in the afternoon. I'd like to report I took the time to overcome his every objection, however, I'm like you, sometimes! I don't always take the time (or have the time for these hard heads). So with this leader (?) I said, "A test? Great! And, sir, you attend the sales management seminar, then we will let these salespeople test you and see how much you have retained!" See the points? I hope so!

He really didn't like that, however, if I don't confront people with their garbage who will have the courage to do so? Sales people most often need to follow their leader, even when he or she is wrong(?) Why do some salespeople go from job to job? Because of poor sales management, many times.

We *must* have better **sales management education.** We must inspire salespeople and sales managers to desire personal development and improvement. Technoselling is needed.

At the end of one of my consulting assignments, a high tech company had the best month in the 11 year history of the owners work in the industry. Why? This sales manager knew he had not yet arrived, even though he was #1 in sales in his market.

In November of that year, a client company (sales manager) whom I served for 29 hours of intensive consulting and training, had their best month in the companies 27-year history. "Remarkable!," some would say. Others would say, "a coincidence!" Still, someone else would ask, "Thom, what is the secret?"

THE SECRET

In one word . . . DISCIPLINE! Or two words . . . SELF-CONTROL! And, sometimes it seems the Spirit can help you be in the right place at the right time saying or doing the right things. *If,* you are the right person! Think about this:

Recently, a man shared a slide presentation before a large community group. It was not a typical sales presentation, but he did have a message he was trying to sell. One picture had a staircase that simply defied logic in terms of how it was constructed and stood. It was one of those winding staircases, however, this one "has no joints, nails or typical materials of construction to bind it together."

He went on to say that "a carpenter came to build it then left quickly after construction, never to be seen again. It stands despite all laws of gravity and logic that it should not stand."

Then, the speaker showed a slide and described a painting "which has a cross that is seen when the picture is photographed in the dark, only. Otherwise, this cross can not be seen." He said "the darkness could be said to depict those dark times in our lives then only God can be seen or His purposes become clearer."

"Everyone says that these two, the staircase and the painting must be either a . . .

MYSTERY,

MAGIC, or a

MIRACLE

People confirm that I am as pragmatic and logical as the next person. "Thom is much wiser than most." Recent projects for *consulting engineers* and *architects* where I worked in their organizational/business and strategic marketing helps me to know that these principles in this book are appreciated by all business people. But how does one explain providential help? How you can attain it in your selling career? Is it a mystery, magic, or a miracle?

CODE OF PROFESSIONAL ETHICS

Many professionals have a code of ethics to which members subscribe. Along with this, many companies have a certain *culture* which when violated causes red flags to blare in the air. When working for a company or selling to a company, understanding this culture is critical in many cases.

I have a friend who is a member of The National Speakers Association (a group with a published code of ethics), who consults with medical facilities and practices.

He reports that he becomes a mystery patient by admission at the facility with the permission and knowledge of usually only one doctor, when indeed he has no illness. He determines how patients are treated, so he can properly train and consult with management.

Is this ethical? The nurses do not know that he is evaluating so he can structure ideas to help them all improve. You have heard of mystery shoppers who evaluate sales people in stores? In this case he takes it one step further by not just *catching people doing things right* (which is really what we need to do), he also gives the objectivity that is often lacking. GREAT IDEA!

I know on some of my own projects in past years, I have been best received on an ongoing basis only after I walked in the employees moccasins for awhile or observed in depth as a customer. EMPATHY! Have you heard the Indian's prayer? It goes something like this:

LORD, HELP ME NOT TO CONDEMN ANOTHER BRAVE UNTIL I HAVE WALKED IN HIS MOCCASINS FOUR FULL MOONS.

HOW about you and your company? Do you thoroughly understand the culture and ethics of the companies or people you are attempting to sell? Would that help? Since values and ethics shape behavior, I find that sales people most often gravitate to the companies and people who most often reflect their own values and ethics.

Master sales people have firm convictions and stand by their values or a code of ethics. And they respect others who do the same, even if they disagree. In selling you can disagree, however you must never be disagreeable about it!

A 26 year old partner in a security company asked me to assist him with his *company development*. His first need or complaint?

His two partners were, from his view point, unethical. Two years later I checked back with him and found much progress in his company, and still found many inconsistencies in *his* life. He finally had married his girl friend when she was pregnant with their second child, and he still was critical of all organized religions AND consultants AND his two partners. In *truth* he did not like to be confronted with *his own unethical behavior.* He survived because his partners balanced him out, rather than hurt him!

He is another case of a potentially great sales person whose *inconsistencies could be his un-doing.* There is nothing that destroys relationships faster than when one is perceived to be unethical. *The best companies and individuals are values driven.*

Certainly, all of us will face issues in the future where we will not be totally clear, initially, what is the right thing to do. In cases like that it is best to wait. . .do nothing. . .*seek counsel*, if need be. I seek my Heavenly Father many times each day in prayer for His counsel. And I always get it! And, to often the counsel of wise mentors.

For the BEST YET TO BE, we need to continue to: grow, research, attend seminars, read, study, use cassette and video tape learning, monitor relationships, prioritize properly, evaluate and use new ideas and technology, and have disciplined implementation.

SUMMARY

Recently I attended a seminar entitled "Razor Sharp Marketing" which was sponsored by the American Marketing Association. My friend, Dr. Roger Blackwell's keynote speech, **"Global Thinking as a Source of Increased Profits,"** helped attendees realize that in many industries, selling will undergo continued and dramatic change in the years ahead.

How people will buy, when, from whom, and why will change dramatically. Buyers are becoming better educated in nearly every market segment. Salespeople must become better too. Roger confirms that we need to "become more team oriented, like the

The Best Salespeople

Japanese." Individual selling skills will continue to be rewarded, however, maybe not to the degree as before. Salespeople "need new skills" as technology increases, and globalization impacts us all. You need faith to change. You need to think and help others think through important decisions better. Do It Now!

QUESTIONS

1. Do you know salespeople like Charlie, Mike, Linda, Donna and David? _____ What can we best learn from these salespeople? _____

   _____

2. What 4 types of decision are discussed?

   _____

   _____

   _____

   _____

3. How can Sales Managers win more?

   _____

   _____

   _____

4. Why is prescribing to a Code of Ethics important?

   _____

   _____

_____CHAPTER 14_____

LIFE BEGINS AT 40

TIPS, THE TELEPHONE, SALES PLANNING, PROPOSALS AND MORE!

Or. . .TODAY. . .at your age! Although, some employers continue to discriminate based on age. We can prove you can learn new disciplines, technology, selling or marketing methods and skills at ANY age.

When I turned 40, my sister, Sally, gave me a birthday card picturing some comical rats in running uniforms at the starting line on a track. Have you ever felt like one of those rats? Ever been in a maze (and not know it)? Or felt like you were going around in circles?

Remember. . .YESTERDAY DID END LAST EVENING!

You no longer need to spin your wheels. **Believe that God is directing you to make the best and right decisions.**

Accept *responsibility for the future* and you will not need to repeat the past. Blame others for the past if you must to rid yourself of any (and forgiven them) and get on with it! Accept God's forgiveness and forgive yourself! YOU ARE SOMEBODY!

Affirm: I am SOMEBODY!

Affirm: I will not settle for second place!

Affirm: I realize to become #1 I must serve better than I have and better than all others.

Affirm: I am committed to doing all the right things in life. I am born to Become #1 in SELLING!

You are selling yourself, now continue to sell others! The ideas in this chapter are vital for most salespeople.

The bible asserts "he who will be first will be last, and he who is last is first." Think about it! ***To become #1 you must be willing to put yourself last by serving all others.***

TIPS AT ANY AGE!

Murphy's first law:

Nothing is as simple as it seems! (Simplify)

Murphy's second law:

Everything takes longer than it should! (Plan ahead!)

Murphy's third law:

If anything can go wrong, it will. (So be prepared!)

O'Toole's commentary:

Murphy was an optimist! (WRONG!)

Parkinson's first law:

Work expands so as to fill the time available for its completion. (give deadlines and stick to them)

Douglas's law of clutter:

Clutter expands to fill the space for its retention! (Unclutter your work spaces so you can stay focused and save time. Throw away what will not be needed.)

Corcoran's law of Packrattery:

All files, papers and memos saved will never be needed until such time as they are disposed of when they will become essential and indispensable. (Start new. . .what will never be needed dispose of A.S.A.P. If you haven't looked at it recently, you probably will not. This includes computer files.)

Segal's Law:

A man with one watch knows what time it is: a man with two watches is never sure. (develop a plan. . .one master plan and, have a backup if needed. Stick with it!)

Parkinson's telephone law:

The effectiveness of a telephone conversation is in inverse proportion to the time spent on it. (Unless you are in tele-marketing, or interviewing, or courting, or catching up with a friend, use the phone to set appointments. *K*eep *i*t *s*imple and *s*hort. . .K.I.S.S.)

TELEPHONE SELLING KEYS

A. BE PREPARED.

Decide what your objective is and what you want to say before making a call.

B. Speak directly into the receiver.

The only impression you can make is with the way you speak and with the words you use.

C. Ask for a minute to talk.

"Is this a convenient time to talk?"

D. Identify yourself and

"Ms. Smart, I am following

.your company.

up with some exciting and profit producing ideas; this is Thom . . . Lisk." (. . . = pause).

E. State the facts.

Do not waste the persons time. Do be friendly. . .do smile, your voice is more pleasant.

F. Sell your prospect on your objective.

And, set up a definite time to meet.

G. Use the person's name.

The sweetest sound to a persons ears is his or her own name. Use it often!

H. Listen carefully.

Do not get wrapped up in what you are saying. You can learn a lot; listen.

I. Take notes

Keep a tablet handy and jot down key points of the conversation.

J. Let your prospect hang up first.

Your prospect may have an after thought. If you hang up first, he/she might let the thought go rather than call back.

K. Restate the day, date and time of the appointment.

"Let's see, I've got Monday at 8:30 A.M., April 10. Mr. Smart, is that what you have on your calendar?

THE INCOMING PHONE CALL:

Life Begins at 40!

If in your job you accept incoming phone calls, you can follow a set format in accepting these calls. This is not the format for a receptionist or secretary who is attempting to screen you out. It is a format for someone that is trying to sell by phone.

1. Express your interest
2. Listen to the customer or caller carefully
3. Ask fact-finding questions
4. Make a decision, make a "pitch," ask them to decide
5. Overcome any objections
6. Close the conversation and/or the sale; determine the next best step *"where do we go from here?"*

(if additional information is needed on how to develop a script or the fact finding questions, please inquire)

THE OUTGOING PHONE CALL:

Some rules to follow if you must set appointments by phone are helpful. The first 8 years of my sales career this was not needed, but when I had to set appointments, I found this helpful, and I hope you will too!

What is your batting average by phone? Commit to improve!

1. Decide the *objective* of your phone call.
2. Make a list of all ideas and thoughts that relate to the purpose of your desired conversation BEFORE calling.
3. Arrange your ideas in the appropriate order of importance, but remember to ask questions, first, and relate the ideas around the known needs of the prospect or customer.
4. Eliminate weak points in your presentation. Audio taping yourself, listening and critiquing will help.
5. Pick your strongest point to use as a greeting.

6. Write out an action desired close (alternate of choice may be the best) "Mr. A, is Wednesday at 3:00 best for you or would you prefer 4:00 pm?"

There are companies that do nothing but sell *list management* services. This is a direct mail, pre-approach letter service to create interest before contacting the prospect by phone. . Of course, you could also do this in house; however, a computerized service might be valuable to expedite and facilitate this. Sometimes you can *generate leads* with a postage-paid return postcard.

Develop your *letter system* step-by-step. Guidelines can be given and customized further, however, remember what your prospect may be thinking.
Consider:

"Who is this person?"

"Whom does she/he represent?"

"What does he want from me?"

"Why did she call me?"

"What is he trying to sell me?"

"Will she really help me?"

"How does it work?"

"Is it as good as he says?"

"Is it too complex for me to understand and use?"

"Will I be able to use it and understand it after he is gone?"

"Is he really telling me the truth?"

"Why does she want me to buy it right now?"

"Would it be wise to examine a competitive brand?"

"What is my real reason for not buying today?"

These and many other questions surface in the mind of any customer or prospect during a typical presentation. Can you anticipate them better in the future? Then. . .

NEW SALES LIFE BEGINS TODAY!

And, you can. . . affirm: I can . . .

BECOME #1 IN SELLING!

Human nature is such that you really can come to understand how people will react (negative) or respond (positive) to your offers or recommendations whether in person or by phone.

PASSIVE? AGGRESSIVE?

It is said some salespeople are passive/aggressive and others aggressive/aggressive. Which are you? The best boxers "float like a butterfly and sting like a bee" to quote Mohammed Ali. They know when to close the sale! This may not be the best analogy because you must not sting people. And, in your selling you both need to *feel* you are winning.

PLANS

Not long ago I was putting together a business plan, and I asked a pastor to pray for me. He reminded me of Proverbs 16:9. You might want to look that up. How many sales people have long range written goals, and the accompanying plans? Sometimes a new career plan is needed. We must overcome living for money and from pay check to pay check to have the long range vision and goals we spoke about earlier in this book. Strive for a *life of significance*! Significance is better than success.

There are great tools for anyone needing help in planning. If you were wanting to begin a new business, as an example, you might want to refer to Touche Ross' (CPA's) guide to writing a business plan. Why reinvent the wheel!? Nightingale Conant has created a number of wonderful audio and video cassette learning programs. One of them is on how to start a new business. *Beginning anything is half finished.*

In developing a business, personal, marketing, or *sales plan*, one must consider finances, (sometimes do *financial projections*, and *forecasts*). I mention this here because even if you do not need to do these things, your prospects may be going through this process. They many create an objection that speaks to the fact!! "It does not fit into the budget." Or, you receive a delaying tactic, inferring we are planning and you will have to check with me later." Can these objections be over come? Of course! Marketing experts (and psychologists) advise not to start certain plans unless you *feel confident you can finish.*

On a personal level, *each sales person* most usually needs to calculate how much activity is needed to fulfill their specific plan and reach their sales goals. Or, you must accept what your mentor or sales manager determines is the right plan for you.

ACTIVITY BREAKDOWN

You need to determine how you will reach your goals (sales, income or otherwise) by the judicious use of your time. For the sake of clarity, we will here concentrate on specific income objectives.

Since you are in some capacity of sales and/or marketing, the activities which relate most *directly* to earning an income are:

1. Prospecting for more business through existing accounts or new prospects.
2. Conducting sales presentations to close sales.
3. Traveling to appointments or preparing for them.
4. Doing paperwork that pertains to making sales or serving customers.
5. Using the phone with prospects or customers or influences.

The following activity breakdown will help you to determine or *define what you must do* each week to reach your income objectives. I know many sales people who are #1 in their companies or industries who know these statistics. They have their plan and the discipline to keep working it.

(fill in the blank places as you proceed)

The Sales Doctors 23

1. How much income do you *want* to earn this year? (want is different than need)_____

2. What is your average net income per sale?_____

3. Divide your net income per sale (line 2) into your gross income (line 1) to get the total number of sales you need to reach your goal._____

4. How many prospects do you need to contact in order to get one selling interview?_____

5. How many interviews do you need to make to obtain one sale?_____

6. Multiply line 3 times line 5 to get the total number of interviews needed to reach your goal._____

7. Multiply line 6 times line 4 to get the total number of prospects needed to reach your goal._____

8. Divide line 6 by 244 to get your daily prospect goal.

   _____

9. Divide line 7 by 344 to get your daily prospect goal.

   _____

10. How long does it take you to give an interview or make a first presentation?_____

11. Multiply line 6 by line 10 to get your daily time invested in selling interviews._____

12. Divide line 11 by 244 to get your daily time invested in selling interviews._____

13. How much time do you invest in pre- and post- interview preparation, etc.?_____

14. Multiply line 13 times line 6 to get the total time invested in sales preparation._____

15. Divide line 17 by 244 to get your daily time invested in prospecting._____

16. How much time do you invest getting an interview? (Example: 3 minutes on the phone)_____

17. Multiply line 16 times line 7 to get the total time invested prospecting. Divide by 60. (3000 prospects times 3 minutes = 9000. Divide by 60=15 hours) _____

18. Divide line 17 by 244 to get your daily time invested in prospecting._____

19. How much time do you invest traveling to and from a selling interview?_____

20. Multiply line 19 times line 6 to get the total hours invested in traveling._____

21. Divide line 20 by 244 to get your daily time invested in traveling._____

22. Total lines 11, 14, 17, and 20._____
This will give you the total hours for the year in selling time.

23. Divide line 22 into line 1 to get the dollar value for your selling time per hour._____

SUMMARY OF ACTIVITY BREAKDOWN

My name: _____

	PROSPECTS NEEDED	SALES PRESENTATIONS	SALES
Each year	_____	_____	_____

	TIME PROSPECTING	PRESENTATIONS	TRAVEL TIME
Each year	_____	_____	_____

	PROSPECTS	PRESENTATIONS	TRAVEL TIME
Each day	_____	_____	_____

	PROSPECTING TIME	PRESENTATION TIME	SALES
Each day	_____	_____	_____

	PROSPECTS NEEDED	PRESENTATIONS	SALES
Each week	_____	_____	_____

	PROSPECTING TIME	PREP. TIME	TRAVEL TIME
Each week	_____	_____	_____

PREPARATION TIME:

_____	_____	_____
Each day	Each week	Each year

If you are (A) servicing and selling existing customers, as well as (B) prospecting for new business, determine what time must be invested for the maximum return for both customers and prospects. Be *certain to keep your customers #1.*

WHAT MORE DO YOU NEED?

THAT WAS A QUESTION, WASN'T IT?

You now have most of what you need to structure your sales activities to serve customers and create new customers so well that you can BECOME #1 IN SELLING! Throughout this book I have asked a lot of questions, haven't I?

Some have been *tie down questions* as in this sentence and in the last one, HAVEN'T THEY? You can tie down most statements with a *positive question*, WOULDN'T YOU AGREE?

The positive tie down question is a good technique you conclude, DON'T YOU? You can use these more, CAN'T YOU?

Have you identified which of my questions were *open ended* and which were *close ended?*

And what are the *benefits of using each type question*? That was an OPEN ENDED question. You knew that!? The last one was CLOSE ENDED because I knew how you would respond.

YOU CAN CRAFT YOUR OWN QUESTIONS! DO IT NOW! Ask your prospects the most thought provoking questions(s), positioning you above your competition: and you will compel business your way, won't you?

PROPOSALS

To BECOME #1 IN SELLING! you may need to master the art of written correspondence, including the fine art of creating proposals that are accepted. Proposals usually need to be brief and to the point. Often a summary of what was said in your discussions and/or a definition of the problems would be written after an appropriate greeting.

"Sam, *based on what we discussed,* you stated that you have the following problem (or need): This proposal, along with the support materials and documentation, will present an effective and affordable solution. The time frames are left to your discretion for implementation, however, we suggest phase one begin _____(date). Let's discuss these options. Please give us your feedback and questions as we proceed."

The above could be paragraph two in a written proposal or shared verbally when the proposal is given. Note, I used the words *"based on what. . ."* These words trigger active listening and replaying of what was said which generated the proposal or letter. This is a great idea. This we label a **PRESCRIPTIVE STATEMENT**.

The basic steps of many written proposals are:
(Always master the Basics!)

1) introduction/greeting
2) prescriptive statement
3) summarize needs or problems
4) identify possible solutions
5) best recommendation(s)
6) suggested timetable, costs or fees
7) call for action: specific follow up or next step.

YOUR FIRST SALES PRESENTATION

The seven steps in a professional sales presentation were described in earlier chapters. Sometimes it may take several sales calls before you can prepare a full blown presentation, or written proposal. Some professionals charge for the fact finding time, during which they demonstrate their capabilities.

Professionals place a *high value* on their time. Architects, Doctors, Lawyers, Dentists, Consultants, Engineers, Service Technicians. . .we pay for their problem solving abilities. You do not expect something for nothing. . .nor will *your* customers or prospects.

Those that are not willing to pay for the time investment to have their problems solved may never receive the best advice. I think of a very well prepared and informed Certified Financial (Professional!) Planner. . .a friend of mine. He, in one hour, could give someone advise that would gain much more than the $125 he asks per hour, however, most would prefer to invest 30 of their own hours, which may be worth $10-$75 per hour to get the same answer. Doesn't make sense, does it?

DEMONSTRATIONS

I have *given* many "free" speeches to Rotary, Kiwanis, Jaycees, The Lions Club, and in house to companies to demonstrate my capabilities or the value of my message. I always expect something good to come out of this service, some return on the investment of my time. It is not always immediate or direct. As a Rotarian, I identify with their slogan one year. ."REAL HAPPINESS IS HELPING OTHERS." And another BELIEVE IN WHAT YOU DO! DO WHAT YOU BELIEVE IN!

If you really feel you have something that will help others, you will want to share it with them. Demonstrate better.

Remember, your expectations will shape your future! Making a group presentation before a group of decision makers can be a wise use of time IF you *give* value and are believable, and memorable. At the conclusion, ***always call for some kind of action.*** Remember, also, ...

THE LOWEST BIDDER

It is unwise to pay too much, but
    it is worse to pay too little.
When you pay too little, you
    sometimes lose everything
    because the thing you bought is
    incapable of doing what it was
    bought to do.
The common law of business
    balance prohibits paying a little
    and getting a lot: it cannot be done.
If you deal with the lowest bidder,
    you must add something for the
    risk you run. If you do that
    you will have enough to pay for
    something better.

    . . . John Ruskin

BOOK REVIEW

May I suggest you go back through the book and review, briefly? What have you received in each chapter? Make some *written notes*. I realize I asked this of you before. Did you do it then? If not, please DO IT NOW!

CLOSING THOUGHTS

You can oppose your Sale Doctor, however, let's be sure to never oppose God! Salespeople like to be in charge to the point of sometimes shortening the life of relationships. You can redeem bad choices, statements and much in life if you simply will remember the famous prayer . . . "Lord, not my will but Your will be done." God wants you to sell better and more; so do I! Who prevents you from doing so? Take a deeper look in the mirror tomorrow morning and see the person you can become. Then, affirm: More profitable sales are mine today! Sales Are Mine Today! Thank God in advance for the desired outcome and it will be soon appearing.

CHAPTER 14

REVIEW QUESTIONS

1. What tip was most helpful to you?

_____

2. How can you improve your use of the telephone?

_____

3. Did you complete the blanks for your activity breakdown? Please do so.

_____

4. What are some of your favorite open or close ended questions?

_____

5. What words were suggested to begin a prescription statement?

_____

CHAPTER 15

YOU MUST COMPLETE THE SALE

A NEW BEGINNING!

What book about selling would be complete without a few standard tried and proven closing the sale "techniques," methods, or ideas? As you evaluate a few ideas, please consider how you can customize them to fit your situation.

I have been asked to help sales managers and sales people at times to customize their verbiage. At other times, I have listened to salespeople attempt to close sales, and then gave constructive advice once we were alone. When was the last time YOU asked someone to evaluate your attempt to close? Or, tape recorded your message so YOU can evaluate it and improve?

BLUEPRINTS FOR BUILDING YOUR BUSINESS

This is the name of a seminar in which we role play how to make sales presentations, and close sales. I customized it and gave it in 8 hours for The Ohio Association of Realtors. Two state representatives (Congressmen) were in the audience all day. Both were Realtors and needed to acquire their 30 hours of continuing education credit. One man, the minority, then later, majority leader of the Ohio House of Representatives, nearly took over the seminar with his *charismatic power* (dominant verbiage). What a closer he was!! He knows how to connect with people!

In selling, the stronger personality often takes over, and wins. Don't allow yourself to be abused because someone has *position power*! There are different kinds of power in this world, and one is *personality power*. In my experiences, personal or personality power will win over position power, if you are in the right. However, do you have the staying *power to persevere?*

This book is a good support text for our seminars and other training programs as you build your business. Persons attending our:

> BLUEPRINTS FOR SUCCESS,
> BLUEPRINTS FOR BUILDING BUSINESS,
> SUCCESS IN SELLING,
> SUCCESS THROUGH SERVICE,
> BLUEPRINTS FOR LIFE
> BEYOND SUCCESS TO SIGNIFICANCE (New)

seminars offered know that to have success they must ask. *Close the sale!* People from all walks of life attend these seminars, some writing me about the benefits for their personal and business life. Their *dreams are coming true*!! And so can yours, if you close more sales! And you can have more significance if you believe and act accordingly.

Shaping our behavior to be better closers can often be learned by modeling behavior and verbiage after other closers. You can see how important that is, can't you? *Adapt* it to fit you! You need not adopt it word for word.

CLOSING THE SALE

Develop some *trial closes* of your own on the next page.

Start your sentence with the word. . ."**If**. . . . . ."

Here is an example:

"If you could double your sales by learning and using some new words or improving beliefs, *you would be interested,* wouldn't you?"

You Must Complete the Sale

This trial closing question includes a *positive tie down* question, doesn't it? Please note I have planted what I want to take place in advance by using the phrase. . .*you would be interested.* That is exactly what I want. . .and what you want too, isn't it?

Please use this space. . . . write your best trial closes!

If. . .

If. . .

If. . .

If. . .

If. . .

If. . .

MOTIVATIONAL CAUTION

Please never use the combination of . . . IF ONLY. . .This signifies regrets! You can not change the past. You can learn from it, and improve! REMINDER. . .BE THANKFUL THAT SOME ASPECT OF YOUR CAREER IS SELLING! Selling is an *honorable profession* when performed correctly. Salespeople are the highest paid if at the top of their industry.

CLOSING CAUTION

Actually, if you are selling correctly, often you will NOT NEED TO ASK FOR THE ORDER!

How can that be? We are helping people to make decisions and choose. We present our products and services, and if done professionally, and they have a need, or you surface a need, they are going to express (verbally or nonverbally) that they want what you offer! This is *nonmanipulative selling*.

The caution with some of the techniques I listed earlier. . .the tie down questions, etc. . .is that they are designed to lead people to YES responses. You need to *give people permission* to say. . .

NO!

I would much rather receive NO than the uncertainty that ends many sales calls. You would too.

BUYING SIGNALS

You can often tell a prospect is sold and ready to buy by carefully listening to his or her words and the way in which they are chosen, or strung together. You can tell more, however, many times, by watching the *non-verbal* expressions, gestures, and the like. If someone is giving you many positive responses, it can be a good idea to simply STOP TALKING, and ask for the order or allow appropriate action.

Prospects and customers reveal their thoughts and feelings nonverbally. . .remember! If you are first concerned about the commission rather than the buyer, you will lose sales and maybe not know why. Your nonverbals give you away too!

Earlier in the book I shared some stories. Here is one I love to share which will make my point.

Several years ago, I was speaking at a large convention as a Keynote speaker and seminar leader at the Disneyland Hotel in Anaheim, California. Dr. Robert Schuller of the Hour of Power and the Crystal Cathedral fame was the other primary speaker, as I recall it. His magnificent testimony to *possibility thinking* is just a short distance from Disneyland. Talk about someone who has mastered the expression of positive nonverbals! Study this great salesperson.

You Must Complete the Sale

During my seminar I asked the group. . ."How many of you would admit to procrastinating once in awhile?" Every hand it seemed went up. Then I requested: "Please write this prescription to yourself. . .I. . .WILL. . .NEVER. . .PROCRASTINATE AGAIN!. . .in the form of an affirmation."

Every one of the approximately 300 people was writing except a woman in the front row. So I walked over to her, kneeled down so I would be at eye level with her. I. . .

> LOOKED HER IN THE EYE,
> SMILED,
> NODDED MY HEAD IN A YES MOTION,
> LOWERED MY VOICE,
> LEANED FORWARD

and I said, "Miss, I notice you are not writing and participating. May I ask you why you are not writing the statement "I WILL NEVER PROCRASTINATE AGAIN?" She said,

"I WILL IN A MINUTE!"

She was even procrastinating about that! I do hope you will not procrastinate, and you will **DO IT NOW**. There is negative and positive procrastination, and it would be a negative for you to not become determined to learn better how to read buying signals, and MIRROR AND MASK, to bring people to your side.

You can add to the list, however, know *A FEW FAVORABLE NON-VERBAL RESPONSES TO LOOK FOR SO YOU CAN WRAP UP THE SALE.*

WHEN THE PERSON. . .

. . .nods his or her head in agreement to your statements.
   (And not just because you structure questions so they must say YES.)

. . .easily volunteers favorable comments or information.

. . .smiles at much of what you say.

. . .becomes animated or excited with noticeable body actions and/or facial expressions. They will be more likely to do these if you are excited and offer positive facial expressions.

. . .asks about the price or financing non verbally. It can be a good idea to ask them: "How much do you think this sells for?" They may quote a price higher than you were about to ask!

. . .states realistic objections with expression (or verbally).

. . .has eyes that are sparkling, or brow raises.

. . .shows signs of impatience and wants to get to the bottom line.

. . .asks pertinent questions, often first non verbally.

If the person you are attempting to sell flashes any of these or other buying signals, it is then your responsibility to be **perceptive**, and respond accordingly. Again, you must pay *close attention* to each word or action.

At times it is not easy to *mirror their nonverbals* and build rapport. When they put their hand in their pocket, so do you. They fold their arms then so do you. This is a demonstration of empathy, if done correctly. It can be carried overboard to become a sympathetic manipulation, which I, of course, do not recommend. Once you *open* your folded arms, your prospect will, too, and this is why you mirror or mask negatives only briefly.

DIFFERENT CLOSES

Completing this book feels very much like the closing of many sales to me. When you reflect on all that you have discussed, and make a summary statement you are closing. Here is a laundry list

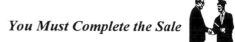

of 15 closing the sale methods. There are others. When have you or can you use these?

1. THE ALTERNATE OF CHOICE CLOSE

"Do you want one or two scoops of ice-cream on your delicious apple pie?"

"Mrs. Sharp, would Wednesday in the afternoon or morning be best for you? . . . Fine, morning looks good to me, how about 9:00 am or would 11:00 am suit you better?

2. PHYSICAL ACTION CLOSE

"Will you please stand if you want to commit yourself."
"Simply put the YES sticker in the box highlighted and return it in the self-addressed stamped envelope."

3. MINOR POINT CLOSE

"The completed recreation room and wood burning fireplace in the basement more than makes up for the lack of a first floor laundry room. Do you agree with this?"

"Mr. Clinton, would you like to use your pen or the one specially prepared for today to sign this agreement?"

4. ASSUMED CLOSE

"Thank you in advance Sam for providing a deposit today so we can schedule the seminar for you in three weeks. You can make it out for 50% of the total to THE THOM LISK GROUP."

"Our delivery truck is in your area every Thursday. Will there be someone available to receive it next Thursday?" (If he says yes,

you can assume the sale is made and simply give him a copy of the paper work, unless a signature is required).

5. EMERGENCY CLOSE

"Mr. company President, if you act today on this recommendation, you can receive an additional 5% discount. Since you said price was very important to you, then this is our best price, I'll simply need your initials here. Thank you."

6. HARD TO GET CLOSE

"Mr. & Mrs. SALE, my computer shows this house has a contract or an offer on it already. If it were still available, would you be interested?"_____"Ok, in that case what would be your best offer, keeping in mind this is a great buy at the asking price?"

7. OPINION CLOSE

"In your opinion, Mr. Miracle, is there any reason why we cannot go ahead today?"

8. MORAL OBLIGATION CLOSE

If the prospect asks, "Do the tapes come with the seminar?" You ask, "Do you want the tapes?" If she says YES, she is now obligated. You need only to work out the details.

9. THE ORDER BLANK CLOSE

MANY SALES PEOPLE WISELY WRITE FIGURES AS THEY DISCUSS THEM ON WHAT SOME CALL A TALKING PAD. THEY REMEMBER THE VISUAL IMPACT AND THAT BELIEVABILITY INCREASES. While casually slipping an order blank out, you ask, "Let's see, Mr. Jones, your middle initial for our paper work is A, isn't it?"

10. THE COURAGE CLOSE

"I know it takes a great deal of courage for you to consider taking action at this time, and I am encouraged by your willingness to proceed with my proposal. You will not regret it, as others have said. You will be pleased!"

11. FIRST CLOSING SUMMARY

You can add to, change and improve upon these to fit your specific needs, can't you? You can be closing throughout your presentation or conversation, isn't that true? Remember, PLEASE, do not be forced, "canned," or unnatural if you use these methods and words. Build relationships for the long-term not just sales for today.

12. THE BOTTOM LINE

You must believe in your heart that what you are selling is best for your customer. Would you own it and use it yourself? SELLING IS NOTHING MORE THAN A TRANSFERENCE OF FEELING OR BELIEF! DO UNTO OTHERS AS YOU WOULD LIKE OTHERS TO DO UNTO YOU. I recently leased an auto where the sales person did not do this, however. The finance man and sales manager did not really meet my needs. It must be a *team effort to develop repeat business!*

13. SUMMARY CLOSE

"That's about it, Michael. So you can begin classes next week, we will complete this paperwork, and finish with a few questions for these enrollment forms. Now let's see, you spell your middle name. . . ."

14. THE "T" CLOSE

Some sales trainers label this the "Ben Franklin Close" because it was a technique Ben used for decision making. What ever you chose to call this procedure, it can help the indecisive to weigh the options, and then get on with it! You may not use this often, however, over the years I have found it to be helpful, and I hope you will too.

There are. . .

NINE STEPS TO HELP TIP THE SCALE IN YOUR DIRECTION TO BRING A DECISION.

a. INTRODUCTORY PHRASE_____
    Example: You can say, "I can see you are undecided, so let's think on paper. Let's draw a line down the middle of this piece of paper, and another across it at the top. We'll label both sides."
b. DRAW THE "T."
c. "We will list the ideas against on one side."
d. ASK THREE TIMES FOR THE IDEAS AGAINST THE PURCHASE OR DECISION.
e. NEXT, LIST YOUR AND THEIR IDEAS IN FAVOR OF THE PURCHASE ON THE OTHER SIDE OF THE PAPER.
f. The last big idea listed is to APPEAL TO THE PERSON'S DOMINANT BUYING URGE. . .THE HOT BUTTON.
g. CHECK BOTH SIDES. (Work to list 2-1/2 times as many IDEAS FOR compared to ideas against to tip the scales.
h. PUT YOUR HANDS UP IN THE AIR AND WEIGH THEM VISUALLY.
i. ASK FOR A FAVORABLE DECISION. "It seems the ideas for the purchase outweigh the ideas against, so it is a good idea to proceed today, isn't it, Bob?"

They still may hesitate, however, if they helped you develop the ideas for and agreed to each one as you listed them, then, they cannot dispute this logic. Maybe they have not given you the REAL objection if they will not now buy.

You can succeed when you think WIN/WIN or GIVE/GIVE. This is not a technique as much as it is a *philosophy for selling.* You may need to give something to tip the scale. Most people will reciprocate.

15. THE TAKE AWAY CLOSE

This method some sales people believe is the most fun to use. And I do recommend it when it develops WIN/WIN relationships. I have witnessed masters in many sales fields use this technique. One friend would say when selling franchises: "Mr. Jones, we only want the most qualified people in our organization. Based on what we know about you so far, I cannot see how you can qualify. Can you *give* me more reasons why you must be considered?"

You *reverse the process* and the prospect begins selling you!!

This can work best sometimes when you do not need to make the sale. Otherwise, you might get too anxious. Some sales people use this method almost exclusively to close sales.

As an example, I once had an automotive salesperson say to me: "Mr. Lisk, this is an expensive and beautiful car. We cannot tell whether or not you will qualify for financing or not. So, to save you (and me) time, let me ask you a few questions for the application, just in case you do qualify. Then you can decide to proceed. Your annual income last year was approximately how much?" If the prospect gives the amount that means he is serious about buying!

In selling seminars I sometimes have said something like:

"Larry, I can see you are hesitating to enroll your people in the program. That is expected. You are a man of wisdom and want to be certain you are making the right decision. Whatever is best for you and your people is what I want, too. We are nearly out of seats for this event, and I do have another company who I believe will take the last seats. Unless you can commit now, I am afraid you will be left out, so why not give me back the brochure, I certainly do not want you coming if you do not believe you will greatly benefit. Many other people believe, according to their testimonials. that this is a great investment in time and money.

Take the form back from the prospect and begin to leave. He may stop you. If not, you can turn just as you are exiting and say:

"CAN YOU GIVE ME ONE GOOD REASON WHY YOU CANNOT GIVE ME A CHECK TODAY?" (or approval to go ahead today?)

This may get the *real reason finally out on the table!* In this example, one might continue by saying "Since that is the only reason, I will _____(action to eliminate objection). Now, you can benefit from this product immediately! I know you will look back on this decision and be glad you decided to go ahead! "Congratulations!"

Recently I had a graduate of one of my seminars sell me a one-write checking and bookkeeping system I did not think I needed or wanted. After buying my breakfast, he presented his idea for making me more efficient after finding out about my current system. He literally took my checks and objections away by *giving* me a rebate out of his own pocket for my old checks. He located and *took away* every objection! And, you can too!

Now, devise "my own take-away" statements in this space:

THE BEST IS YET TO BE!

Remember POSITIVE SELF TALK? YOU ARE TERRIFIC! Since the greatest gift we can *give* another is to see them as the person they can become, I want to share with you what I shared with a large group of direct sales people one recent Monday evening:

"I SEE YOU AS BORN TO BE #1. . .HOW DO YOU SEE YOURSELF?"

Can you see me as a champion? Can you say to me: "Thom, congratulations! You now have documented your doctorate in selling. Thom really does stand for INTEGRITY! You have given me a guideline and blueprints for HOW TO:

BECOME #1 IN SELLING!"

If you can see others better too, this will lead to more sales or your becoming a great champion. IF IT IS TO BE, IT IS UP TO ME! *YOU. . YOU. . .YOU!*

Rewrite your MOST important goals on purpose:

Example: To help as many people as possible move beyond
success to significance and closer to God.

DO IT NOW!

Become 🏃 in Selling!

.Remember how I became THOM TERRIFIC. What will your positive nickname be in the future? Write it out NOW please:

_____

If we meet, you may ask me to autograph this book. What does your signature say about you? Please sign on the dotted line now:

X_ _

YOU HAVE COMPLETED THE BOOK. COMMIT TO BE YOUR BEST.
". . .he who endures to the end will be saved." Matt. 10:22

Endure is a positive word which means INCH BY INCH ANYTHING IS A CINCH! When I heard Dr. Robert Schuller say this, I thought of YOU. Sales people everywhere and all the world over need this kind of book. At times I have fought the fact THAT IF my Becoming #1 in Selling IS TO BE, IT IS UP TO ME! What great thing can God trust YOU to do?

START NOW, where you are today, and for the next 21-30 days to gradually make a difference, to do it better. You will see...YOUR SUCCESS THROUGH SERVICE ATTITUDE: You *first* must be the best servant of all!"

"Until one is committed, there is hesitancy, the chance to draw back, always ineffectiveness, concerning all acts of initiative (and creation). There is one elementary truth the ignorance of which kills countless ideas and splendid plans: That the moment one definitely commits oneself, then providence moves too. all sorts of things occur to help one that would never otherwise have occurred. A whole stream of events issues from the decision, raising in ones favor all material assistance which no man could have dreamed would have come his way. Whatever you can do or dream you can, begin it. boldness has genius, power, and magic in it. Begin it now!"

. . . Jonann Wolfgang Von Goethe

364

CERTIFICATE OF COMPLETION

_____ (Your Name) has
completed *"Become #1 in Selling,"* the book dedicated
to *YOU,* below the salesperson affirms that he/she has
answered at least 75% of the questions in this sales
course successfully. The author encourages you to
continually apply what is taught, most importantly,
to always make your Customer #1.

X̶̶̶̶̶̶̶̶̶̶̶X _____
Author   Salesperson
Thomas (Thom) Lisk, LHD

X _____
Date Completed

'I am The Alpha and The Omega, the first and the last, the
beginning and *the end*." Revelation 22:13

Bibliography

Chapter One

Golden Rule, Matthew; Platinum Rule, Fettig: 2
Dr. Otto H. Reese, Founder/President 50 year old Christian College and Seminary: 3-4
Frank Wobst, Chairman, Huntington Banc Shares, Inc.: 6
Focus or Die, Juanelle Teague Seminar: 7
King David, proverbs quote: 8
Tom Peters books: "A Passion for Excellence," "In Search for Excellence": 8
Marine Motto, "Semper Fideleus": 14
Robert Louis Stevenson quote: 18
Horatio Alger, Rags to Riches Fraternity: 21
25 Years of Research, equivalent to Ph.D.: 23
Tom Terrific, popular cartoon on Captain Kangaroo Show: 24
Roger Dawson book, "You Can Get Anything You Want (But You Have to do More Than Ask)": 25

Chapter Two

"Win with People", "3 Yards and a Cloud of Dust," book by Woody Hayes: 29
Mark Spitz, Gold Medal Winner: 30
Rudy, Notre Dame football player and movie: 30
NCR study: 31
Walt Disney on Success: 32
Bear Bryant, Woody Hayes were strategists: 33
Mickey Mantle, Lou Gehrig, Babe Ruth: 34
Dennis Waitly, Nightingale Conant: 36
National Speakers Association: 39
Dress for Success, book by Malloy: 40
Psychology Today Magazine and Sales Marketing Digest: 43
Roger Maris, Roger Banister, Carl Lewis: 43
Leon Royer, 3M and Blake Roney, Nu Skin: 44
Abe Lincoln quote: 45
Dr. Herbert Greenburg's Caliper: 46
Napoleon Hill, "Going the Extra Mile": 49
Socrates, Woody Hayes, quotes: 49-51
Jack Nicklaus: 51
Patrick M. Morley, book "The Man in the Mirror": 54

Plato, Rings of Influence: 55
Robert Lewis Stevenson, quote: 56

Chapter Three

Will Rogers: 59
George Washington: 60
Dr. H. Greenburg: 63
Fred Astaire, A legend: 66
Ben Franklin attributes: 66
Ronald Reagan comment: 67
Zig Ziglar, "Young": 69
W. Clement Stone, Napoleon Hill books, "Think and Grow Rich," "Success Through A Positive Mental Attitude": 72
Maslow's Hierarchy of Needs: 76
Elbert Hubbard, quote on Loyalty: 77

Chapter Four

Personal Selling Power: 80
Al Walker, The Art of Mastery: 81
Dr. Herbert Greenburg, Predetermine Sales Aptitude: 82
Carl Stevens, Coach and Mentor: 83-84
Wall Street Journal quote: 84
Henry Ford quote: 91
Cavett Robert, OPE: 91
Paredo Principle: 92
Apostle Paul quote: 92
Thomas Edison, quote: 93
Elvis Presley, story: 94
Walter Dill Scott, memory tests: 95
The Salesman, poem by John Wolfe: 95
Possibility Thinker, phrase popularized by Dr. Robert Schuller: 99
Dr. Richard Restak, Brain: 102
Life magazine article, 1994: 103
E.E. Cummings, Hardest battle quote: 103

Chapter Five

Runners World Magazine, Rod Dixon: 105
Readers Digest article, issue unknown: 107
Dan Evans, CEO, Bob Evans Farms Restaurants: 110

Bibliography

Zig Ziglar, quote from See You at the Top: 111, 124
Realtor: 113
Ben Franklin, technique: 115
Americas "#1 Sales Architect," Carl Stevens: 115
Tom Hopkins, J. Douglas Edwards: 117
Vince Lambardi quote: 108
Harry Truman, quote: 120
J. Veronica Biggins letter: 121
The Waltons TV show: 124
Forbes Magazine, Wealthiest People: 124
Consumer Reports: 126
Prentice Hall, survey: 127
Harold Lisk, Scholarship: 129
Jesus, The Solution: 129

Chapter Six

Dale Carnegie: 136
Susan Silver, "Organized to Be Your Best" book: 137
HER Realtors: 138
Abe Lincoln, quote: 144
Tom Winninger, NSA: 145
Socrates, quote: 148
Johann Wolfgang Von Goethe, quote: 155
The Bible, quotes: 156, 157, 161

Chapter Seven

Art Bartlett, story: 168
Domino's Pizza: 168
Fiesta Beauty Salons: 168
Heavy Weight Champs: 169-170
Drummond Gaines, Mentor: 177
The Peter Principle: 183
Betty Lisk, Mother: 187
Dr. Norman Vincent Peale, quote: 189
"The Magic of Thinking Big" book: 191
Marsha Sinetar, "Do What You Love, The Money Will Follow!": 191
Columbus Dispatch, Blue Chip: 192
"How I Raised Myself from Failure to Success in Selling"; book by Frank Bettger: 193
Dan Evans, CEO, Bob Evans: 195

Bibliography

Able Lincoln, Woodcutter quote: 269
President Harry Truman, The Buck Stops Here: 272
Dr. Marilyn Manning, Comments on Conflict: 273
67% of All Sales Approaches, Unknown source: 277
Books recommended on prospecting; Truax, Boyan: 279
J.C. Penney, quote: 284
Anne Boe book, "Is Your Net-Working?": 285
Franklin D. Roosevelt, Habit of Success: 285
Dr. Charles Swindoll, quote: 287
Dr. Roger Blackwell, quote: 287

Chapter Eleven

AT&T, quote from ad: 289
Neil Armstrong, Moon quote: 289
Art Linkletter book, "Yes, You Can!": 290
Prentice Hall study and quote: 296
Bear Bryant, quote: 298
Charles Atlas example: 298
Bob Wellard and Steve Newman, determined walkers: 298
Kyle Rote, Jr. example: 298
Peter Druker, quote: 299
Dean OSU business school, quote: 300
Elihu Root, quote: 301

Chapter Twelve

Marriott Corp, quote: 304
Survey Results, leading sales magazine: 308
Joel Weldon, quote: 310
Ingredients: 311
Bible quote new testament, Apostle Paul: 311
Dr. Robert Schuller, Hour of Power, books: 312
Peter Druker, quote: 314
Day-Timer, Franklin Planner, recommendation: 315
Experts recommend include: Merrill Douglas, Harold Taylor: 316
Highlights for Children: 316-318, form
The Best Servant of All, bible quote, Proverbs; and Proverbs 4:7 quote: 320
John Locke quote: 320

Chapter Thirteen

Charlie, Mike, Linda, Donna, David; actual people: 322-323
Robert Schuller, "Life is Not Fair, But God is Good!": 324
President of Iraq, decisions example: 324
SMEI, Sales Management for year 2000 . . . Now!: 328
Mans comments with "Miracle" slide show: 330
Roger Blackwell, Ph.D., speech and quote: 332

Chapter Fourteen

Quotes from bible, Murphy, O'Toole, Parkinson, Douglas, Corcoran: 335
Quotes from Segal, Parkinson: 336
Mohammed Ali, quote; Touche Ross, Nightingale Conant, Corp., Chicago, IL: 340
Rotary International, yearly themes: 347
The Lowest Bidder, John Ruskin: 348

Chapter Fifteen

Ohio Association of Realtors, client: 351
Hour of Power, Schuller: 354
One write checking system-McBee: 362
Jonann Wolfgang Von Goethe, quote: 364
Revelations, quote from last chapter of The Holy Bible: 365

Index

Index

Service / Product Order Form

Book	Retail
BECOME #1 IN SELLING!	$40

Quantity Discounts

(Suggested that companies purchase for all salespeople and use each chapter as a weekly sales training session.)

3-7 copies	$35 each
8-14 copies	$30 each
15-21 copies	$25 each
22 or more, please inquire	

Cassette tape album

Live 6 hour seminar by Thom Lisk with much of this material presented.

BECOME #1 IN SELLING!

6 tapes, 12 lessons and workbook	$70
3-7 copies	$65 each
8-14 copies	$60 each
15-21 copies	$55 each
22 or more, please inquire	

Book store prices for single copies may be less due to their quantity purchases.

Services

Thom Lisk...Keynote speeches, banquets, workshops, seminars, training, consulting honorariums, fees, etc., based on location and time. Travel expenses added and reimbursed.

BECOME #1 IN SELLING!
by
Thom Lisk

Phone Thom Lisk: (800) 705-0079 or Fax: (614) 846-1377
Phone Fairway Press: (800) 537-1030 or Fax: (419) 228-9184

Name:_____

Street Address:_____

City:_____State:_____Zip:_____

Phone:_____

A.   When ordering from the author, please send check or money order to:

Thom Lisk
1112 Firth Ave.
Worthington, OH 43085

B.   When ordering from Fairway Press, please send check or money to:

Fairway Press
517 S. Main Street
P.O. Box 4503
Lima, OH 45802-4503

Quantity Ordered _____

Please add proper shipping, tax and handling:

1 copy	add $2.91	6-9 copies	add $5.93
2-5 copies	add $4.37	10-15 copies	add $8.17

Sub-total $_____
Shipping & Handling $_____
Total $_____

❏ check or money order enclosed   ❏ charge to MASTERCARD
❏ charge to VISA

Card Number _____

Expiration date_____ Signature_____